3 00
G

many great dinners and
conversations!

Kathleen ☺

Political Women

Political Women

Language and Leadership

Edited by
Michele Lockhart
and
Kathleen Mollick

LEXINGTON BOOKS
Lanham • Boulder • New York • Toronto • Plymouth, UK

Published by Lexington Books
A wholly owned subsidiary of The Rowman & Littlefield Publishing Group, Inc.
4501 Forbes Boulevard, Suite 200, Lanham, Maryland 20706
www.rowman.com

10 Thornbury Road, Plymouth PL6 7PP, United Kingdom

British Library Cataloguing in Publication Information Available

Library of Congress Cataloging-in-Publication Data

Political women : language and leadership / edited by Michele Lockhart and Kathleen Mollick.
pages cm.
Includes bibliographical references and index.
ISBN 978-0-7391-8203-1 (cloth : alk. paper) -- ISBN 978-0-7391-8204-8
1. Women--Political activity--United States. 2. Political oratory--United States. I. Lockhart, Michele.
II. Mollick, Kathleen.
HQ1236.5.U6P653 2013
320.082'0973--dc23

2013023727

Printed in the United States of America

Table of Contents

Introduction

Diane M. Blair

When I look at the issues we face, and when I think of the changes we need, I am convinced as I have ever been that our future depends on the leadership of women—not to replace men but to transform our options alongside them. — Marie C. Wilson, *Closing the Leadership Gap*

The 113th Congress includes the largest number of women ever elected among its membership. According to the *Center for Women and Politics*, women now occupy twenty seats in the U.S. Senate and seventy-seven seats in the House of Representatives.[1] With the 2012 election, five states have elected women to the Senate for the first time in their histories (Hawaii, Massachusetts, Nebraska, North Dakota, and Wisconsin). Among these women representatives are the first openly gay senator and the first Asian American senator, and in the House the first Hindu representative and two combat veterans. Thirteen of the women elected to the House of Representatives won open seats. New Hampshire is the first state to have an all-women delegation in its top political positions of the Governorship, U.S. Senate, and House of Representatives. Such gains were rightly heralded as important achievements toward our ongoing efforts to close the gender leadership gap.[2]

At the same time, it is important to acknowledge that even with these celebrated gains, women are still woefully underrepresented in our political leadership. The United States still only ranks seventy-seventh in women's political participation around the world.[3] Overall, women make up 18 percent of our congressional representatives, with minority women making up less than 5 percent of the total membership of Congress. With the recent gains made by women in Congress, including the election of Tammy Baldwin and Elizabeth Warren in closely watched competitive races, and the high profile political careers of women like Hillary Clinton and Sarah Palin, public perceptions of women as active participants in the political process have clearly broadened. Yet it is also important to consider the various factors that continue to restrict political leadership opportunities for women as well as some of the ways in which individual women have strategically sought to enact political power and leadership for themselves.

THE GENDERED NATURE OF POLITICAL LEADERSHIP

Although well-covered territory in academic circles, it bears repeating that political leadership has historically been defined as a masculine trait. Karlyn Kohrs Campbell argues that when women first began "to speak outside the home on moral issues and matters of public policy, they faced obstacles unknown to men."[4] One of those obstacles was the need to address the cultural assumption that "femininity and rhetorical action were seen as mutually exclusive."[5] That gendered legacy reverberates still in performances of political leadership. Marie Wilson argues that "[w]hen it comes to women's leadership, we live in a land of deep resistance, with structural and emotional impediments burned into the cultures of our organizations, into our society, and into the psyches and expectations of both sexes."[6] Susan Carroll and Richard Fox argue that in many ways political leadership is still highly gendered: "We want our leaders to be tough, dominant, and assertive— qualities much more associated with masculinity than femininity in American culture."[7] In addition to the deeply gendered nature of our political ideologies, the language politicians, the media, and the public employ creates our political society at any given point in time. In other words, "those who control [political] discourse control society."[8] As such, if women are to make meaningful contributions to the shaping of our political reality, their voices must be included not only the national discussion of political affairs but also in our critical analyses of political leadership and performances. The study of the political discourse employed by the women who have found their way into state and national politics and whose voices have been included in the political dialogue are central to advancing women's opportunities and our own understandings of how their leadership is transforming the political landscape. Finally, it is important to point out that a generic woman's style of political leadership does not exist because other factors like race, ethnicity, age, sexual orientation, and political affiliations/commitments play important roles when determining the context of one's actions or behaviors in the political arena. When trying to understand women's political leadership, a case study approach like those featured in this book reminds us that political leadership is always socially embodied and culturally situated.

ORGANIZATION OF THE BOOK

Part I of this book, "Initial Women Moving Forward: A Fight for Language," includes three essays that explore some of the innovative ways women carved out political leadership roles for themselves prior to the twentieth-century women's liberation movement. In each case, the women sought to build upon their earlier leadership experiences and/or celebrity, at the same time they sought to negotiate and in some cases exploit traditional gender expectations. Kristie Fleckenstein examines Frances Willard's supposed non-political, personal memoir as an act of feminist rebellion. Willard's leadership in the women's suffrage movement and as President of the Woman's Christian Temperance Union (WCTU) made her a national political figure, and she built the WCTU into the largest all-female reform organization of its time. Fleckenstein argues that even in writing her personal reflections about learning to ride a bike, Willard advocates and performs a new spatial activism for women's equality and a celebration of feminist communal virtues. In the next chapter, William Carney writes about Aimee Semple McPherson, who was probably best known for her religious leadership as founder of the first mega churches, the Angelus Temple of Los Angeles. According to Carney, McPherson's blending of her established evangelical ministry with her ambitious political involvement in California gubernatorial politics established her as a forerunner, for better or worse, of the rise of contemporary organizations like the Moral Majority and the Christian Coalition. Finally, Sara Hillin argues that child movie star Shirley (Temple) Black sought to build upon her former celebrity and establish herself as a legitimate political figure as a United Nations representative and international diplomat. Relying on strategies reflective of an invitational rhetoric, Black established her own political credibility and also increased the visibility of women in high-profile, national political careers.

Part II of the book, "A Shift to Modern Day: A Look at Leadership," provides several case studies that explore more current women leaders and what their political performances and rhetorical representations communicate about the larger political and social culture. Rebecca S. Richards explores how nationalistic belief systems (doxa) emerge and circulate to constitute executive political leadership as inherently masculine. As such, when women, like Hillary Clinton, enter this political realm as leaders and potential leaders, the nation's "readiness" to elect a woman head of state becomes central to the popular and mediated discourses of the culture. Richards' analysis examines how several women leaders across geo-political positions have the potential to both subvert and affirm the doxa of the nation-state with their rhetorical performances. Returning attention to our own nation-state, both Michele Lockhart and Kathleen Mollick take a closer look at the rhetorical performances and portrayals of the only two women nominated on a major party presidential ticket. Lockhart's chapter explores the rhetorical performances and language choices of both Geraldine Ferraro and Sarah Palin, while Mollick analyzes the satirical portrayals of both candidates on *Saturday Night Live*. Lockhart's discourse analysis of speeches by Ferraro and Palin suggests a possible shift toward more assertive and direct language strategies on the part of women involved in national politics. She argues that the rhetorical strategies of both Ferraro and Palin emerge within a larger presidential discourse community and that their discourse in turn shapes that discourse community. Her analysis leads her to conclude that the credibility and success of women political candidates will depend on the rhetorical continuity of their own language strategies within this larger discourse community. Mollick, with regard to how high-profile political women are portrayed and satirized in late-night comedy, sees very little change in the twenty-four years separating Ferraro's and Palin's run for office. Such prominent portrayals suggest that with every crack in the political glass ceiling, there is still much work to be done. Finally, the last chapter in this section focuses on the public advocacy of Meghan McCain, especially as it relates to her public criticism of certain aspects of the Republican party's political ideologies and positions. Nichelle D. McNabb and Rachel B. Friedman investigate the rhetorical strategies McCain employs to debate conservative politicians and pundits, and they also explore how her strategic responses enable her to successfully negotiate and confront the common double binds for women leaders.

The chapters in the Part III, "Women and Politics: 2012 and the Future of Women Leaders in America," speculate about what our most recent experiences with women's political leadership might mean for our future, especially when it comes to women and the U.S. presidency. Alison Novak and Janet Johnson set out to understand the role of prominent women leaders in the most recent presidential campaigns of Barack Obama by examining the role of women in online presidential campaigning. The authors argue that First Lady Michelle Obama, Jill Biden, and Caroline Kennedy were strategically employed to appeal to women voters during the Obama re-election campaign. While the email campaign appears to recognize the importance of women as a voting constituency, the rhetorical topics and strategies featured in the emails reinforce gender stereotypes about women's political interests and concerns, and also continues to cast women in supporting roles when it comes to presidential leadership.

The remaining chapters in this section are devoted to providing insight into the successes and failures of one of the most prominent woman leaders of our times, Hillary Clinton. These chapters trace Clinton's emergence as a controversial first lady to a national and international political leader. Nancy Myers explores some of the challenging issues that emerge when women leaders from the United States seek to exert their political influence on a global level. Myers addresses transnational feminists' important critiques of the Western "savior" narrative and the politics of representation whenever a Western woman of privilege seeks to speak on behalf of other women. Using Hillary Clinton's speech to the 1995 United Nations fourth World Conference on Women, Myers analyzes the construction the *ethos* of the rhetor, those spoken on behalf of, and the audience within a discursive act. She argues that multiple *ethē* enabled Clinton to advocate on behalf of women around the world at the same time her discourse acknowledged differences among women and her own social location. Mary Tucker-McLaughlin and Kenneth Campbell seek to understand the potential legacy for Clinton's historic run for the presidency through a theory of collective memory. In their chapter they argue for an understanding of collective memory that gives more weight to the role the news media play in shaping society's collective memory of women as political leaders. They argue one of the biggest obstacles female presidential candidates face is media coverage that emphasizes their novelty as a candidate due to their gender, which tends to diminish their significance as a serious contender. As an innovative first lady and popular U.S. senator from New York, Hillary Clinton was well positioned to finally overcome the gender novelty obstacle. Despite her advantages over previous female candidates, Tucker-McLaughlin's and Campbell's analysis suggests that the news media once again focused primarily on Clinton's novelty as the first wife of a former president to run for the presidency, which once again emphasized the gender novelty of Clinton's campaign. Finally, Maria Daxenbichler and Rochelle Gregory turn their attention to Clinton's presidential campaign and they argue that Clinton acquiesced to the "gender regime" of presidential politics. According to the authors, Clinton engaged in a masculine rhetorical style and relied heavily on militaristic rhetoric as her primary campaign strategy to prove she was fit for the office of the presidency. Given that the office of the presidency is still heavily gendered a masculine role, such a strategy hardly seems surprising. What may be surprising is the authors' concluding speculations that the political electorate might actually be ready to embrace a female presidential candidate with a more feminine rhetorical style.

NOTES

1. "Facts on Women in Congress 2013," accessed March 28, 2013, www.cawp.rutgers.edu/fast_facts/levels_of_office/Congress-CurrentFacts.php.
2. Ibid.
3. "Women in National Parliaments: World Classification," accessed March 28, 2013, www.ipu.org/wmn-e/classif.htm.
4. Karlyn Kohrs Campbell, *Man Cannot Speak for Her: A Critical Study of Early Feminist Rhetoric*, Vol. 1 (New York: Praeger, 1989), 1.
5. Ibid., 9.

    6. Marie C. Wilson, *Closing the Leadership Gap: Why Women Can and Must Help Run the World* (New York: Viking, 2004), xiii.
    7. Susan J. Carroll and Richard L. Fox, *Gender and Elections: Shaping the Future of American Politics* (Cambridge: Cambridge University Press, 2006), 3.
    8. Christ'l De Landtsheer, "Introduction to the Study of Political Discourse," in *Politically Speaking: A Worldwide Examination of Language Used in the Public Sphere*. Ed. Ofer Feldman and Christ'l De Landtsheer (Westport, CT: Praeger, 1998), 4.

I

Initial Women Moving Forward:
A Fight for Language

Chapter One

Epideictic Memories

The Argument for Spatial Agency in Frances E. Willard's A Wheel within a Wheel

Kristie Fleckenstein

POLITICS ON A BICYCLE

Despite suffering "from the sedentary habits of a lifetime," in her fifty-third year, Frances E. Willard mastered the safety bicycle,[1] a new and radically improved version of the ordinary that initiated "bicycle passion" during the Gay Nineties in America and abroad.[2] Leader of both national and international organizations of the Woman's Christian Temperance Union (WCTU), the largest and most politically influential mass mobilization of women in the nineteenth century, Willard was no stranger to breaking new political and social ground for women. At the height of her political powers, lured by the "swiftness of motion which is perhaps the most fascinating feature of material life,"[3] Willard defied the counsel of her loved ones and the limitations of a "careworn and inelastic" body[4] to conquer "the most remarkable, ingenious, and inspiring motor ever yet devised upon this planet."[5] By doing so, she recaptured the joy she had experienced as a child running wild like a "young human colt" before she was encased in long skirts, corsets, and high heels.[6] As she practiced for ten to twenty minutes per day over a three-month period with various helpers, this political activist recorded her experiences in her journal and dictated them to her stenographers.[7] These musings of the woman celebrated as "the greatest woman orator living"[8] and an "outstanding nineteenth-century women's leader"[9] served as the basis for the modest seventy-five-page memoir, *A Wheel within a Wheel. How I Learned to Ride the Bicycle, with Some Reflections by the Way*, published in 1895.

1

A lively account of Willard's struggles with Gladys, the name Willard assigned the safety bicycle purchased for her by Lady Henry Somerset, her friend and host in England, *A Wheel within a Wheel* provides an engaging narrative of Willard's triumph over the challenges presented by Gladys to a fifty-three-year-old in poor health. It was, as one reviewer notes, "a good book to while away an hour with."[10] But, while Willard might have shown "pluck" in learning to ride at fifty-three,[11] the book itself, reviewers conclude, offers little of substance to either the cyclist or the reformer.[12] However, I argue that by advocating and embodying physical mobility in her memoir, Willard also advocated and embodied political mobility in her readers' lives, an important dimension of the fight for women's equality. Much more than an aesthetically pleasing story with a spirited, if aging, heroine, Willard's memoir functions as a performance of epideictic rhetoric, one subtly designed to praise women's expanded spatial agency.

The goal of transforming spatial boundaries for *fin de siècle* women certainly warranted Willard's attention and rhetorical ingenuity. Defined as a woman's ability to act in a range of private and public venues, spatial agency in one guise or another constitutes a key element in Western feminist activism from the Seneca Falls Convention to the current post-feminist moment, nowhere more hotly contested than in the final years of the nineteenth century. During the waning decades of the 1800s, American women experienced a cultural backlash. With their increasing participation in the public sphere through burgeoning women's clubs and professionalization and with the rise of the New Woman icon threatening traditional gender roles, cultural pressure on a variety of fronts sought to funnel women back to the confines of domestic spaces. Writing in 1905, Grover Cleveland exemplifies the draconian nature of this spatial redistribution. Particularly concerned with the rising popularity of the club movement, which drew women out of the home into public spaces, Cleveland excoriates mobile women as "perversions of a gift of God to the human race."[13] As the longtime president of the national and international WCTU who reigned as "America's uncrowned queen," Willard served as a potent spokesperson to rebut this pernicious trend.[14] Her memoir, an ostensibly non-political publication, presented the right opportunity for such rebuttal. She undertook both the bicycling and the memoir, Willard claims, not only to improve her health but also "to help women to a wider world."[15]

With its focus on Willard's adroit use of epideictic rhetoric to argue for women's mobility, this chapter makes three contributions to disciplinary understanding of and appreciation for the rhetoric of political women. First, and foremost, it highlights the importance of spatial agency in gendered politics especially within emancipation efforts. Political activism for nineteenth-century women required social activism in that enlisting women in the service of political change, such as suffrage, necessitated social change in the ideology circumscribing women's entry into the public sphere and public spaces. As the "Queen of Speech,"[16] Willard asserts and performs a new spatial activism for women, who, like herself, were all too frequently "slaves of public opinion"[17] and thus quailed before the prospect of participation in the public sphere. By so doing, she supports a political revolution by championing a social revolution, directing attention to the importance of both space and mobility for women's equality. Second, the chapter sheds light on a little examined aspect of Willard's rhetorical prowess: the novel way in which she employs a quaint memoir to change social attitudes and beliefs as a prelude to changing political attitudes and beliefs. While her effectiveness as a political rhetor has been acknowledged—for instance, famed Unitarian minister Edward Everett Hale claimed that he awaited Willard's WCTU's president's address with more anticipation than the president's state of the union[18]—less attention has been paid to the political ramifications of the book frequently described as a self-help manual.[19] That omission is redressed here. Finally, in emphasizing the epideictic function of the memoir, this chapter forwards recent efforts in rhetorical studies to recuperate epideictic rhetoric from its status as "meaningless display" serving only to reify not change the status quo.[20] Traditionally defined as ceremonial speeches of praise or blame, epideictic rhetoric represents the fusion of aesthetic and rhetorical elements as well as the fusion of praise and persuasion. Willard's memoir aligns with this speech type, proposing and arguing for a new set of beliefs about women's spatial agency, beliefs that then become the premises for future action. Therefore, analyzing Willard's memoir for its persuasive strategies complements disciplinary efforts to re-theorize epideictic rhetoric as integral to public and political discourse. In view of those aims, I begin with an examination of the memoir genre as a matrix for epideictic rhetoric, establishing *A Wheel within a Wheel* as a "vehicle through which communities can imagine and bring about change."[21] Next, I turn to the ways Willard celebrates women's expanded spatial agency, a process that brings together images of the real and the imaginary, thereby enabling the audience to envision different realities.[22]

MEMOIR AS A VEHICLE FOR EPIDEICTIC

Unlike her political speeches and articles that overtly endorse specific reform issues and actions, Willard's memoir implicitly endorses a far more subtle argument in favor of *a* woman's movement as a synecdoche for *all* women's movement thus furthering *the* woman's movement. "A reform," Willard writes, "often advances most rapidly by indirection,"[23] and her memoir of her experiences learning to ride the safety bicycle provides evidence of her effective use of indirection as a tool of persuasion. During a moment when the woman's suffrage was suffering from decreasing membership and waning influence, Willard's epideictic memoir invites a transformation of socially conservative attitudes and beliefs about white, middle-class women's spatial mobility. "Let us live the life of action, which is the only true and happy life," Willard commands.[24] Because "God is ACTION," she claims, "let us be like God," implicitly asserting a role for women dependent on an expanded spatial agency.[25] Thus, as its title suggests, *A Wheel within a Wheel* functions rhetorically as a wheel within a wheel: an epideictic argument about spatial agency spinning within the circle of an entertaining narrative of Willard's personal struggles to break Gladys, her steed of steel, to the bit.

Willard's rhetorical goal—articulating and redefining women's circumscribed spatial agency—is particularly congruent with epideictic rhetoric in that it focuses on a pattern of existence rather than a particular action. Traditionally denigrated as the least important of Aristotle's three categories of oratory, epideictic rhetoric consists of speeches that praise or blame "existing qualities"[26] with the aim of reinforcing the "honorable or disgraceful."[27] A category of ceremonial speeches designed for specific occasions, such as funerals, epideictic has been historically subordinated to the deliberative discourse of the assembly and the forensic discourse of the courts, scorned for its lack of political significance or direct impact on the *polis*.[28] It existed by virtue of its artistic merits rather than its pragmatic worth, valued for its aesthetic display rather than its response to an exigent circumstance within a community requiring action on the part of its membership. However, Jeffrey Walker contends that this disparaged discourse genre actually constitutes the framework from which all persuasive discourse arises, emphasizing epideictic's—and rhetoric's—roots in poetry, and oral culture's first public speech.[29] Drawing from sophistic traditions, Walker recuperates epideictic rhetoric, arguing that it not only celebrates communal virtues, but it also "calls its audience to acts of judgment and response."[30] Epideictic, he claims, invites the audience to witness, contemplate what they witness, and transform their beliefs on the basis of both witnessing and contemplation.[31] More importantly, while epideictic is not a response to a specific urgent matter within the culture or community, it is a response to "'permanent' or chronic issues in a society's pattern of existence."[32] By giving voice to this pattern, which may only exist as tacit, rather than explicit, knowledge, epideictic seeks to redefine the "entirety of the pattern itself."[33] Such is Willard's agenda—changing the pattern of women's spatial agency—and the vehicle for her epideictic performance is the memoir itself. Two elements common to both epideictic and memoir—constructing a virtuous *ethos* and oscillating between public and private—function in tandem to ensure that *A Wheel within a Wheel* exists as something more than a pleasant way with which to while away an hour.[34]

The first element of memoir germane to epideictic rhetoric consists of a mutual emphasis *ethos*, exemplified by Willard's own considerable political and cultural cachet and her evocation of that cachet in the memoir's text. *Ethos* is the epicenter for both memoir and epideictic. Defined by Aristotle as persuasion through good character, *ethos* consists of speech "spoken in such a way as to make the speaker worthy of credence,"[35] a crucial element in any rhetorical situation because an audience finds it easier to believe "fair-minded people" than it does those who are not.[36] A similar logic operates in memoir, where the character the memoirist creates via the text is fundamental to the memoir's success. Without using the term *ethos*, Ben Yagoda in *Memoir: A History* traces the genre's preoccupation with a textual persona, one who strips bares internal and external turmoil for the reader's gaze. Dating from Augustine in the fourth century CE, whom Yagoda identifies as the first memoirist in the West, memoirs chronicle an individual's inner transformation, serving as a map of that individual's character. A similar privileging of *ethos* is evident in epideictic.[37] While *ethos* is a crucial invention strategy for both deliberative and forensic rhetorics, it is particularly pertinent to epideictic. Like memoir, a considerable component of epideictic's effectiveness ensues from what Dale L. Sullivan calls the authority of the rhetor's "positive image."[38] Epideictic's goal, Sullivan claims, is to define and foster adherence to communal values, and the rhetor's construction of a good character is essential to this endeavor. If audience members do not embrace the goodness—the high merit (or the struggle to be meritorious)—of the rhetor, they will be less inclined to embrace the goodness endorsed by that rhetor. Sullivan points out that the construction of epideictic *ethos* is critical to creating the "sense of communion" necessary to persuade the audience to emulate the virtues celebrated by the rhetor.[39]

A Wheel within a Wheel illustrates the centrality of *ethos* in the memoir-epideictic interface, for Willard's credibility as its author—both inside and outside of the text—is integral to her efforts to persuade readers to espouse an expanded spatial agency for women.[40] Prohibitionist and suffragist, Willard brings to her memoir considerable national renown, a reputation for high virtue that existed external to the memoir's text. By the end of the nineteenth century, she was perceived as "the embodiment of 'character,'"[41] an indispensable element in creating an epideictic *ethos*. In 1893, almost fifteen years after assuming leadership of the national WTCU, Willard was America's, if not the Western world's, leading female political figure, described in one eulogy as "the woman of the century, the woman of Christendom."[42] Over her fifty-three years prior to mastering the bicycle, Willard had mastered a variety of professional and leadership positions, facts well known to the American public. Following stints as elementary, high school, and college teacher and principal, she served as the president of Evanston College for Ladies, and then as Dean of Women, as well as professor of rhetoric and aesthetics, when the college merged with Northwestern University. After leaving the higher education, Willard served in local, state, and national chapters of the WCTU until she was elected president of the national organization, a position that she held throughout the next nineteen years. In this role, she crisscrossed the nation speaking and writing prolifically in support not only of temperance but also various linked reforms, including suffrage, public kindergartens, child labor, and wage parity.[43] Under her leadership, the WCTU grew from 27,000 to over 200,000 members, becoming the first mass mobilization of women in the world.[44] By the end of her life, one eulogist lauded her "purity of character, the self-sacrificing devotion of her life, and the splendor of her achievements" even while censuring her positions on suffrage and prohibition.[45] Furthermore, Willard subtly invokes within the memoir itself her reputation as the "personification of a principle."[46]

In an effort to render women's spatial agency praiseworthy to her audience, Willard constructs a persuasive *ethos* within the text by gently gesturing to her own status as a woman of sterling character.[47] More specifically, Willard works to position herself and the controversial spatial agency she supports under the aegis of two culturally validated identities: the loving daughter and loving mother/world leader. Willard tethers her discursive *ethos* to womanly roles embraced by the culture at large to present herself as virtuous and thus, by association, to present the spatial agency she advocates as virtuous. She underscores her identity as loving daughter within the opening pages of her memoir. Willard explains that it is the emotional distress of her mother's death, in conjunction with a mental and physical life "out of balance," that motivates her to "learn the bicycle."[48] Willard describes herself as blessed by her mother's companionship, endowed with the gift of a parent who understood Willard's need to have her "own sweet will" as a child and run wild during her youth.[49] In response, Willard adorates Mary Willard, an adoration that reaches its fullest expression in an effusive tribute, *A Great Mother*, published the year after Willard learned to ride the bicycle.[50] That filial devotion surfaces at different intervals throughout the memoir attesting to Willard's continued reliance on the absent mother, one who supports and sanctions her spatial adventures. At one point, as Willard struggles to balance herself on Gladys, she conjures up the image of her mother. She defeats her wobbling will and the cycle's wobbling wheel by picturing her mother above her steadily holding a pair of balances, verbally assuring her that "of course you'll do it; what else should you do?"[51] Willard explains that this mental apparition was "palpably helpful in enabling me to 'sit straight and hold my own' on my uncertain steed."[52] The loving daughter thus solicits her departed mother's aid in acquiring her expanded spatial agency, acquiring at the same time the mother's authorization for that agency.

Congruent with Willard's depiction of herself as a doting daughter, whose efforts with her nickel-plated steed are anointed by an equally doting parent, is Willard's depiction of herself as a devoted world leader who shapes herself and her organization according to "organized mother love."[53] Willard notes in "The Dawn of Woman's Day" that "mother-love works magic for humanity, but organized mother-love works miracles. Mother-hearted women are called to be the saviors of the race,"[54] and she constructs an *ethos* in the text of her memoir that resonates with this mother-hearted love. For instance, although grief and nerve-wear propel her to master Gladys, her primary reason for writing about her struggles grows out of a desire to help women, to promote their well-being just as her own mother promoted hers. She emphasizes the bicycle would improve "physical development of humanity's mother-half,"[55] forward dress reform,[56] and foster gender equality.[57] Thus, grappling with Gladys, risking physical injury through falls, and jeopardizing her social stature by undertaking a pursuit not universally accepted for women are all undertaken because of her devotion to the betterment of women. Such devotion encompasses the betterment of the home as well. As Willard points out in her final pages, the increased spatial agency represented by cycling will multiply the chances of a happy home; "for the more interests women and men can have in common," she argues, and thus, by implication, the more spatial mobility they share, the more harmony in the home.[58] Her three months of physical travail therefore reflects her loving leadership of women and her loving commitment to the needs of a successful home. Willard secures her audience's adherence to her expanded spatial agency by securing their adherence to her identity as loving daughter and leader. Thus, Willard's epideictic goal of reshaping spatial agency as virtuous—"the basic code of value and belief by which a society lives"[59]—is furthered by her construction of this virtuous character.

The second key element that renders the memoir a pliant vehicle for epideictic is its poetic roots, the same matrix from which epideictic issues. Walker argues that epideictic evolves from ancient poetry, especially lyric poetry, an origin story that places epideictic on the cusp between pragmatic discourse (rhetorical prose) and poetry. Memoir is similarly situated between creative writing and non-fiction; it evolved in the West as a form of creative non-fiction designed to recount and reflect on a specific set of events or experiences in one's (or even another's) life, inviting a similar reflection from the reader.[60] It inhabits that anomalous realm between the facts of one's life and the truths of one's life, between the reality of one's life and the memory of one's life. Like epideictic, it operates with one foot in poetry and one foot in prose. In addition, Margery O'Rourke Boyle underscores explicitly the connection between memoir and rhetoric, arguing that all autobiographical genres in general function as epideictic rhetoric, using as her illustration Augustine's *Confessions*.[61] Augustine illuminates not only the me-

moir as epideictic, but also the historical intertwining of memoir with rhetoric. For even as the Bishop of Hippo Regius initiates the memoir as a saga of
spiritual struggle, he simultaneously works to rescue classical rhetoric from
the stigma of paganism, reclaiming its considerable power for the service of
God and Church. Out of the wealth of aesthetic elements shared by memoir
and epideictic, particularly salient to the *A Wheel within a Wheel*, is the
oscillation between the public and private.

   Both memoir and epideictic dance between private and public domains.
While memoir resurrects private moments for public reflection, epideictic
evokes virtuous individuals and deeds for public commemoration. The nest-
ing of the private within the public provides an effective vehicle for Willard's epideictic argument about spatial agency. The emotional intimacy afforded by scripting the private for the public "epitomizes Willard's way of
participating in public life" and in her mobilization of women as social
activists.[62] Willard achieves her political success by framing women's public
work as an extension of their private work, an integration exemplified by
WCTU's rallying cry of "Home Protection," which justifies (and motivates)
women's social activism on the grounds of increasing the private well-being
of women and children through public, or political, means.[63] Work in the
public sector essentially constitutes work for the private sector. Furthermore,
Willard shaped WCTU's conventions themselves as a blend of public forum
and private home. One tribute following Willard's death claimed that "all of
our meetings, including our great conventions when women came together
from the ends of the earth have always been homelike," a reflection of
Willard's devotion to home, even in the public sphere, for her life, including
her political life, "was preeminently for the home."[64] That oscillation inevitably marked the text of her memoir as well. She makes her grief public, her
illness public, her failures and successes public. She shares details of emotional and physical struggle, flaws and virtues, selecting elements of her
private life for public consumption. In one telling anecdote, Willard points to
an incident with a tricycle in which, without proper training, she races around
the garden of Rest Cottage, her home in Wisconsin, in a friendly effort to
beat the time achieved by her personal secretary and niece. However, by
taking a turn too sharply, she crashes and breaks her arm. Ruefully, Willard
points to both her pride and her competitive spirit, using that honesty to
forward her agenda for spatial agency thoughtfully enacted. The private becomes the public in an effort to position spatial agency as a public outgrowth
of private mobility. Given this concatenation of elements linking memoir to
epideictic, *A Wheel within a Wheel* constitutes more than a self-indulgent
narrative designed for readers to while away a pleasant hour admiring Willard's pluckiness. Instead, it exists as a performance of epideictic rhetoric
conveyed through the vehicle of the memoir and serving political goals.

A MODEST REVOLUTION: TURNING THE WHEEL ON SPATIAL AGENCY

A Wheel within a Wheel responds to a pattern in women's spatial agency to transform that pattern and effect a modest revolution. This goal has direct political implications, for without spatial agency women would be discouraged from participating in the very reforms that call them from the confines of their parlor. Willard uses her memoir epideictically to advocate an expanded spatial agency for women as a tool for political agency, and she does this by calling her readers to witness, contemplate, and then transform their beliefs about women's mobility in public venues. By combining the qualities of a memoir with those of epideictic, Willard first enacts a "showing-forth," which subsequently invites contemplation and ultimately shapes "opinions and desires on matters of philosophical, social, ethical, and cultural concern."[65] Thus, *A Wheel within a Wheel* grapples covertly with efforts to limit women's mobility by overtly showing forth new avenues for and performances of mobility. In so doing, it invites a contemplation of that mobility and the possibility of re-shaping opinions about and desires for a new spatial pattern of existence that embraces political activism. Willard accomplishes this end through three nonlinear moves: she relies on amplification to enact new spatial agency, she solicits reflection through an extended metaphor, and she regenders space and mobility to transform spatial agency.

The first move in Willard's epideictic rhetoric is a showing-forth, or calling the readers to witness a new pattern of existence. Integral to this goal is amplification, which in classical rhetoric "signified intensification, raising the emotional or ethical level of discourse."[66] Aristotle assigns amplification to epideictic as a primary mechanism of persuasion;[67] he notes that epideictic uses many forms of amplification, such as adding details from an individual's deeds or background to illustrate the exercise of a particular virtue or extending a concept beyond its original mention to add depth and complexity to a virtue.[68] Without necessarily calling her techniques amplification, Willard intensifies her argument in two ways: by narrating vivid details about her cycling experience and expounding on the virtues of cycling for all people, especially women. Willard devises no more persuasive mode of amplification than that of calling her readers to witness her own successful efforts to learn the bicycle. Despite age and illness, Willard reschools her body to enact the mobility she desires for all women, thus using her body as a site of persuasion. To begin, she narrates how she literally retrained her body to grasp the spatial agency afforded by "this new implement of power."[69] Essaying Gladys endowed Willard with "new intelligence in the muscles"[70] as she learned through endless repetition "how to sit, how to pedal, how to turn, how to dismount."[71] Even more draconian, Willard humorously recounts relearning how to see: "Do not look down like an imbecile upon the steering wheel in front of you. . . . Look up and off and on and out; get forehead and foot into line."[72] By providing such vivid imagery of the physiological changes Gladys required of her, Willard invites her readers to identify with her and experience vicariously their own physiological transition into a new spatial agency. Via an array of concrete details, she makes visible a new way of being in the world for women, thereby underscoring its veracity. In addition, Willard links the rewards of her new intelligent muscles with specific spatial rewards. Two months into her experiences, Willard rejoices in the moment when she could pedal with "judicious accuracy" to enjoy the "swift motion round a bend, ascend Priory Rise, avoid the hedge on one side as well as the iron fence on the other."[73] She celebrates her "consoling degree of mastery over Gladys" in terms of the spaces she can now navigate with grace and speed, inextricably weaving pleasure in riding with pleasure in the new environs she enters.[74] Thus, as the audience witnesses Willard's learning experience, they witness both its embodiment and its rewards, sharing Willard's joy in the gains accrued from a new pattern of existence. Finally, Willard explicitly poses her spatial agency as an adventure open to all women: "Nor could I see a reason in the world why a woman should not ride the silent steed so swift and blithesome."[75] Her response to an English naval officer who pities women because they "have no idea of the new realm of happiness which the bicycle has opened to us men" is for all women to enter into that new realm.[76] Her amplification of the details of her own entry into that realm trail blazes the way for them.

Amplification also operates in *A Wheel within a Wheel* through extension—the process of elaborating on cycling as a concept, not merely an experience. Such extension responds to the entrenched cultural resistance to women cycling that dissuaded women from embracing the new mobility, just as that resistance dissuaded women from directly influencing political change. Despite the "tens of thousands" who had discovered the joy of swift motion via cycling,[77] conservative social forces continued to disapprove of women cyclers using medical and moral arguments. Willard counters this antagonism by gesturing to established practices, citing medical support, and acknowledging emerging patterns of women's mobility. Willard's first extension aims to accrete virtue to spatial agency by connecting cycling to its popularity among both the masses and the social elites. Willard begins with a concession, admitting that she had not been tempted to master the bicycle when Bertha von Hillern first gave cycling demonstrations in America on the dangerous two-wheeled ordinary with its enormous front wheel and small stabilizing rear wheel. Then a woman riding was perceived as "a sort of semi-monster," and Willard confesses that she would "certainly have felt compromised, at that remote and benighted period."[78] But now, with the advent of, first, the tricycle and then, in 1886, the safety bicycle, women no longer risked such acute social condemnation for cycling. In addition, she points out, cycling has received the imprimatur of royal patronage: both British princesses, Louise and Beatrice, "ride the tricycle at Balmoral,"[79] a state of affairs that Willard herself, as well as "the great mass of feminine humanity," finds socially validating.[80] Furthermore, Willard argues in a neat logical turn that "where the tricycle prophesies the bicycle shall ere long preach the gospel of the outdoors,"[81] justifying her own forays on Gladys by anchoring it to the royal patronage of the tricycle. She reinforces this position by pointing to the French aristocracy among whom riding the safety bicycle, not the tricycle, is the "current craze."[82] Thus, Willard amplifies the virtue of bicycling by noting its popularity and aligning it with royal acclaim and aristocratic uptake; she evokes her own patron in a similar spirit, for Isabel, Lady Henry Somerset—daughter to an earl and daughter-in-law to a duke— not only purchases Gladys for Willard but also supports Willard's political agenda. Her readers, then, witness not only Willard, but, by extension, many women of high station enjoying the pleasure of the wheel and of politics. Furthermore, Willard intensifies witnessing by incorporating medical experts who proclaim the benefits of cycling for women. In the face of such dire prophesies as poor posture, heated blood, asymmetrical development, and depleted energies,[83] all designed to render the bicycle taboo for women, Willard garners an array of medical experts attesting to mental and physical benefits of women riding the steed of steel. Cycling lifts the rider, including the female rider, out of the "thoughts and cares of daily work;" it develops "his will, his attention, his courage and independence" at the same time that it distributes physical development over the whole body.[84] Admittedly, the woman cyclist will only accrue these benefits if she will "use judgment and not overtax herself."[85] If she is judicious in her practices, the bicycle will be a boon to mental and physical health. Finally, Willard amplifies spatial agency by providing evidence of radical changes in women's mobility through her allusions to Nellie Bly and Elizabeth Bisland,[86] two American women journalists who, in 1890, raced around the world alone in fewer than eighty days. Willard points out that, while a trip around the world a mere quarter decade ago would have been considered scandalous for a woman, now "young women of the highest character and talent are employed by leading journals to whip around the world."[87] By referring to these two women, who were universally lauded for their spatial agency and, in the case of Bly, her reform efforts, Willard establishes ongoing changes in the pattern of women's mobility, a pattern the bicycle merely replicates. Bly and Bisland join Willard as exemplars of women who have already embraced a new spatial agency, finding it virtuous and worthy of emulation.

Through the combination of concrete details and conceptual extensions, amplification functions to make spatial agency both vividly real and praiseworthy. Willard's next goal is to draw her readers from witnessing that reality to contemplating its new pattern of existence as a prelude to judgment and transformation. As Walker explains, epideictic's audience is to be a "*theoros*, that is, one who is to make 'observations' (*theoriai*) about what is praiseworthy."[88] The observations then lead the audience to thoughtful consideration, the important process whereby they shape new ideologies and imageries.[89] To move her readers from observing her display of personal spatial agency to reflecting on that display, Willard makes use of an extended metaphor linking cycling and life, noting that "as I have said, in many curious particulars the bicycle is like the world."[90] She uses the "imageries" of that metaphor to shape a new philosophy of life as an object of reflection for her readers. The first component of her extended metaphor shifts the stakes of the memoir from an amusing tale of a plucky heroine to a disquisition on an ideology: "Indeed," Willard claims, "I found a whole philosophy of life in the wooing and winning of my bicycle,"[91] and she offers various components of that ideology for her audience's consideration. To begin, the philosophy of the wheel illuminates the necessity of balance in riding, in spatial agency, in life, and, by extension, in reform efforts. The sense of balance, so hard to achieve and maintain in cycling, is the key criterion to a fruitful life and to virtuous mobility, Willard claims, for cycling relies on "a part of that equilibration of thought and action by which we conquer the universe in conquering ourselves."[92] To ride a wheel, one must match thought and action; too much of either one or the other endangers stability, resulting in painful tumbles in cycling, life, and reform efforts. So in pursuit of reform or any goal in life, a woman must balance the need for mobility in new spaces with a careful examination of goals that mobility affords as well as of the means of enacting that mobility. Spatial agency—action—without thought is as dangerous as thought without spatial agency. Achieving that balance requires the second and third elements of her belief system: self-knowledge and self-mastery.

The philosophy of the wheel that Willard learns through her intimate association with Gladys includes the ability to assess her own character and exercise self-discipline on the basis of this assessment, for in these linked qualities one finds social and political triumph or catastrophe. Self-knowledge comes before self-mastery, for without knowledge one cannot determine where discipline is needed. Thus, grappling with the challenges presented by Gladys required Willard to audit her own character, both the good and the bad, an audit she thus implicitly invites her audience to imitate. So she tidily accounts for the strengths she brings to cycling, to life, and to reform efforts—her hardy spirit, her persistence, and her patient tenacity,[93] all qualities that secured her success in politics as well as with the wheel. Willard observes, "That which made me succeed with the bicycle was precisely what had gained me a measure of success in life."[94] But her tally of characteristics also includes her less admirable traits for "that which caused the many failures I had in learning the bicycle had caused me failures in life;

namely, a certain looking for of judgment; a too vivid realization of the uncertainty of everything about me; an underlying doubt."[95] The balance sheet of her human qualities invites readers to contemplate the way such qualities intersect with the decisions one makes in life, especially in terms of one's mobility. Like cycling, spatial agency too is learned, and it too relies on the compendium of character traits a woman brings with her to any instance of movement, to any opportunity to enter spaces from which she is traditionally barred. Decisions about when, where, and how to move in public spaces to achieve a particular end must be weighed against a woman's knowledge of her own character strengths and weaknesses. Without such consideration, one risks painful social and political failures.

Finally, the last component of Willard's new ideology concerns self-mastery: "She who succeeds in gaining the mastery of such an animal as Gladys will gain the mastery of life, and by exactly the same methods and characteristics."[96] Once one has a tally sheet of characteristics—the requisite self-knowledge—one must also possess sufficient self-discipline to curb the less admirable traits and to spur on the more admirable traits. To illustrate, if Willard had not mastered her fear of adverse judgment, her fear of failure, and her doubt in her own abilities to succeed, she would never have undertaken the challenge presented by Gladys. Similarly, if she had not mastered these fears, she would never have expanded her own spatial agency as a public speaker or as leader of the largest organization of women in the world: "Just so, I felt, it had been all my life and will be doubtless, in all worlds and with us all. The totality of native forces and acquired discipline and expert knowledge stands us in good stead for each crisis that we have to meet."[97] Self-mastery facilitated by self-knowledge provides the basis for balancing thought and action, for determining what constitutes that balance on the seat of a bicycle or on the dais of a public forum. Through her extended metaphor of "cycling is life," Willard presents a new ideology, a philosophy of spatial agency in life and politics for her audience's contemplation, concluding that, perhaps, the value of the bicycle itself is in the new philosophy it inspires: "And so I found high moral uses in the bicycle and can commend it as a teacher without pulpit or creed."[98] The cumulative weight—the final accounting of that philosophy   results in not only a new spatial agency, but a new political identity: "I began to feel that myself plus the bicycle equaled myself plus the world, upon whose spinning-wheel we must all learn to ride, or fall into the sluiceways of oblivion and despair."[99]

By inviting her readers, first, to witness her enactment of spatial agency, and, second, to think deeply about what they witnessed, Willard sets the stage for the final move in her epideictic rhetoric: transforming the spatial conventions restricting women's lives and their political participation. Walker notes that the realm of epideictic is the realm of values and codes by which a culture organizes itself. Operating between the binaries of conservation and

revolution, epideictic possesses the power to "challenge or transform conventional beliefs"[100] as well as the power to reinforce those beliefs. Willard
seeks transformation, and she attempts to effect this transformation by overtly and covertly regendering space. Perhaps the most explicit expression of
this regendering is Willard's claim that the bicycle supports women's equality: "We rejoiced greatly in perceiving the impetus that this uncompromising
but fascinating and illimitably capable machine would give to that blessed
'woman question' to which we were both devoted."[101] That impetus is far
ranging. First, Willard argues that the act of cycling itself erodes the male
sense of innate superiority: "the comradeship of women who are as skilled
and ingenious in the manipulation of the swift steed as they themselves"[102]
will inevitably cause men to question long held assumptions about the traditional gender hierarchy. In addition, that comradeship regenders the space of
public byways: there is "great advantage in good fellowship and mutual
understanding between men and women who take the road together," she
notes.[103] As a result of this good fellowship and mutual understanding, public spaces are no longer marked as a male domain but as one shared by men
and women who are both equally proficient on this marvelous new machine.
Eventually, Willard claims, that change in spatial equality in public will
result in a change in spatial equality in private, enhancing mobility between
the public and private. When girls demonstrate facility on the wheel, she
foretells, young men will brag about being "that girl's brother" rather than
girls deriving pride from being "that boy's sister."[104] Thus, women's mobility will be something men celebrate rather than something they condemn.
Mobility itself is regendered. Finally, as women become more equal to men
within public spaces, men themselves will undergo a transformation: "We
contend that whatever diminishes the sense of superiority in men makes them
more manly, brotherly, and pleasant to have about."[105] Spatial agency, then,
is certainly a desirable change in the pattern of the culture's existence.

Regendering also operates covertly from a subtle shift in pronouns to the
dress reform, both of which emphasize a transformation in male-marked
spaces. Perhaps one of slyest and most delightful instances of regendering
occurs in Willard's celebration of self-mastery as integral to success on the
wheel and in life. With the remarkable change of a masculine pronoun—the
universal "he" with the implied referent of "all people"—to a feminine pronoun, Willard feminizes mastery of the wheel, the space one enters via the
wheel, even life itself. She writes: "*he* who succeeds, or, to be more exact in
handing over my experiences, *she* [emphasis added] who succeeds"[106] will
master life in the process of mastering the wheel. By changing pronouns,
which occurs nowhere else in the book, Willard stealthily transforms agency,
including spatial agency, regendering both as a female as well as a male
prerogative. That covert transformation is supported by a second equally
subtle argument: dress reform. The spatial agency afforded by the bicycle

reaches far beyond the regendering of public parks and public thoroughfares, of country lanes and city streets, important as that regendering might be. It encompasses as well the far more wholesale spatial transformation emblemized by dress reform. Spatial agency proceeds from the skin out; to regender space, one must regender the clothing that restricts a woman from enacting spatial mobility. A bicycle costume is a prerequisite, Willard asserts.[107] A woman with bands on her hips, with a dress snug around the waist and choking the throat, with heavily trimmed skirts dragging her down, "heating the lower part of the spine," and with agonizingly tight shoes epitomizes the spatial limitations of her existence, one that prevents her from enacting spatial agency.[108] Willard vividly describes this incarceration only to cleverly regender the inequality. "She ought to be as miserable as a stalwart man would be in the same plight,"[109] she says, implicitly suggesting that apparel appropriate for a woman's mobility will resemble the apparel the "stalwart male" sees as appropriate to his own mobility. Transformation, then, in patterns of women's spatial agency begins with and proceeds from a regendering of the most quotidian component of their confinement: their clothing.

RIDING THE REVOLUTION

Through the construction of a virtuous *ethos*, through the oscillation between public and private spaces, through the invitation to witness, contemplate, and transform, Willard in *A Wheel within a Wheel* crafts an epideictic performance that invites a reformation in her culture's patterns of existence. As a combination of belief and desire, Willard's memoir underscores the reciprocity between the political and the spatial in the nineteenth century at the same time that it illustrates Willard's own subtle use of rhetoric. In addition, *A Wheel within a Wheel* highlights the memoir as a form of epideictic, one that reconfigures and then celebrates the new feminist virtue of spatial agency as an essential foundation of women's political activism. By means of her epideictic memories, Willard creates not only a new space for women but also a new woman, and a new man, for that space. Perhaps her goal is best exemplified not by her words but by the last photographic image of the book, positioned just a few short pages from Willard's final lines instructing her readers to "*go thou and do likewise.*"[110] In that black-and-white halftone, Willard rides her bicycle into the photographer's lens, pedaling gracefully down the middle of a pebbled lane with fall foliage surrounding her. In the distance, on the side of the road, one foot on the lane itself, one foot on the grassy verge, stands a motionless man, who, with arms dangling at his side, watches Willard wheel away from him, out of the frame into the viewer's world. Indeed, go thou and do likewise.

NOTES

1. Frances Elizabeth Willard, *A Wheel within a Wheel. How I Learned to Ride the Bicycle with Some Reflections by the Way* (New York: Fleming H. Revell Co., 1895), 19.

2. "Topics of the Time," *The Century,* July 1895, 474. moa.library.cornell.edu/.

3. Willard, *Wheel*, 11.

4. Ibid., 38.

5. Ibid., 75.

6. Ibid., 10.

7. Carolyn De Swarte Gifford and Amy R. Slagell, eds., *Let Something Good Be Said: Speeches and Writings of Frances E. Willard* (Urbana, IL: University of Illinois Press, 2007), 207.

8. "Fine Figures," *The McCook Tribune*, September 12, 1898, 1. chroniclingamerica.loc.gov/.

9. Marian D. Tomlinson, "Frances E. Willard Centenary," *ALA Bulletin* 33 (1939): 518. www.jstor.org/.

10. "The National Vehicle," *The Courier*, July 20, 1895, no page. chroniclingamerica.loc.gov/.

11. "Fashion, Fact, and Fancy," *Godey's Magazine*, April 1896, 435. www.proquest.com/.

12. Despite the tepid response of these reviews, the memoir "was a best seller and probably encouraged many a sedentary woman to take up the cycle." Ruth Bordin, *Frances Willard: A Biography* (Chapel Hill, NC: University of North Carolina Press, 1986), 208.

13. Grover Cleveland, "Woman's Mission and Woman's Clubs," *Ladies Home Journal* 22 (1905): 3. www.proquest.com/.

14. "Nation's Uncrowned Queen. Eloquent Tribute to Memory of Frances E. Willard," *Kansas City Journal*, March 21, 1898, 6. chroniclingamerica.loc.gov/.

15. Willard, *Wheel*, 73.

16. "Fine Figures," 1.

17. Willard, *Wheel*, 14.

18. Gifford and Slagell, *Let Something*, xxiii, xli.

19. Ibid., 208.

20. Michael F. Carter, "The Ritual Functions of Epideictic Rhetoric: The Case of Socrates' Funeral Oration," *Rhetorica* 9 (1991): 211. www.jstor.org/.

21. Cynthia Miecznikowski Sheard, "The Public Value of Epideictic Rhetoric," *College English* 58 (1996): 771. www.jstor.org/.

22. Ibid., 770.

23. Willard, *Wheel*, 39.

24. Frances E. Willard, *What Frances E. Willard Said*, ed. Anna A. Gordon (Chicago: Fleming H. Revell Co., 1905), 7.

25. Ibid.

26. Aristotle, *On Rhetoric: A Theory of Civic Discourse*, trans. George A. Kennedy (New York: Oxford University Press, 1991), 1.3.4.

27. Ibid., 1.3.5.

28. See Jeffrey Walker, *Rhetoric and Poetics in Antiquity* (Oxford, UK: Oxford University Press, 2000), vii.

29. Jeffrey Walker, "Aristotle's Lyric: Re-Imagining the Rhetoric of Epideictic Song," *College English* 51 (1989), 9. http:/www.jstor.org/.

30. Walker, *Rhetoric*, viii.

31. Walker, "Aristotle's Lyric," 8.

32. Ibid.

33. Ibid.

34. "The National Vehicle," no page.

35. Aristotle, *Rhetoric*, 1.2.4.

36. Ibid.

37. Ben Yagoda, *Memoir: A History* (New York: Riverhead Books, 2009), 15.

38. Dale L. Sullivan, "The Ethos of Epideictic Encounter," *Philosophy and Rhetoric* 26 (1993):118. www.jstor.org/.

39. Ibid.

40. Although Aristotle claims that *ethos* is a creation of the speech itself (1.2.4), Sullivan, following Isocrates, notes the importance of the rhetor's reputation within the community at large (118).

41. Gifford and Slagell, *Let Something*, ix.

42. "In Memory of Miss Willard," *Kansas City Journal*, February 25, 1898, no page. chron iclingamerica.loc/gov/.

43. Bordin, *Frances*, 131.

44. Suzanne M. Marilley, "Frances Willard and the Feminism of Fear," *Feminist Studies* 19 (1993): 123. www.jstor.org/.

45. "Frances E. Willard and Her Work: The Outlook," *Current Literature*, April 1898, 317. www.proquest.com/.

46. "Miss Willard," *The Times*, February 19, 1898, 4. chroniclingamerica.loc.gov/.

47. Excluded from this analysis are the six photographic halftones and one engraving illustrating the memoir.

48. Willard, *Wheel*, 11.

49. Ibid., 10.

50. Bordin, *Frances*, 213.

51. Willard, *Wheel*, 51.

52. Ibid.

53. Mary Aline Brown, "Organized Mother Love," *Arthur's Home Magazine*, April 1897, 244. www.proquest.com/.

54. Frances E. Willard, "The Dawn of Woman's Day," in *Let Something Good Be Said: Speeches and Writings of Frances E. Willard*, ed. Carolyn De Swarte Gifford and Amy R. Slagell (Urbana, IL: University of Illinois Press, 2007), 127.

55. Willard, *Wheel*, 38.

56. Ibid., 39.

57. Ibid., 41.

58. Ibid., 73.

59. Walker, *Rhetoric*, 9.

60. See Yagoda, *Memoir*, 31.

61. Margery O'Rourke Boyle, "A Likely Story: The Autobiographical as Epideictic," *Journal of the American Academy of Religion* 57 (1998): 24. www.jstor.org/.

62. Gifford and Slagell, *Let Something*, ix.

63. Bordin, *Frances*, 100.

64. "Temperance Topics," *Natchitoches Populist*, June 10, 1898, no page. chroniclingamer ica.loc.gov/.

65. Walker, *Rhetoric*, 9.

66. Brian Vickers, *In Defense of Rhetoric* (Oxford, UK: Clarendon Press, 1988), 242.

67. Aristotle, *Rhetoric*, 1.9.4.

68. Ibid., 1.9.38.

69. Willard, *Wheel*, 73.

70. Ibid., 23.

71. Ibid., 22.

72. Ibid., 17.

73. Ibid., 50.

74. Ibid., 52.

75. Ibid., 13.

76. Ibid., 11.

77. Ibid.

78. Ibid., 13.

79. Ibid., 14.

80. Ibid.

81. Ibid.

82. Ibid., 16.
83. Robert A. Smith, *A Social History of the Bicycle: Its Early Life and Times in America* (New York: American Heritage Press, 1972), 68–69.
84. Ibid., 56.
85. Ibid., 54.
86. Ibid., 15.
87. Ibid.
88. Walker, *Rhetoric*, 9.
89. Ibid.
90. Willard, *Wheel*, 23.
91. Ibid., 25.
92. Ibid., 26.
93. Ibid., 28.
94. Ibid.
95. Ibid., 22.
96. Ibid., 28.
97. Ibid., 47.
98. Ibid., 28.
99. Ibid.
100. Walker, *Rhetoric*, 7.
101. Willard, *Wheel*, 38.
102. Ibid., 40.
103. Ibid.
104. Ibid., 41.
105. Ibid.
106. Ibid., 28.
107. Ibid., 74.
108. Ibid., 39.
109. Ibid., 40.
110. Ibid., 75.

Chapter Two

"Shall America Retain the Faith of Our Fathers?"

Aimee Semple McPherson and the California Gubernatorial Campaign of 1934

William Carney

In many ways, the California Governor's race of 1934 ushered in many aspects of the modern political campaign. Both major parties featured primary campaigns with several candidates, even though the Republican incumbent was running for election. Mass media in the form of radio advertisements featured "attack ads" and appearances by celebrities and "surrogates" designed to create interest in the candidates, themselves. There was national media attention on the race and a Democratic President who struggled with the decision about whether or not to endorse his party's candidate in an important election in a populous state. In the middle of all this stood Aimee Semple McPherson, founder of both the first "mega-church," the Angelus Temple, and of a denomination, the Church of the Foursquare Gospel, and, arguably, the most popular (and controversial) evangelist in America. A female evangelist who paved the way for later successful ministries such as those of Kathryn Kuhlman and Joyce Meyer, she preached a gospel that mixed patriotism, popular culture, and scripture. In 1934, she would influence the outcome of the race for Governor in California.

In 1934, at the height of the Great Depression in California, Lt. Governor Frank Merriam ascended to the Governor's office following the death of Governor James Rolph. Rolph's sudden death from heart failure placed Merriam, a Republican, in the state's highest office at a time of unprecedented difficulty in the state.[1] The International Longshoreman's Association (ILA) authorized a series of strikes and shut down the ports of San Francisco and

Oakland in a violent confrontation with state and municipal authorities over issues such as a six-day workweek and closed shop bargaining.[2] Following Department of Labor intervention that yielded no settlement, Merriam activated the California National Guard to settle the strike. This action culminated in a confrontation on July 5, later termed "Bloody Thursday."[3] Despite the Teamsters and other unions joining the ILA in what organizers hoped would be a general strike in San Francisco, the National Guard and local law enforcement quelled the strike after more than two weeks and forced the strikers to accept arbitration. California business owners praised Merriam's actions to settle the strike and many conservatives in the Republican Party started to encourage Merriam to run for Governor in the November elections. But, while California boasted a relatively low unemployment rate of 11.5 percent, compared to other states, large urban areas such as Los Angeles and San Francisco were much harder hit by the Depression and the influx of unemployed workers from other parts of the country created a perception that California's unemployment rate was much higher than it actually was.[4] Although his putting an end to the strike was widely viewed with relief, Merriam's reputation suffered in the weeks that followed. A progressive third party movement, akin to Theodore Roosevelt's 1912 "Bull Moose" party, organized by Frank Height, attempted to woo more moderate Republicans and centrist Democrats away from a GOP that was starting to be viewed as being too sympathetic to wealthy interests.[5]

Meanwhile, the California Democratic Party nominated Upton Sinclair as its choice for Governor. Sinclair, a journalist and film-maker, was, of course, best known for *The Jungle*, his 1906 exposé of conditions for workers in Chicago's meat-packing industry. He had gone undercover to investigate the rather horrific and dangerous conditions in slaughterhouses and, upon publication, the book cemented his reputation as an investigative reporter. In the 1920s, Sinclair moved his family to Monrovia, California and formed a chapter of the American Civil Liberties Union there.[6] He ran for several elective offices on the Socialist Party ticket. He became a nationally known spokesperson for radical causes, championing, for example, the First Amendment rights of groups such as the International Workers of the World.[7] Thus, it was surprising to many in late 1933 when Sinclair announced that he would seek the Democratic gubernatorial nomination on a platform he termed End Poverty in California (EPIC), a platform with ideas such as an "urban homestead" program, allowing those who needed housing to move into abandoned structures for very little money and a promise to pay property taxes.[8] While Sinclair's ideas were certainly progressive, they were hardly the stuff of his earlier activism. The platform, however, proved attractive enough to garner him the nomination in a very crowded primary field. Sinclair was the best known (and best financed) of the left-leaning primary candidates with a platform that seemed to drain votes from George Creel, a lifelong Democratic stalwart and fellow investigative journalist, but with far less name recognition than that of Upton Sinclair.[9] Indeed, Creel seemed to be more or less a relic of the Wilsonian days of the Democratic Party. Sinclair took the nomination with slightly over 54 percent of the vote and began his campaign for Governor immediately after the August 28, 1934 primary election.[10] Frank Merriam himself beat a crowded field in the Republican Party that included an effort to have disaffected Republicans cast write-in ballots for Upton Sinclair.[11]

Thus, the stage was set for a rather unique gubernatorial election. With Frank Merriam as the Republican standard-bearer, the party had nominated an experienced political operative who had held elective office as a legislator in his native Iowa and later as Speaker in the California Assembly. A successful politician, he was, however, not known for being a dynamic campaigner. Upton Sinclair, on the other hand, while also lacking in political charisma, had friends and contacts in the mass media (although the heads of motion picture studios were solidly Republican). His platform seemed far more moderate than his previous radical activism would have suggested. While suspicions about his true ideology persisted, Sinclair and the California Democratic Party attempted to depict EPIC as a proposal very much in line with the sorts of things President Franklin Roosevelt proposed in the New Deal legislation.[12] Along with the homesteading idea, EPIC proposed that idle factories and farmland could be run and managed by collectives in an effort to create employment for the unemployed.[13] Third-party candidate Raymond Haight, a veteran of Theodore Roosevelt's "Bull Moose" party attempted to attract what he saw as the political center in both major parties.[14] What initially started out to be an interesting and probably close campaign soon became the first campaign influenced in a significant way by mass media. In this rather dynamic and divided electoral milieu, the evangelist Aimee Semple McPherson would soon step forward to take a significant role in the outcome of the campaign. "Sister Aimee," as her followers referred to her, was arguably the first major religious figure to make extensive use of radio, film, and advertising in her ministry and the role she played in the 1934 California Governor's race in many ways provides a model for the role of religion in modern political campaigns.[15] How McPherson attained this influence is itself an interesting story and her biography allows a glimpse at California in the 1920s and 1930s, at the height of a great migration to the state and how the state becomes in many ways the epicenter of American mass media.

Aimee Semple McPherson was born Aimee Elizabeth Kennedy on a farm in Ontario, Canada in 1890. Her mother, who worked for the Salvation Army took Aimee to the Army's soup kitchens as a child and, although raised in a household that held dear the sometimes rigid doctrine of that denomination, hers was a relatively normal childhood and adolescence.[16] In 1907, at a revival meeting, she met Robert Semple, a Pentecostal preacher from Ireland, and, in 1908, the two married. Her husband died of malaria on a mission to Hong Kong and the young widow Aimee Semple began her own ministry, barnstorming throughout the southern and western United States.[17] Her fame as an evangelist grew, as a result of her rather unusual approaches to preaching the gospel. At one revival, she spoke in a boxing ring (a fight was scheduled after her sermon) and spent her time during the bout dressed as a "ring girl" marching around the ring with a sign exhorting those in attendance to accept Christ. Her fame was considerable and, during World War I, the Wilson administration made use of her unique appeal and fund-raising talents in an effort to sell War Bonds.[18] Almost constant traveling took its toll on her health, however, and on her second marriage. The couple filed for divorce in 1918 and, following a rather bitter series of legal actions, the marriage was dissolved in 1920. McPherson, however, retained her second husband's name.[19]

Because of the constant travel, McPherson decided to alter her ministry in a rather novel fashion. She and her mother (who served as business manager for the ministry) were impressed with the way southern California had been transformed into a tourist destination.[20] During 1920, they toured potential sites throughout Los Angeles, finally purchasing a large plot of land on Glendale Boulevard. Her vision, according to Matthew Avery Sutton, was to erect a temple to rival that of Solomon. Lacking funds, however, she embarked on a national tour to raise funds at her revival meetings. Additionally, she sought funds from California business leaders and sold chairs in her church to potential congregants.[21]

The decision to build a church in southern California was, in hindsight, an incredibly shrewd move by McPherson. With the Dust Bowl storms of the early 1930s, the state was experiencing a great influx of people from the Midwest whose farms and businesses had been decimated by the unprecedented bad weather conditions. Uprooted, families made the trek to California to try their luck in a different place. When many arrived, however, what they found was high unemployment and, for those who could find work, low wages and the absence of the social and family structures they had been accustomed to. Additionally, bad economic conditions across the country led to a migrant working class of people from many states and of many different racial and ethnic backgrounds traveling to California in search of employment. In the midst of such anomie, McPherson created an institution open to all, regardless of race or social class, which could meet spiritual, social, and even physical needs for people who, frankly, had few choices. Although she downplayed the Pentecostal roots of the Angelus Temple (preferring instead to call it nondenominational), the Christianity of the new church featured the opportunity for more democratic participation in church affairs (historically, a hallmark of the Pentecostal churches) and "old time religion," even as it sought to coexist with and even embrace modernity.[22] Unlike many other preachers in the Pentecostal ranks, McPherson recognized the material aspects of the Great Depression and sought to alleviate them for her followers.[23]

In 1923, construction was completed on the Angelus Temple, a magnificent structure by any standard. With a huge space for services and revivals, it also contained offices and classrooms and a commissary that fed the needy and, in a move quite radical for its time, invited people of all races and ethnicities.[24] Soon, her ministry included unabashed boosterism for Los Angeles and the city's Chamber of Commerce rewarded her by advertising Angelus Temple as a recommended sightseeing destination.[25] McPherson also bought a share of a radio station so that she could broadcast her sermons. Later, she bought the station, KFSG, outright.[26] By 1924, church records showed that over 30,000 people attended services at Angelus Temple each week, although, certainly, a large percentage of these people probably attended multiple meetings.[27] Although derided in the local and national press as a huckster and charlatan (mostly due to her claims that she could heal the sick and disabled as well as for the opulence of the church), Aimee Semple McPherson was fast becoming a figure of national influence. Indeed, by 1925, the church had become its own denomination, the Church of the Foursquare Gospel, and satellite churches began to spring up across the country.[28]

Services in the Angelus Temple were lavish. The main stage of the temple was large enough to accommodate a pulpit, a large choir, and an orchestra. McPherson wore figure-flattering vestments to services and her sermons contained many popular culture references, particularly references to Hollywood movies. She employed props and costumes. One sermon, entitled "Arrested for Speeding," discussed how, when Christ returns, he will talk about things familiar to Christians today such as automobiles and speeding tickets. Following an introduction, a recording of a loud police siren sounded and McPherson used the story of how she received a ticket to exhort her listeners to obey God's laws.[29] In other sermons, McPherson dressed in specially designed costumes (her favorite was that of a milkmaid, which she wore when she preached about her rural upbringing) to highlight the theme of a particular sermon.[30] Throughout the 1920s and 1930s, visitors to southern California were drawn to her spectacular sermons at Angelus Temple and, when she went on the road, her revivals usually sold out. Her use of mass media and "show business" technique made her by far the most influential and popular religious figure of the time. In many ways, Angelus Temple was the fore-runner of the modern "mega-church" with glitzy and exciting services, weekly classes, the radio stations, and special events such as opportunities to take a vacation and "cruise the Pacific with Sister Aimee."[31]

McPherson's theology was deceptively simple. Her interpretation of scripture was decidedly pre-Millenialist. The Bible was the inerrant word of

God and the Holy Ghost worked in the present day and age in much the same way as it did in the Book of Acts.[32] Thus, speaking in tongues and experiencing other religious ecstasies were gifts given to believers. Grace was available to all.[33] Worldly pursuits such as alcohol consumption and card playing were distractions and should be avoided, although movies were not specifically prohibited.[34] She preached against the evils of teaching evolution and, indeed, William Jennings Bryan was a very vocal supporter of McPherson's ministry. But, even in her fundamentalism, McPherson attempted to create an image of inclusion.[35] Advertising flyers for church activities often depicted a feminine god-figure, which served as a reminder that this particular pastor was a woman and that feminine qualities were themselves godly.[36] Her political beliefs were just as sophisticated and nuanced. She was a registered Republican, but an advocate of the domestic and foreign policy of Woodrow Wilson during his Presidency.[37] Pentecostalism in America had always had pacifist tendencies but McPherson supported military readiness and a strong national defense. In sermons, she often equated the Holy Bible and the U.S. Constitution.[38] McPherson, however, took a more progressive stance on other issues. During the 1920s, she opened Angelus Temple to African Americans and Latinos.[39] By 1936, the temple's commissary was open around the clock serving meals to the homeless, regardless of race or religion. After the stock market crash of 1929, McPherson spoke in support of Roosevelt's New Deal, particularly those aspects of it that created employment opportunities.[40] She admired Huey Long's tenure in Louisiana and had met with him on occasion to discuss issues such as old-age pensions.[41]

Indeed, McPherson's interest in the plight of the poor and unemployed in California led her to share the stage on a couple of occasions with Upton Sinclair himself. One such occasion involved mock debate over prohibition between McPherson and the actor Walter Huston with Sinclair as the moderator.[42] The other was a rally advocating assistance to the poor. McPherson was clearly sympathetic to much of Sinclair's EPIC platform and many of her views on these and other social issues (women's rights and pay inequity) were at odds with the Republican Party bosses in the state. While we often think of McPherson today as a "social conservative," Sutton and other historians remind us that Pentecostalism was essentially a populist movement that attracted the poor and the lower middle class in America and clearly shared many of the same concerns about social betterment as did the Progressive Movement of 1870–1930.[43] Michael McGerr's book on the Progressive Movement, *A Fierce Discontent*, shows a number of parallels between the two. Both attempted to co-opt radical ideas but shared a distrust of radicalism, per se, and, indeed, viewed socialists and communists with suspicion as both schools of thought were seen as atheistic and, thus, at odds with the American *ethos*.[44] Because of Sinclair's previous Socialist Party affiliations (and his dalliances with homeopathic medicine and theosophy), President

Roosevelt did not offer an endorsement, despite California's importance in the Electoral College.[45] Sinclair, however, was a popular figure in California with a national reputation as an advocate for the American worker.

Sinclair actually believed that McPherson would endorse his campaign as they, after all, saw eye-to-eye on so many important issues and McPherson was an advocate for cooperative farming and industry. The endorsement, however, never materialized. A year after the election, Sinclair claimed that McPherson had been pressured by leaders within the film industry such as Louis B. Mayer to withhold her endorsement. He claimed that his enemies promulgated the "Big Lie" about EPIC being a socialist program, yet elsewhere in the same letter to Norman Thomas about the campaign, Sinclair does call it socialist and discusses how to market socialism to the American people.[46] While his assertions about McPherson's relationship with the movie industry may be true, the refusal to endorse Sinclair (and, finally, to work for his defeat) was the result of a host of other factors, some personal and some ideological.[47] Two of these factors involved Sinclair in one case making light of a scandal surrounding McPherson and, in another case, his rather liberal and unsympathetic use of McPherson's persona and biography in one of his best-selling novels.

Sinclair made light of an incident that occurred in 1926 when Aimee Semple McPherson disappeared after swimming at Venice Beach. Days later, she reappeared claiming to have been kidnapped. The Los Angeles Police Department found much of her story impossible to verify; a grand jury indicted her (and her mother) with obstruction of justice.[48] The newspapers and the radio stations suggested that McPherson had either vanished to spend time with a lover, had had an abortion, had undergone plastic surgery, or had engaged in an elaborate publicity stunt.[49] Public sentiment, however, was decidedly in McPherson's favor and, in 1927, all charges were dropped.[50] Still, McPherson remained an object of ridicule among the academic elite and among wealthier and better-educated Americans.[51] Upton Sinclair was among these people and published a sarcastic bit of doggerel in the *New Republic* that contained lines about her "magic radio" and "magic microphone."[52] The poem itself, faintly mocking in its tone with an elevated style, was little different than much of what appeared in national newspapers. But, Sinclair's derision did not end here. He had also drawn heavily from McPherson's own biography to create the character of Sharon Falconer in this 1927 novel *Elmer Gantry*. The book was the best-selling novel of that year and was widely denounced in churches across the country for its depiction of evangelism.[53] But, more than the thinly veiled characterizations of McPherson or the mocking tone of the poetry, there was genuine mistrust among many California church-goers about Sinclair's disdain for organized religion. Still, Merriam was a poor campaigner and the unemployment rate seemed immovable.[54]

The California Gubernatorial election, then, became one of the first major national elections to employ mass media and the use of what are termed "surrogates," in the contemporary vernacular. The heads of the movie studios were particularly opposed to Sinclair, whose views regarding popular entertainment were surprisingly prudish, given his radical views on other issues. Louis B. Mayer and Samuel Goldwyn, for example, sent various contract players to events where Governor Merriam would be in attendance in an effort to give his campaign a more contemporary feel. They also produced a "newsreel" showing a train full of supposed immigrants who were, in actuality, Hollywood extras, arriving to "enjoy the good life in California—if their hero Sinclair is elected."[55] These contract players were also frequent special guests at McPherson's Angelus Temple but, McPherson herself was absent from the campaign as she was touring the country, speaking and visiting other Foursquare churches.[56]

Indeed, McPherson had embarked on a national tour in 1934 to raise funds for the ambitious outreach projects at Angelus Temple. She titled it her "America, Awake!" tour and her sermon during all of her appearances concerned the threat imposed by Communism and Socialism to the American way of life.[57] The Great Depression itself led to great interest in left-wing ideas and even those religious leaders with sympathy for progressive social legislation, such as McPherson herself, were concerned about the atheism and "godlessness" that they saw at the heart of these ideologies.[58] McPherson's sermon was a more general warning to the nation as a whole and reflected the anxieties of more mainstream Republicans and Democrats about how a combination of economic hardship and an unraveling of the nation's Judeo-Christian heritage offered a recipe for disaster. Her sermon was well-received wherever it was delivered and, in October 1934, she returned to California just in time for the election.[59]

Just prior to McPherson's return to California, the *Los Angeles Times*, which had supported Merriam, published an editorial calling on religious leaders to speak out against Sinclair. McPherson claimed to be surprised that her one-time ally now embodied the evil she had spoken about on her recent national tour.[60] On the Friday before Election Day, McPherson headlined a rally at Los Angeles Shrine Auditorium featuring the choir and orchestra from Angelus Temple and other religious leaders from across the city. Her message was essentially the "America, Awake!" sermon, but, in this setting, the people who packed the auditorium were only too aware that the Communist evil she described was embodied by Frank Merriam's opponent.[61] On the Sunday before the election, however, her attack was much more explicit. The title of the sermon was "EPIC—Epic Power Invades Christianity" and, while it was delivered as part of the regular Sunday service at Angelus Temple, thousands of listeners heard it broadcast live on her radio station.[62] She told the crowd that, despite America's tradition of separation of church and state,

"Never again can American political issues be separated from the cause of the gospel" and that we must serve "God, the Bible, our country, and our national principles."[63] From the pulpit she recognized the anti-Sinclair guests in attendance, which included Clark Gable, Jean Harlow, Norma Shearer, and Jeanette MacDonald.[64] The service was repeated again in the afternoon. She took great pains as well to compliment President Roosevelt as a leader who attempted to guide through Biblical principles, thus attempting to create distance between Roosevelt and Sinclair. She asked, "Will America retain the faith of our fathers?"[65]

The sermon was a jeremiad that took great pains to avoid naming Sinclair explicitly. Much of the sermon took the shape of an allegory in which an Eagle was subject to the punishments suffered by other animals (the bear and the bull, for example).[66] She warned that, unless the eagle returned to the ways of God, the Lord himself would return, not as a lamb but as a lion. It was the special duty of Christians to hold fast to the ways of the Lord, even in desperate times.[67] While not different from the sermon she preached on her national tour, the timing of the address, the special celebrity guests in attendance, the proximity to the election, and the fact that it was broadcast on her own radio station seemed to suggest that McPherson was no friend to the left-leaning Upton Sinclair.

On Election Day, Frank Merriam was elected Governor in his own right by a very comfortable margin. Sinclair made the unfounded accusation in a letter to Norman Thomas that every African-American preacher in the state had received $50 from unnamed sources to preach against him and that McPherson was hired to put on a pageant. Still, he felt somehow vindicated. He advised Thomas to avoid the term "socialism" in any future electoral efforts and stated, "Running on the Socialist ticket I got 60,000 votes, and running on the slogan to 'End Poverty in California' I got 879,000. I think we simply have to recognize the fact that our enemies have succeeded in spreading the Big Lie."[68]

Sinclair, however, failed to recognize several factors that ultimately led to his downfall. First, running a secular campaign could be a successful move, but hostility to religion is certainly not a winning formula. Sinclair had written numerous articles criticizing and ridiculing religion and religious believers.[69] Sinclair made no attempt to reconcile his atheistic writing in the past with his candidacy for Governor and his plan for California's economic recovery.[70] Without the backing of the national Democratic Party and an endorsement from the very popular President Franklin Roosevelt, his failure to address this part of his past seems to show a rather poor understanding of the influence of religion in the United States. This is rather baffling given Sinclair's interest in and analyses of socio-economic issues.

Second, in a campaign that used the media of film and radio, Sinclair was ill-equipped to communicate well in these venues. Garrulous and lacking in humor, he was a candidate who desperately needed surrogates to campaign for him. A review in *Time* magazine called him a man in possession of every conceivable gift "except humor and silence."[71] Unfortunately, most of his influential friends were from outside the state of California and many were viewed by Californians as quite radical. His background as a socialist, a dabbler in the occult, and a proponent of open marriage were the things many California voters focused on in making their electoral choices.[72]

Finally, Upton Sinclair underestimated the impact of his anti-religious writing, the obvious parallels between the character of Sharon Falconer in *Elmer Gantry* and McPherson's own life, and how his poem about McPherson's disappearance might impact whatever relationship they might have had. In his 1935 book about the election, Sinclair expressed surprise about how McPherson had essentially betrayed him and explained it through a theory about a conspiracy between her and the studio heads.[73] For Sinclair, the fact that the both he and McPherson were interested in cooperative production and economic experimentation should have trumped all else. This seems to suggest either a naiveté or, perhaps, a poor understanding of politics and the building of relationships. At any rate, the election marked the end of Sinclair's electoral career, but EPIC went on to field candidates as a sort of unofficial third party in two Los Angeles city races and one statewide contest.[74]

What can be said, too, about McPherson and her significant role in the defeat of Upton Sinclair? A polarizing figure, Aimee Semple McPherson was nevertheless a figure of great influence in religion and politics. Candidates for statewide office actively sought her endorsement following the gubernatorial campaign, which often consisted solely of the candidate being recognized as a guest at an Angelus Temple service. She was not in the habit of giving traditional endorsements as her chief concern was attracting members to the Temple. While Matthew Sutton suggests that her activism during the week before the election stemmed from her being swept up in the general anti-Sinclair fervor among clergy and church-goers in California, she continued to endorse candidates. One, Ernest Debs, a pro-labor Democrat, used his appearance at Angelus Temple to win a State Assembly seat.[75] Senatorial candidate Gerald Winrod did not fare as well, but used the appearance at the Temple to support his candidacy.[76]

For McPherson, political activism had decidedly mixed results. After the 1934 election, many of her followers expressed disappointment that, at least for some of them, she had abandoned the working class. The American Legion, however, made her an "honorary Colonel" and claimed in a press release that her efforts were at least as significant as those of FDR, Cordell Hull, and Douglas MacArthur in both garnering support for the New Deal and, later, in getting Californians behind the war effort.[77] Many historians suggest that her efforts to defeat Sinclair did truly make a difference, but it is noteworthy that, as time went on, McPherson never again became quite so involved in electoral politics, preferring instead to spend time supporting the growth of her Foursquare denomination and speaking out on behalf of issues rather than candidates.

NOTES

1. "The States: Governors," *Time*, November 12, 1934, 19.
2. Paul S. Taylor, "The San Francisco General Strike," *Pacific Affairs* 7, no. 3 (1934): 274.
3. Ibid., 277.
4. Peter Phillips, "The 1934–1935 Red Threat and the Passage of the 1934 National Labor Relations Act," *Critical Sociology* 20, no. 2 (1994): 43.
5. Greg Mitchell, "Upton Sinclair's EPIC Campaign," *The Nation*, November 1, 2010, 18.
6. Anthony Arthur, *Radical Innocent: Upton Sinclair* (New York: Random House, 2006), 102.
7. Ibid., 134.
8. Ibid., 138.
9. Steven Vaughn, *Holding Fast the Inner Lines: Democracy, Nationalism, and the Committee on Public Information* (Chapel Hill: University of North Carolina Press, 1980), 213.
10. John Hollitz, *Contending Voices, Volume II: Since 1865*, 3rd ed. (New York: Cengage, 2010), 130.
11. Greg Mitchell, *Campaign of the Century: Upton Sinclair's Race for Governor of California and the Birth of Media Politics* (New York: Random House, 1992), 53.
12. Ibid., 137.
13. Upton Sinclair, *End Poverty in California: The EPIC Movement. Virtual Museum of the City of San Francisco*. Accessed January 31, 2012. www.5fmuseum.org/hist/sinclair.html.
14. Kevin Starr, *Endangered Dreams: The Great Depression in California* (New York: Oxford University Press, 1996), 202.
15. Charles L. Bartow, "Just Now: Aimee Semple McPherson's Performance and Preaching of Jesus," *Journal of Communication and Religion* 20, no. 1 (1997): 76.
16. Matthew Avery Sutton, *Aimee Semple McPherson and the Resurrection of Christian America* (Cambridge: Harvard University Press, 2007), 8.
17. Ibid., 12.
18. Ibid., 16.
19. Ibid., 11.
20. Ibid., 21.
21. Ibid., 13.
22. Darren Dochuk, *From Bible Belt to Sunbelt: Plain Folk Religion, Grassroots Politics, and the Rise of Evangelical Conservatism* (New York: Norton, 2010), 262.
23. Heather Curtis, "'God is Not Affected by the Depression': Pentecostal Missions During the 1930s," *Church History* 80, no. 3 (2011): 587.
24. Kristy Maddux, "The Feminized Gospel: Aimee Semple McPherson and the Gendered Performance of Christianity," *Women's Studies in Communication* 35, no. 1 (2012): 43.
25. Sutton, *Aimee Semple McPherson*, 22.
26. Maddox, "Feminized Gospel," 44.
27. Sutton, *Aimee Semple McPherson*, 76.
28. Ibid., 24.
29. Matthew Avery Sutton, "Clutching to 'Christian' America: Aimee Semple McPherson, the Great Depression, and the Origins of Pentecostal Political Activism," *Journal of Policy History* 17, no. 3 (2005): 329.
30. Sutton, *Aimee Semple McPherson*, 184.
31. Ibid., 185.
32. Donna E. Ray, "Aimee Semple McPherson and her Seriously Exciting Gospel," *Journal of Pentecostal Theology* 19, no. 1 (2010): 160.

33. Ibid.

34. Ibid., 161.

35. Ibid., 160.

36. Kristy Maddux, "The Foursquare Gospel of Aimee Semple McPherson," *Rhetoric and Public Affairs* 14, no. 2 (2011): 299.

37. Bartow, "Just Now," 73.

38. Ibid.

39. Sutton, *Aimee Semple McPherson*, 212.

40. Sutton, "Clutching to Christian America," 311.

41. Sutton, *Aimee Semple McPherson*, 212.

42. Ibid., 211.

43. Michael McGerr, *A Fierce Discontent: The Rise and Fall of the Progressive Movement in America, 1870–1920* (Bloomington: Indiana University Press, 2003), 24.

44. Ibid.

45. Mitchell, "Upton Sinclair's EPIC Campaign," 19.

46. Upton Sinclair, "Letter to Norman Thomas," *Spartacus Educational*. Accessed December 27, 2012. www.spartacus.schoolnet.co.uk.

47. Ibid.

48. Sutton, *Aimee Semple McPherson*, 39.

49. Ibid., 42.

50. Ibid., 39.

51. Ibid., 40.

52. Upton Sinclair, "An Evangelist Drowns." Accessed February 1, 2013. xroads.virginia.edu/~ug00/robertson/asm/sinclair.html.

53. Kerwin Swint, *Mudslingers: The Twenty-Five Dirtiest Political Campaigns of All Time* (New York: Union Square Press, 2008), 18.

54. Ibid., 19.

55. Sutton, *Aimee Semple McPherson*, 226.

56. Ibid., 227.

57. Ibid., 226.

58. Ibid., 228.

59. Ibid., 230.

60. Swint, *Mudslingers*, 18.

61. Sutton, *Aimee Semple McPherson*, 228.

62. Ibid., 230.

63. Ibid., 231.

64. Daniel M. Epstein, *Sister Aimee: The Life of Aimee Semple McPherson* (Orlando: Harcourt Brace and Company, 1993), 201.

65. Ibid., 202.

66. Aimee Semple McPherson, *This Is That: Personal Experiences, Sermons and Writings of Aimee Semple McPherson* (Los Angeles: Bridal Call, 1936), 646.

67. Ibid.

68. Sinclair, "Letter to Norman Thomas."

69. Swint, *Mudslingers*, 19.

70. Ibid., 20.

71. "Uppie's Goddess," review of *Southern Belle*, by Mary Craig Sinclair, *Time*, November 18, 1957, 120–21.

72. Swint, *Mudslingers*, 18.

73. Sutton, *Aimee Semple McPherson*, 234.

74. Starr, *Endangered Dreams*, 156.

75. Sutton, *Aimee Semple McPherson*, 234.

76. Ibid., 250.

77. Epstein, *Sister Aimee*, 201.

Chapter Three

From the Good Ship Lollipop to the White House

Ethos and the Invitational Rhetoric of Shirley Temple Black

Sara Hillin

Shirley Temple Black, public servant, first female U.S. Chief of Protocol, and former U.S. Ambassador to Ghana and Czechoslovakia, indicated to the public that she had an interest in political activity as early as June 1965 when, in an interview with C. Robert Jennings for the *Saturday Evening Post*, she alluded to her many civic activities "involving hospitals, charities and other good works. The list runs for two mimeographed pages of a self-prepared 'Shirley T. Black Activity Resume.'"[1] Though at this time her fledgling efforts were primarily confined to local concerns, the article makes it clear that Black did possess some ambitions for a wider political sphere. Jennings, who dubs Black a "junior matron of San Francisco society," but also reassures readers that she is a "model mother to her three spritely children,"[2] offers one comment in an otherwise fairly bland "where are they now" piece that portends her later involvement in diplomacy. A few months prior to the interview, Black had visited Russia, where she had been asked to appear on a televised "tribute to cosmonauts Belyayev and Leonov."[3] Black, Jennings, writes, "thoughtfully added her own tribute, in brave Russian, to the American space effort."[4] Jennings takes a jab at Black's political stance when the discussion turns to her views on civic participation: "I don't think of the people around home as being 'society' so much as people who *accomplish something*" she says in the tones of the conservative Republican she is. "We are mostly just young families . . . We just have a sense of community responsibility."[5] This sense of civic responsibility that was alluded to off-

hand in Jennings' article soon supplanted Black's desire to maintain a foot-
hold in Hollywood, and Black forged a new political path for herself that
would take her from grassroots campaigning in California all the way to
working as an ambassador to two foreign countries. Her mastery of rhetorical
skill seemed to evolve with each new situation, presenting an *ethos*-driven,
invitational rhetoric that had overtones of feminism. And although the enduring impact of her former child star image could not be effaced, Black's
rhetoric *should* be considered as a major contribution to women's political
discourse, especially since two of her male co-stars, George Murphy and
Ronald Reagan, had successfully run for office as Republicans in California.
This essay traces Black's rhetoric as a U.N. Ambassador and contributor to
McCall's through her role as Ambassador to Ghana, arguing that in employ-
ing an at times laconic but always empathetic rhetorical style, she functioned
as an effective feminist political force in international politics and on the
home front throughout the late 1960s and well into the 1980s. In doing so, it
pulls from Aristotelian and Ciceronian considerations of the importance of a
speaker's *ethos*, and also from scholarship on power feminism and invitational rhetoric. Specific consideration is given to the articles she wrote for
McCall's Magazine between 1967 and 1973, her participation in U.N. meetings, and her 1976 speech accepting the position of Chief of Protocol. These
particular primary sources help to illustrate Black's evolution from a strictly
conservative Republican, whose terministic screen was shaped primarily by
an insular and affluent lifestyle, into a diplomat to foreign nations who began
to focus her career on humanitarian efforts and social justice.

MCCALL'S MAGAZINE: BLACK'S NARRATIVE, INVITATIONAL DISCOURSE

Black seemed to find a particular niche with *McCall's Magazine*, a popular
women's magazine, in the late 1960s and early 1970s. Her first article for the
journal, "Sex at the Box Office," was published in January 1967 and dealt
with her concern over pornography in film and censorship. At this time she
and Ronald Reagan had aligned themselves with the "Clean Initiative," a
movement to "strengthen the state's obscenity laws."[6] This article, in
contrast to the later ones Black wrote for *McCall's*, followed a more classical
argumentation style, refuting vehemently the claim that Black was in favor of
censoring free speech (in this case the clamor concerned a provocative Swedish film). The previous October, Black had served as Chairman of the Program Division of the San Francisco International Film Festival, and, despite
Black's objections, the rest of the members had decided to include *Night
Games*, a Swedish film whose advocates described it as "a serious attempt to
ennoble one man's search for the roots of his sexual impotency."[7] While

Black had objected to what she saw as the film's crassness as an exercise in commercialized pornography, her critics had jumped to the conclusion that she simply wanted to censor the film due to its sexual content. However, Black asserts, she was not disgusted or outraged by the film, but rather saddened. "It is a melancholy thing," she writes, "to view the debasement of two high estates particularly precious to me, childbirth and sexuality."[8] Her argument amounts to a claim of fact from definition, asserting that pornography and sexuality "are not synonymous," and takes issue with both her critics and her supporters, who, she asserts, are misguided in their assumptions about her motives: "'Pack Shirley off to Sunnybrook Farm!' snarled the in-group. 'Hooray!' shouted the 'out-group.' 'Back to long petticoats!' 'Censorship! Censorship!' shrilled a professional critic. Nonsense, all of it. Sunnybrook Farm is now a parking lot; the petticoats are in the garbage can, where they belong in this modern world; and I *detest* censorship."[9] Although Black uses classical figures of refutation, her argument is an attempt to *clarify* terms at the center of the debate rather than a screed against pornography, so that she can be in stasis with those arguing the issue from different perspectives. One of these figures of refutation is *anthypophora*, a "figure of reasoning in which one asks and then immediately answers one's own questions (or raises and then settles imaginary objections)."[10] In using this tactic, Black comments, "'Won't the new "Suggested for Mature Audiences" rating protect our youngsters from such films?' I don't believe so. I know many forty-five-year-old men with the mentalities of six-year-olds and my feeling is that they should not see such pictures, either."[11]

Black lists previous films with famously sexual themes or content, such as *Tom Jones* and *Dear John*, contending that "[s]exuality in movies can run the gamut from tenderness to hilarity to boredom to poor taste. By my definition, this should not be confused with pornography."[12] Even D. H. Lawrence, Black argues, whose books "now hold a symbolic role in freedom from censorship," stated that he would "censor pornography rigorously."[13] Black was, though, "fed up with . . . those medicine men of movies who create and sell hard-core pornography for profit."[14] The argument is also an attempt to move the argument beyond binaristic thinking about sexual content in film. Black even gives a slight nod to invitational rhetoric in celebrating further debate on the issue: "In my case, I believe that sex is a noble creation and one that should not be debased. There are people who will disagree with me about *Night Games* and about what makes artistic merit. Neither opinion, theirs or mine, need be imposed on the other. Herein lies what seems to be an area of dangerous confusion regarding the concept of censorship."[15]

Black takes care to own her views throughout the piece, using first person wherever possible (in her last sentence, she states, "But I am squarely against pornography for profit.") so as not to coerce her readers into submitting to her perspective. Though she displays clear passion for her views, she concludes the article by acknowledging the dialogue that had taken place and comments that "the rest was and should be left up to the conscience of the community and its intelligence."[16] Black's piece essentially attempts to define the terms of the debate about pornography and move it beyond an either/or stalemate.

Black's later *McCall's* articles showcase an evolving feminist rhetorical stance, which I would argue grew out of her experience with United Nations teamwork and diplomacy. It is interesting to note that Black's initial opinion on the work of the United Nations, which she had originally described to Robert Jennings in early 1967 as "communist propaganda,"[17] did a complete turnaround after she actually became a U.N. delegate in 1969. As Michael Ryan notes, Black was awarded the position as a U.N. delegate due to her support of Republican initiatives, but the work "soon became an obsession as she accepted a series of unglamorous assignments to represent the United States before a variety of international bodies and conferences."[18] "Prague Diary," from January 1969, was a piece in which Black recounted with vivid detail, in personal narrative form, her experience of having been in Prague the day that Russian troops invaded the city. This had occurred in 1968, when "reformist leader Alexander Dubcek was deposed by Warsaw Pact troops."[19] Black had happened to be in Prague on this particular day due to business for the Federation of Multiple Sclerosis Societies (in an attempt to persuade Prague to become the twentieth member of the Federation). This particular article, though it did not overtly argue in favor of the Czechoslovakian people, did convey support and sympathy for their vulnerability, and this piece was remembered by the nation for years afterward. In fact, as Michael Ryan notes, her publication of the Czechoslovakains' plight is one reason that Black was named an Ambassador to Czechoslovakia in 1989: "'People in Czechoslovakia like her because they remember her from before,' says Daniela Mrazkova, a historian of photography . . . Outraged by the brutal repression, she [Black] stayed on for days, as Soviet tanks rumbled through the streets, then went home and helped publicize the agony of Czechoslovakia."[20]

In "Prague Diary," Black invites her audience to share her experience through a use of raw detail and imagery that evokes empathy with the Czechoslovakian people. There are very few interpretive comments throughout the article, and the ones that she does include are seamlessly integrated into the narrative. Early on in the essay, however, Black contextualizes the positive reforms that had been taking place under Dubcek's leadership: "Censorship was being abolished, non-Communist minorities were being brought into the decision making process, and relations with humanitarian organizations such as ours were being encouraged."[21] The initial context Black sets up here makes the stark contrast with the violence that ensued (on the day that she had been scheduled to meet with Dubcek) all the more shocking. She describes "great green tanks, grimy and oily from the long night race from the border, thunder[ing] along Stepanska Street, guns depressed toward the gathering crowds."[22] Though Black powerfully conveys the threat to the public posed by the Russian soldiers—she describes the "charging," "behemoth" tanks and the bodies lying with "flower wreaths propped against their lifeless forms"[23]—she also catalogs the acts of resilience and bravery she witnessed among the Czech people, mentioning one group that had "massed in Wenceslaus Square, carrying Dubcek posters and heaping scorn on the Russian tankmen."[24] Black also recounts the aura surrounding the event: "One overriding impression stands out through all these initial hours of the crump, crump, crump of automatic weapons, the crashing of tank treads across the cobblestones, the rumble of troop carriers, and the heave and surge of the street crowds. It is the air of defiant and undaunted spirit of resistance one senses among the people. The Russians seem to have grasped a nettle."[25] In an act of "reframing," Black uses this piece to choose terms and metaphors to describe the violent political struggle between the two factions which display the dignity of the oppressed Czechoslovakian citizens.

Black's most well-known article for *McCall's* was her February 1973 essay "Don't Sit Home and Be Afraid," which delved with sincerity and explicit detail into her experience with breast cancer. In this piece, Black narrates her experience, beginning with her detection of a lump, through the aftermath of her mastectomy. She offers no easy answers, but offers her thought process on the tougher questions, ones that faced other women dealing with cancer: lumpectomy vs. mastectomy, when to tell family about the diagnosis, how much physical pain accompanies the treatment, and, perhaps most profoundly, the question of the emotional scars left by the diagnosis and treatment. Though it is largely experiential and follows the chronology of her illness and treatment, the piece had a deeper purpose, which was to urge women to educate themselves about the disease and advocate for themselves.

It is easy in 2013, a time in which we all know October as Breast Cancer Awareness Month, to forget that a few decades ago, discussing breast cancer openly and exposing the ugly truths about treatments were all but taboo.[26] Black does not take on a holier-than-thou tone, instructing women to dutifully do their monthly exams and prevent breast cancer. In fact, she does not *directly* attempt to persuade them to do anything other than to listen to *her* story. The article opens with Black's acknowledgment that the subject matter is difficult but that the *exigence* has prodded her to do so: "This is the hardest story I have ever had to write. Yet write it I must. The specter of breast cancer is a universal element of the feminine condition—and it makes sisters of us all, the world over. We need to reach out to one another, to sustain one another through this problem that we all share. I write this story, then, for all of my sisters who have lost a breast, for all of my sisters who fear that they may."[27]

In invoking the concept of a sisterhood of women, Black identifies with her audience of women readers. Although she does not condescend to them by eliminating references to her status as a politician or celebrity to create an I-am-just-like-you façade—various details of her day to day career are necessarily interwoven into the narrative—she does use "strategic essentialism" to convey the gravity of her cause to raise awareness: "Here and now I apologize to the medical profession for trying to be knowledgeable about the details of this most complicated question. At the same time I am a body, and I vigorously defend my right to do with my body exactly what I wish to do. The ultimate decision is mine. As I mused to myself, 'The doctor can make the *in*cision, but I'll make the *de*cision.'"[28] This particular comment was bold, considering that, in the early 1970s, there was much debate in the medical community concerning the number of unnecessary radical mastectomies.[29] Black makes clear that part of her purpose is to raise awareness about choices so that women do not unknowingly sign documents that allow surgeons to remove a breast without their consent, which had happened to one of Black's own friends. Her focus on helping women recognize their choices creates a power, one which "is accessed through realigning the distortions imposed by male supremacist epistemologies, allowing women to see and experience our-selves and our power through the reclamation of that which has been rendered taboo."[30]

Black, undoubtedly, knew the content of her narrative was frightening, and knew that an expressive piece such as this, devoid (as much as possible) of clinical content, except definitions of the different types of mastectomies, would help to spur on a necessary national conversation about breast cancer. Through an invitational rhetoric, in which she recounts conversations with her husband, her children, and her doctors, she asks women to consider doing what they can to prevent their own deaths. For example, in remembering how she broke the news to her son about her diagnosis, recounts how she told him, ". . . I wanted to tell other women about it, to urge them, please, please, not to wait—not to stay home and be afraid. It could be, would be, alright as long as they didn't wait too long."[31]

Black's aim is largely educational, and she identifies with her audience by emphasizing her role as a wife and mother, one who happened to enjoy status as a child star in her earlier life. Granted, as in other examples of Black's rhetoric, there are moments in which her blind spots become apparent. As a white, upper class woman, and certainly as a celebrity, she enjoyed the privilege of access to excellent medical care and also to physicians who were willing to share their knowledge with her so that she might distill it into a neater package for the publication's readers. The comment as she made urging women "not to wait," and, to some degree the concept of sharing a sisterhood with women "the world over," excluded women of color, women without a familial support network, and low income women who had far less hope of successfully detecting and having their cancers treated effectively and in time. Her essay assumes an education on ways of detecting and preventing breast cancer (breast self-exam, mammography), that many women lacked. Her firsthand knowledge of Third World women's struggles for basic medical education and care, for example, would not come into play until at least a year later, when she took the position of Ambassador to Ghana and became involved in initiatives such as the Mother and Child Care Project. One of the most striking elements of Black's article is her willingness to express the ugly mess of emotions and issues with body image that accompanied her treatment; neither of these are glossed over with facile optimism: "I don't want to leave the impression that the whole thing is at all easy. It is an ugly operation, a maiming operation, and there is a certain amount of physical pain. I am not yet comfortable in my revised body. My left arm hurts from the elbow to the shoulder. I seem to be off balance. And as I look in the mirror I feel quite unattractive."[32] Despite the rhetorical blind spots that are apparent in some segments of the essay, Black's article made strides, raising awareness of breast cancer, and its impact is apparent in much of the publicity following its appearance. In "Shirley Black Lauded," an *Evening Independent* article from March 1973, Dr. Walter Alvarez wrote that Black was to be "commended" for courageously sharing her story,[33] but perhaps more importantly, Alvarez used Black's article as a springboard to promote Reach to Recovery and Research to Recovery programs, both of which were designed to aid women seeking knowledge and support during a cancer diagnosis and treatment.

Between 1969 and 1976, Black began to rely more on *phronesis* (practical wisdom) and a sincere effort to project concern for the public good as part of her ethos. In Aristotle's *Treatise on Rhetoric*, he states that the rhetor "should make his audience feel that he possesses prudence, virtue, and goodwill" and that doing so "is especially important in a deliberative assembly."[34] As James McTavish explains, phronesis, according to Aristotle, "is that virtue of the intellect by which men are able to deliberate well about what is good and bad, with a view of achieving happiness."[35] Aristotle, McTavish elaborates, was primarily concerned with moral character as a means of persuasion, and the speaker must project confidence that her or his audience can identify with.[36] However, this confidence "must come about in the course of the speech and not from any preconceived idea of the speaker's character."[37] Cicero, similarly, "stressed the need to gain the good will of the audience" and held that "during the speech itself the orator's character needs to make a good impression on the audience."[38] And Quintillain proposed that "[a] good orator needs necessarily to show hatred of the wicked, emotional involvement in the public interest . . ." as well as show confidence, firmness, and courage.[39]

There are traces of alliance feminism and power feminism present in some of the political activities Black engaged in as well as in her public discourse. Especially beginning with her participation in U.N. meetings, it seems that her rhetorical stance shifts from being one of combatively "playing the game" to one in which she sought to "eliminate relationships of oppression and elitism" and instead create "relationships of equality, self-determination, affirmation, mutuality, and respect."[40] Sonja and Karen Foss offer a definition of feminism that seems applicable to Black's work as a diplomat, ambassador, and *McCall's* author. They define feminism as "the deliberate application of the capacity for the unlimited and resourceful interpretation to engage exigencies for the purpose of creating a desired world," and they emphasize that their definition "has as its purpose to change the world," asking individuals to "disconnect from hegemonic ways of thinking, believing, and acting . . ."[41] The authors also offer several interpretive options within the "feminist rhetorical toolbox:" brainstorming, resourcement, and reframing. It is the last of these, reframing—"choosing different labels for what we are seeing"[42]—that Black seems to have used successfully in her articles and on several occasions during U.N. meetings.

Going further with the Foss's discussion of feminist rhetorical techniques, it could also be argued that some of Black's strategies place her among "power feminists." A power feminist, according to Foss and Foss (in a distillation of the concept from Naomi Wolf's *Fire with Fire*), "seeks power and uses it responsibly," "chooses an identity that is rooted in responsible power rather than victimage," and "knows that a woman's choices affect many people around her and can change the world."[43] The problem with power feminism, Foss and Foss assert (although they agree with its end goals), is that it "focuses on material conditions and how women can use money and other physical resources to create change—or, in the language of our revised definition, to create the kind of world desired."[44] However, in Black's defense, many of the issues she addressed, particularly in U.N. meetings (pollution, incentives for involving youth in government, human rights violations, the treatment of refugees), necessitated policy-based claims touting material resources, such as funding, for solutions. Her praise for UNICEF's Fund for Population Activities is one example; in the December 2, 1969 meeting, she commented that her delegation "welcomed the programmes under-taken by UNICEF, in cooperation with other agencies, in extending traditional forms of assistance to family planning in response to initiatives made by other countries."[45]

One other critique of power feminism, and how it can gloss over the problem of interpretive blind spots, comes from Aimee Carillo Rowe, who argues that "the slippage between authors and audiences . . . risks centering and universalizing 'their' particular experiences, resources, and political investments, thus failing to attend not only to the power differentials among potential 'we's,' but also the ways in which those same sites of privilege may be gained on the backs of other 'we's.'"[46] This slippage is apparent in Black's "Don't Sit Home and Be Afraid," where she remarks that breast cancer "makes sisters of us all" and comments angrily that all women should strive to take care of themselves as a preventive measure. Of course, many populations, especially women of color, did not have access to the health education necessary to do what Black suggests, but her universalization of her experience leads her to suggest that all women could easily take advantage of her suggestions.

Historically, as Foss and Foss explain, rhetoricians (and presumably, this extends especially to those working in deliberative, political discourses) have worked within what they call a "paradigm of constricted potentiality" in which the rhetor must "focus their efforts on the material features of the world," and these include things that are tangible, such as laws, traditions, documents, people, and places.[47] Persuasion, the "effort to reinforce or transform beliefs or behaviors" is always employed by the rhetorician who wishes to effect change but is working within this tradition.[48] But this paradigm is problematic in that it assumes that change can only effectively happen through persuasion and the use of inartistic proofs and not other means, such as invitational rhetoric. Foss and Foss favor, instead, a paradigm of "constructed potentiality," in which the rhetor realizes that "[e]very moment is ripe with linguistic opportunity in that communicators can choose a different word, a different metaphor, and a different story, each of which makes available another set of resources and options."[49] In this paradigm, then, the potential for change is "constructed or invented, then, because it continually is being created from symbolic resources."[50]

One helpful use of this paradigm concerns its ability to alleviate the rhetor's discomfort brought on by the exigence. In such a case, the rhetor can use interpretation to "make another choice about what to perceive, how to interpret that perception, and how to frame that interpretation symbolically to transform those feelings."[51] In 1967, Black had been backed into a corner on pressing matters such as Vietnam due to the dominant paradigm of *constricted* potentiality, which demanded that an effective rhetor use tangible and established means of persuasion. This paradigm of constructed potentiality is closely aligned with invitational rhetoric, which they proposed as an alternative to patriarchal and coercive rhetorics in their 1995 essay, "Beyond Persuasion: A Proposal for an Invitational Rhetoric." Here, Foss and Foss characterize traditional persuasive rhetorical strategies as constituting "a kind of trespassing on the personal integrity of others when they convey the rhetor's belief that audience members have inadequacies that in some way can be corrected if they adhere to the viewpoint of the rhetor."[52] Invitational rhetoric, in contrast, does not have change as its purpose, and is "an invitation to understanding as a means to create a relationship rooted in equality,

immanent value, and self-determination."[53] Change through invitational rhetoric occurs "in the audience or rhetor or both as a result of new understanding and insights gained in the exchange of ideas."[54] Another crucial hallmark
of invitational rhetoric is the rhetor's acknowledgment of the valuable "contributions audience members can make to the rhetor's own thinking and
understanding, and they do not engage in strategies that may damage the
connection between them and their audiences."[55] The invitational rhetor also
makes freedom, the "power to choose or decide," an important element of
her identification with her audience and builds mutual understanding. Freedom is created "when a rhetor provides opportunities for others to develop
and choose options from alternatives they, themselves, have created."[56]
Black's policy based claim concerning pollution would be one example of
providing such opportunities.

The spirit of U.N. meeting discourse focused on delegates finding ways to
meet each other on common ground; Black tactfully employed an approach
that universalized a particular problem and offered possible ways of con-
fronting it, based on ideas put forth by others. In this speech, Black clarifies
that the participants in the upcoming 1972 Conference on the Human Environment would have the power to decide how to ameliorate serious environmental problems: ". . . we must learn a new ethic based on ecological principles. We must abandon apathy and self-absorption. We do not have time for
what I call one-eyed interests. We must set a tone of urgency for which the
world can respond. This Conference is an ideal way of ringing a fire-bell that
all can hear and none can ignore."[57] In identifying with her diverse audience,
Black focuses on the problem of pollution as "our" exigence which "we"
must respond to with solutions that will "entail plans of action that affect the
attitudes and actions of governments and people."[58] Though not informed of
all possible solutions that would emerge at the conference, Black emphasized
the collaborative nature of problem solving related to ecological issues. In
another speech concerning the Draft Declaration on Social Progress and
Development, Black again displays her concern for allowing governments to
implement policies based on choices they deem fitting for their social structures:

> . . . special care should be exercised to ensure that the Declaration . . . would
> have wide appeal and would be readily understood by people in all walks of
> life. She supported the United Kingdom representative's suggestion that it
> should be addressed to those most directly concerned, who should be fully
> consulted on and informed of measures which affected them . . . She agreed
> with the representative of Uganda that account must be taken of national
> policies, so that Governments could strive toward the goals set forth in the
> Declaration in a manner consistent with local customs and policies . . . [59]

Black, whether representing her own views of those of her delegation, often stressed that solutions to problems, whether pollution, human rights violations, or a panoply of other exigences, should be as inclusive as possible and founded collaboratively on carefully considered choices.

There is one element of invitational rhetoric that is not adhered to in Black's discourse. Foss and Foss claim that "in invitational rhetoric, the audience's lack of acceptance of or adherence to the perspective articulated by the rhetor truly makes no difference to the rhetor" and either rejection or acceptance are amenable outcomes to the rhetor, who is "not offended, disappointed, or angry if audience members choose not to adopt a particular perspective."[60] Black's rhetoric was deliberative, and concerned exigencies on a national and international scale that seemed to demand action and resolution, so there was, realistically, a limit to how much a rhetor in her position could table her concern over whether an audience listened to or accepted her position. In some cases, such as her U.N. speech concerning pollution, it is clear that Black very much did care whether or not her audience agreed with her perspective that environmental concerns were an exigence in need of a response. However, she does not follow her plea to raise awareness with a litany of concrete solutions that her audience needed to acquiesce to, as one would see in a typical claim of policy. Still, the elements of invitational rhetoric, alliance feminism and power feminism which I have identified in her discourse are prevalent enough to warrant consideration.

Beginning in about 1969 and onward, Black's rhetorical posturing began to also take on elements of what Rowe terms an "alliance frame" of feminism, in which the feminist rhetorician "take[s] responsibility for her own complicity in contemporary and historic relations of ruling, not to feel bad or guilty, but to truly heal the violence through which our ancestors, and by extension, our current generation, relate to one another through segregation and separation."[61] The alliance framework forces the Western feminist to question the idea that she is advanced, civilized, and pure[62] and "deconstructs this subject of feminism, whose power and well-being is imagined as separable from the suffering and victimization of others" and is "built upon an imaginary of the West as the model of progress."[63] In Black's U.N. meeting discourse, it is apparent that her concern for refugees stems from an acknowledgment that similar supremacist forces, Western ones, were responsible for the displacement of people.

When Black did draw attention to her gendered, raced, or classed location, she, for the most part, eschewed references to her child star image, the image that further inscribed the trope of the pure, obedient, civilized white child, an "every girl," as a standard for all children, regardless of ethnicity, onto American culture. And in a way, it is no wonder. Black was not necessarily culpable for the impact of her persona, having been three years old when she entered the limelight at the urging of her mother, Gertrude. Having to answer for or somehow atone for this impact would have been a weighty endeavor, but in some instances she does remind the press that that aspect of her career was something she wished to leave in the past. She commented to Jennings that she "classed" herself with "Rin Tin Tin," explaining, "People in the Depression wanted something to cheer them up, and they fell in love with a dog and a little girl . . . I always think of *her* as 'the little girl.'"[64] Her U.N. commentary on refugees, pollution and other issues showed her effort to align herself with the global community and work diplomatically with diverse populations, not just as an individual, to create the common good. Still, she did not believe that total world peace was achievable. In a 1972 interview with Michael Parkinson, she replied to his question of whether she thought the world was "going to the dogs" by showing that her hopes and her beliefs about what was *possible* were in conflict with each other:

> I don't think that the world will ever know peace . . . complete peace in all countries . . . I think that's perhaps not in our makeup to do this although we can pray for it and work for it. But I think that the building blocks of peace are moving into shape and I think that the world is going to be a better place . . . a calmer place and I hope for dignity in man, you know, so that people can achieve dignity and not suffer from hunger and want . . . (*Parkinson* BBC One)[65]

These comments are in keeping with the theme that ran through much of her U.N. commentary, regardless of the issue on the table: Black sought a world in which everyone could, through "self-determination" work for the betterment of humanity and benefit from each other's efforts.

GHANA AND BEYOND: BLACK'S EFFORTS TO CREATE CO-CULTURE

In 1974, Black was named an Ambassador to Ghana, a post that she recalled later as being her favorite position in her entire career of public service. An article in *Ebony Magazine* from 1976 illustrated that Black's humanitarian efforts had endeared her to the people. Hans Massaquoi writes that the *Ghanian Times* described her as "a capable, wonderful person who is determined to work for the good of others."[66] He also comments that her popularity was not confined to those within tribes but also "cuts across class and cultural boundaries to members of the country's establishment," most notably Ghanian women's groups.[67] Black comments in the article that her interest in third world problems:

> was awakened while I served as a U.S. delegate to the United Nations . . . mainly because I was seated between [the delegates of] Upper Volta and the

> Republic of Tanzania. . . . From contacts like that, I became convinced that our
> country was not giving enough attention to Africa and Latin America. I made a
> vow to myself to concentrate on Third World countries and to see where we
> could mutually benefit each other. [68]

In recognizing and attending to her perceived privilege and desire to act in response to it, Black was creating what Rowe terms "co-culture." In acting, speaking, and writing "in alliance" with others, Black illustrated her understanding that "the individual is embedded, inseparable, gracefully poised within a web of interrelations." [69]

Black's last highly publicized political post, that of the first female Chief of Protocol, was one that she accepted in 1976. In her inauguration speech, she makes a jab at President Ford (and in some sense, all previous presidents) for the fact that she was the *first* woman to be offered the position:

> It's a high honor indeed that you've bestowed upon me. It's a great honor to be
> the first woman Chief of Protocol for the United States of America. I don't
> know why, Mr. President, it took two hundred years for one of us to get the
> job, but I'll do all my very best work to fill all the various sizes of shoes of the
> distinguished men who have been Chief of Protocol. [70]

This was one moment in which Black's former childhood persona, the irreproachable "Little Shirley Temple," may have been slyly invoked, as calling out a masculinist political tradition in an inauguration speech might have been too bold for any other woman who did *not* have the enduring (however much she may have pushed it into the background at various points during her career) image of the child star to use as rhetorical leverage.

Ghana, as described by Black's daughter Susan, in her article "Shirley Temple Black in Africa," was a "matrilineal society," and one in which the power of women "as an important national resource" [71] was just being recognized. Black masterfully used her keen diplomatic skills in the private and public sphere, working twelve- and fourteen-hour days and often attending social functions that were routinely "a continuation of work begun at the office." [72] In commenting on her mother's "human touch diplomacy," [73] Susan Black describes one evening during which Shirley played a spirited Ping Pong match with the ambassador to the People's Republic of China and later played a game of chess with the counselor of the Soviet Embassy. She remarks that one beneficial outcome of this event was "an improvement in the relationships between the U.S. Embassy and the Soviet Union as well as with the People's Republic of China." [74] This particular example of Black's ability to build community through seemingly lighthearted play reflects Susan's comment that ". . . her means of accomplishing the ends do not always follow tradition." [75]

Susan also mentions her mother's involvement in several civic projects in Ghana, including the Mother and Child Care Project, her hand in helping oversee U.S.-Ghana business relations, and the Danfa Project, a feasibility study to determine the benefits of a group of rural clinics.[76] She also instituted monthly business meetings at her residence in which Ghanians "representing Ghana-based U.S. firms" and businessmen from the United States discussed needs and problems with the embassy's Chief Commercial Officer.[77] Another milestone accomplished during her stint as ambassador was her being the first ambassador ever invited to speak before the Market Women's Association in Accra, an event at which she "praised the women of Ghana for their fortitude, ingenuity, and enterprising spirit."[78]

In the "Afterword" to *Reclaiming Rhetorica: Women in the Rhetorical Tradition*, Cheryl Glenn comments on the typical difficulties women have faced in trying to be agents for change in the political sphere:

> . . . women have traditionally had little or no access to public display, to competition, to intellectual talk with other men. Women who wanted to contend with other women were most usually denied an audience; women who contended with men were denied respectability. No wonder so many women have resorted to the topoi of modesty and humility; to present themselves otherwise would be to present themselves sluttishly, brazenly.[79]

Black *did* certainly have the upper hand in terms of access to media and her culturally privileged status as a white, heterosexual, upper-middle class woman. Although it may seem bizarre to those who assume that Temple's 1930s golden child persona would open every possible door for her politically, the truth is that she found herself entrenched in the same quagmire of contentious discourses that did not welcome a woman's *ethos* as a mother and wife. She also found herself expected to participate in the paradigm of constricted potentiality that characterized most late 1960s and early 1970s political discourse, a paradigm that demanded "fighting" and labeled women such as Black as overly feminine interlopers, too dainty to seriously address issues of national concern. The development of Black's rhetoric between 1969 and 1976 illustrates her keen awareness of rhetorical situations, her understanding of how she could successfully manipulate her *ethos* by focusing on virtue and dedication to public service, and her concern for harnessing the means available to her to create a desired world.

NOTES

1. C. Robert Jennings, "Her Eyes Are Still Dancing," *Saturday Evening Post*, June 5, 1965, 96.
2. Ibid., 95.
3. Ibid., 97.

4. Ibid.

5. Ibid., 95.

6. Rodney Kennedy-Minott, *The Sinking of the Lollipop: Shirley Temple vs. Pete McCloskey* (Diablo Press, 1968), 31.

7. Shirley Temple Black, "Sex at the Box Office," *McCall's Magazine*, January 1967, 45.

8. Ibid., 110.

9. Ibid.

10. Silvae Rhetoricae, s.v. "anthypophora," accessed April 29, 2013, rhetoric.byu.edu/figures/a/anthypophora.htm.

11. Shirley Temple Black, "Sex at the Box Office," 110.

12. Ibid.

13. Ibid.

14. Ibid.

15. Ibid.

16. Ibid.

17. C. Robert Jennings, "Her Eyes Are Still Dancing," *Saturday Evening Post*, June 5, 1965, 97.

18. Michael Ryan, "As Ambassador to Prague, Shirley Temple Black Watches a Rebirth of Freedom," *People*, January 8, 1990, date accessed April 30, 2013, www.people.com/people/archive/article/0,20116493,00.html, 2.

19. Ibid.

20. Ibid.

21. Shirley Temple, "Prague Diary," *McCall's Magazine*, January 1969, 75.

22. Ibid.

23. Ibid.

24. Shirley Temple, "Prague Diary," 91.

25. Ibid.

26. For more context about the lack of knowledge concerning women's physiology and reproductive issues, one might consider that within this same issue, there is a brief article by *McCall's* doctor William A. Nolen on "Premenstrual Tension" in which he mentions having read (though no citation for this information is offered) that 62 percent of violent crimes committed by women occur during the week before their period. William Nolen, "What Men Don't Understand About Premenstrual Tension," *McCall's* 100, February 1973, 12.

27. Shirley Temple Black, "Don't Sit Home and Be Afraid," *McCall's* 100, February 1973, 82.

28. Ibid., 114.

29. Ibid., 82.

30. Ibid.

31. Ibid., 116.

32. Ibid.

33. Walter C. Alvarez, "Shirley Black Lauded," *The Evening Independent*, March 5, 1973, 15-A.

34. Aristotle, *Treatise on Rhetoric*, Book II, Chapter I.

35. James McTavish, "The Ethos of the Practice of Rhetoric," *Philippiniana Sacra* XLV.133 (January–April 2010): 69.

36. Ibid., 68.

37. Ibid.

38. Ibid., 74.

39. Ibid., 75.

40. Sonja K. Foss and Karen A. Foss, "Our Journey to Repowered Feminism: Expanding the Feminist Toolbox," *Women's Studies in Communication* 32.1 (Spring 2009): 39.

41. Ibid., 45.

42. Ibid., 51.

43. Ibid., 56.

44. Ibid.

45. Shirley Temple Black, Commentary on "AGENDA ITEM 12: Reports of the Economic and Social Council (UNICEF)," United Nations General Assembly, Twenty-Fourth Session, Official Records, Third Committee, 1721st Meeting, December 2nd, 1969, New York, 413.

46. Amy Carrillo Rowe, "Subject to Power—Feminism without Victims," *Women's Studies in Communication* 32, no. 1 (Spring 2009), 21.

47. Sonja K. Foss and Karen A. Foss, "Constricted and Constructed Potentiality: An Inquiry into Paradigms of Change," *Western Journal of Communication* 75.2 (2011): 208.

48. Ibid.

49. Ibid., 213.

50. Ibid.

51. Ibid., 214.

52. Cindy L. Griffin and Sonja K. Foss, "Beyond Persuasion: A Proposal for an Invitational Rhetoric," *Communication Monographs* 62 (March 1995): 3.

53. Ibid., 5.

54. Ibid., 6.

55. Ibid.

56. Ibid., 12.

57. Shirley Temple Black, Commentary on "AGENDA ITEM 21: Problems of the Human Environment," United Nations General Assembly, Twenty-Fourth Session, Official Records. Third Committee, 1278th Meeting, November 12, 1969, New York, 7.

58. Ibid.

59. Shirley Temple Black, Commentary on "AGENDA ITEM 48: Draft Declaration on Social Progress and Development," United Nations General Assembly, Twenty-Fourth Session, Official Records, Third Committee, 1664th Meeting, October 10, 1969, New York, 94–95.

60. Cindy L. Griffin and Sonja K. Foss, "Beyond Persuasion: A Proposal for an Invitational Rhetoric," 12.

61. Amy Carrillo Rowe, "Subject to Power—Feminism without Victims," 22.

62. Ibid.

63. Ibid., 22–23.

64. C. Robert Jennings, "Her Eyes Are Still Dancing," *Saturday Evening Post*, June 5, 1965, 95.

65. *Michael Parkinson Show*, Interview with Shirley Temple, *BBC One*, June 1972. Date accessed April 30, 2013, www.youtube.com/watch?v=M02C-aubxLY.

66. Hans J. Massaquoi, "Ghana's Love Affair with Shirley Temple Black," *Ebony* 31 (March 1976): 116.

67. Ibid.

68. Ibid., 123.

69. Amy Carrillo Rowe, "Subject to Power—Feminism without Victims," 32.

70. Shirley Temple Black, "Chief of Protocol Inauguration Speech," July 20, 1976, date accessed, April 30, 2013, www.youtube.com/watch?v=x4Yfm0pdtDk.

71. Susan Black, "Shirley Temple Black in Africa," *Ladies Home Journal* 92, October 1975, 72.

72. Ibid.

73. Ibid., 74.

74. Ibid.

75. Ibid.

76. Ibid., 75.

77. Ibid., 145.

78. Ibid.

79. Cheryl Glenn, "Afterword," in *Reclaiming Rhetorica: Women in the Rhetorical Tradition*, edited by Andrea A. Lunsford (Pittsburgh: University of Pittsburgh Press, 1995): 329.

II

A Shift to Modern Day:
A Look at Leadership

Chapter Four

Averting Crisis

Women as Heads of State and Rhetorical Action

Rebecca S. Richards

Prior to the election of President Barack Obama, the U.S. presidency was a position built around a tradition of white masculinity. During the 2008 U.S. Presidential election, however, voters had other options; not only were people of color running for office, but there were also several high-profile women vying for the position of President and Vice-President: Sarah Palin, Hillary Clinton, Rosa Clemente, and Cynthia McKinney. As a voter and a rhetorician, I found it fascinating to observe the ways in which candidates performed their identity-based political *ethos*, especially with Clinton using the Internet to announce her candidacy in a living room-like setting. Clinton's decision to use a cyber-living room was analyzed, criticized, debated, and lauded. Likewise, throughout these women's campaigns, the media relentlessly focused on their gendered performance of candidacy—most visibly focusing on the acceptability or the readiness of the white female body for leadership in the form of Clinton and Palin. These two women's ethical appeals were routinely scrutinized, which was no surprise for a political candidate. However, the focus of scrutiny tended toward their gendered performances.

For one notable example, National Public Radio (NPR) ran an interview between correspondent Michele Norris and former U.S. Representative Pat Schroeder of Colorado about whether or not the country would be "ready" for a "woman President" in 2008.[1] Schroeder had briefly considered running for executive office, and Norris investigated if Schroeder decided against running because she is a woman. During the interview, Schroeder expresses that she realized that she could not win and that she did not want to run if she could not win. Two political analysts explain the political conundrums that

Schroeder experienced firsthand: what to wear, how to appear as a military leader, and how to appear tough but not "that other word we don't like to say."[2] While Schroeder's personal experience sheds some light on the issue of gender and U.S. politics, it is the supplementary material of the radio show that gives a broader perspective on how women are perceived on the U.S. political stage.

To begin the segment, Norris provides a sound byte from then-Senator Hillary Clinton; in it Clinton states the real litmus test of national readiness for a woman to "step into that arena" can only come when a woman *actually* enters this traditionally masculinized space. In sum, her answer is a non-answer, and Clinton seems to genuinely laugh at the ridiculousness of her ambivalence to the question of women, leadership, and U.S. politics. It might be surprising to hear an ambivalent response from a woman actively pursuing political power. However, her answer mirrors the sentiments her constituents express in the rest of the NPR segment. Following Clinton's response, Norris continues with sound bytes from people "off the street" in the United States who share a similar ambivalence to the citizenry's readiness for a women in a position of leadership. For example, one unidentified man responds that "I don't know. I guess—men [unintelligible] that thing of power, you know, of a man being in charge type of deal and—when I vote for a woman. You know, it would have to be something like where the candidates were really—they're horrible maybe or the country was going downhill. Or a woman who had maybe good military experience."[3] To show that there is a not a gender bias in this individual response, the segment also provides quotations from two women—one who expresses that she is "ready for a woman president," the other expressing that she "would not vote for a woman president ever."

To back up the anecdotal nature of the off the street responses and Clinton and Schroeder's personal experiences, Norris gives quantitative support for women in leadership such as poll numbers that indicate that over 80 percent of the country says that they would—in theory—vote for a "woman president" and how there have been "dozens" of women elected as heads of state all over the world.[4] In all, the segment says little about women and leadership, and it leaves the listener with no tangible explanation as to why the United States has yet to elect a woman into the Oval Office. What this clip effectively does, however, is model typical, unproductive discussions about how to talk about women seeking political power: focus on voter readiness, the candidate's gendered performance (e.g., "woman president"), and other nations' successes at electing a "woman president."

But it is not just NPR that follows this discursive formula. Many other media outlets followed this type of reporting on the readiness for a "woman president" for the next two years, eventually drawing the attention of the popular television news satire show *The Daily Show with Jon Stewart* on

September 17, 2007. For those unfamiliar with the show, Stewart acts as a news anchor, with a variety of other actors as "on the scene" correspondents. One such correspondent, Samantha Bee, takes on the question of "readiness" for a "woman president" in a segment that spoofs the HBO television series *Sex in the City* (*SITC*).[5] In this segment, Bee plays a version of the *SITC*s protagonist, Carrie Bradshaw, a journalist who writes a column about issues pertaining to women, relationships, money, and sex. Instead of researching those topics, Bee's character sets out to find out if U.S. voters are "ready for a woman president."[6] Again, like the earnest NPR report, Bee finds credible interviewees such as the then-president of the National Organization for Women (NOW), Kim Gandy, and *Washington Examiner* columnist, La Shawn Barber, to express the nation's ambivalence on women in positions of leadership.[7] Barber parrots the gendered stereotypes of leadership, for example, "women are the weaker sex" and "a leader should radiate confidence— *manly* confidence" (emphasis added), while Gandy highlights that it is "silly" to even be asking the question because "all around the world women have been leaders of countries."[8]

To emphasize the scope of the discourses employed by Bee, Gandy, and Barber, the satirical segment opens with a montage of the actual news reports commenting on the readiness of the United States for a woman president, featuring clips from Fox News, NBC, CNN, ABC, and daytime talk shows. While this comedic piece does not provide answers as to why media discourse focuses on readiness, Bee's segment effectively calls attention to the ambivalent discourses that circulate in the U.S. media about women in leadership.

With the defeats of Clinton in the Democratic primaries and the McCain/Palin ticket in November 2008, it would have been reasonable if the discourses surrounding women in U.S. politics subsided. However, this was not the case. For example, the television coverage of the April 7, 2010 Minnesota political rally showed two similar looking women front and center. Palin was in Minnesota to "take the stump" for a congressperson, Michele Bachmann.[9] Bachmann was pretty; well-manicured with polished nails, neat shoulder-length brown hair, and pink lipstick; well-dressed in traditionally feminine upper/middle class attire of a flowery, knee-length ruffled skirt, dark shirt, and yellow jacket; and maternal in the way she embraced, made eye contact with, and communicated affection with members of the audience and Palin. From the enthusiasm of the audience at the rally, it seems as though Bachmann—much like Palin—is a very familiar and likeable presence to the rally's attendees.

Video coverage of the rally shows Palin speaking on Bachmann's behalf, regurgitating the double bind of gender in the political arena: gender is both irrelevant and a defining characteristic of political women. Palin recites Thatcher's quotation, "In politics, you want something said, ask a man. You want something done, ask a woman."[10] The crowd applauds in approval. But in the following minute, Palin rescinds her joke saying, "Now you know I'm just kidding about this gender thing. I'm just joshing about the gender thing. Gender is no issue. Neither is the color of one's skin. It's not a measuring . . . that's not a measuring issue either. It is character, what's inside, and Michele has this."[11] No sooner does Palin tell her audience that "gender is no issue" than she recapitulates again to talk about the "pink elephant of the GOP"— which she defines as the invigorated voting base of conservative women and candidates who are women. She shouts, "Well someone better tell Washington that, warn them that that Pink Elephant is on the move, and 2010 is shaping up to be the year that conservative women get together and help to take back this country. And Michele is leading the stampede!"[12] To this day, the continued national focus on Palin, Bachmann, and other Tea Party conservatives, not to mention the debate over women's health and reproductive rights, keep the question of gender and political representation on the nation's radar.

Palin has been an all too easy target of critique because of her rhetorical style, factual errors, political inconsistencies, and hyper-visibility, for example, *Sarah Palin's Alaska*. But Palin's 2010 Minnesota speech in conjunction with the media buzz from the 2008 presidential election shows how in the past eight years, U.S. political discourse has focused on the issue of gender in political participation and leadership. In these three examples, as well as many others, the same questions and issues continue to be brought up, but the most obvious ones are:

1. Whether gender is an issue for a person's presidential candidacy,
2. Whether the electorate is "ready" for a woman to gain access to positions of power,
3. The replication of gender norms through dress and personality characteristics, and
4. The over-statement of or reference to the extent of women's political participation in other nations.

It does not seem to matter whether the rhetorical situation occurs on the left or the right of the political spectrum, in earnest or in jest, or through the voice of a candidate or a journalist—the United States is clearly ambivalent about the potential of women in positions of national executive leadership. While alleging ambivalence, I contend that these media representations also show that people are curious about the possibilities of women in positions of executive leadership. Most people are aware that there are women who lead other nations, and this seems to either make voters anxious or incredulous—anxious because it means that other nations might be more progressive than the United States, thereby challenging the ideologies of American exceptionalism—or incredulous because many of these nations are labeled as "developing" or even more problematically, "Third World." Nevertheless, there is the gesture to look across borders even if speakers cannot identify or name many of the women who have held executive national office. I open with this brief but critical description of a several media segments not to belittle the journalists' or politicians' work, but to highlight the rhetorical moves that are often made when journalists, citizens, politicians, and political analysts discuss the potentials and pitfalls of women and national leadership—especially within a U.S. context.

In spite of their varied rhetorical strategies and audiences, the underlying assumption of discourses about women running for and holding executive office is that something is about to change or shift with her election or appointment. Using classical and contemporary rhetorical theory with sociological theories, I argue that this "something" is the doxa[13]—the unstated belief in the eternal, inevitable, and patriarchal nature—of the nation-state. In the remainder of this chapter, I highlight how the rhetorical moves listed above are the direct attempts to suture nationalistic doxa that are called into question when breaking (or attempting to break) the masculine tradition of national executive office. Sociologist Pierre Bourdieu asserts that *doxa* are the unarticulated values, social structures, and assumptions that constitute a group of people.[14] *Doxa*, however, is a contested term among rhetoricians and philosophers, beginning with a debate between ancient Greeks about the rhetorical value of using commonly held beliefs in knowledge production. Because there is little consensus as to the use of *doxa*, I examine how this term has been used in contemporary rhetorical studies in order to better situate Bourdieu's sociological understanding of *doxa* within the ancient Greek tradition. Primarily, I explore how nationalistic doxa emerge and circulate to constitute leadership as inherently masculinized in order to maintain the appearance of the stability for the nation-state. This doxa has been maintained through what Carole Pateman calls a "fraternal patriarchy" of male leadership, meaning that the election of a woman into executive national leadership puts this doxa into crisis.[15]

After establishing how the nation-state's doxa functions, I conclude this chapter by analyzing how women in executive national leadership positions hold the potential to both subvert and affirm the doxa of the nation-state. This chapter highlights what Inderpal Grewal calls "transnational connectivities" or linkages across geo-political positions and time.[16] The goal of this analysis is to show how various rhetorical strategies employed by women as national leaders, as well as other rhetors speaking about such politicians, can fall on a broad spectrum of rhetorical action. This spectrum spans from reinforcing the status quo and reinscribing the ideology of the nation-state as an inevitable, eternal patriarchal construction to creating a space for radical democracy and equitable political participation.

In contemporary culture, community through national identity is accepted as commonplace if not *compulsory*, as if the nation has always been the signifier of a unified large, heterogeneous group of people.[17] But this is not the case. Anderson cites the mechanical reproduction of text, "print capitalism," in the 1500s as the shift from "imagined" religious communities to these "imagined" national communities.[18] He calls a national community "imagined" because "the members of even the smallest nation will never know most of their fellow-members, meet them, or even hear of them, yet in the mind of each lives the image of their communion."[19] In Anderson's consideration, national horizontal solidarity resides not in actual interaction of its members, but instead through the symbolic interaction of a shared language, national narratives, for example, fictive ethnicity and the potential of a limitless future of the nation.[20]

However, in order to participate in this imagined community, one must also be a recognized member and granted national citizenship—a process that is simultaneously empowering, oppressive, and reductive. The nation-state, as conceived of with borders, citizens, and commodities, is a limited entity because it cannot account for those who elide the national census due to their lived realities (e.g., migrations, immigrations, and multiple belongings). Furthermore, the nation-state is limited in its conception because it never actually strives to be "coterminous with mankind [sic]."[21] The nation-state would cease to exist if everyone were a part of its structure; it only exists because it stands in opposition to an Other.

Political structures that comprise the nation-state ensure that people recognize legal authority, and such structures exclude and oppress people. Or as Arjun Appadurai cautions, "one man's imagined community is another man's political prison."[22] This means that when examining the nation-state and its functions, one must be careful not to obscure the material consequences of governments and organizations that are granted power through the construct of a nation-state. Because of this reality, academic scholarship cannot simply discount the "imagined" or narrative aspects of a nation-state.[23]

One such material consequence of the nation-state is the subjectification of "women" into a homogeneous category that perpetuates nationalisms and ensures the continuity of the nation-state. By studying the histories of women's role in the evolution of various nation-states, it is clear that at best the nation-state has been ambivalent toward women and at worst they have been oppressive and violent. Even in nation-states that conceptualized their nationalism through metaphors of glorified womanhood, that is, the motherland, or an "abstract 'she'" (e.g., nation-states claiming to be metaphorical wives of colonial powers), women's reproduction, labor, and participation in the nation-state have been strictly regulated and scrutinized.[24] Edited collections such as *Scattered Hegemonies: Postmodernity and Transnational Fem-*

inist Practices[25] and *Between Woman and Nation: Nationalisms, Transnational Feminisms, and the State*[26] provide critical research into how specific nation-states have historically constructed and controlled the category of "woman" to limit specific gendered and racialized bodies' access to the public sphere and to deny women leadership in governments.

As a category and a discourse of nationalism, the category of "women" becomes problematic because it recognizes the female bodies it interpellates as vital subjects of the nation-state while simultaneously restricting participation and mobility. Nira Yuval-Davis writes that "women's membership in their national and ethnic collectivities is of a double nature. On the one hand, women, like men, are members of the collectivity. On the other hand, there are always specific rules and regulations, which relate to *women as women*" (emphasis added).[27] I argue that the double-natured position of woman functions simultaneously as an orthodoxy, a discourse or practice that sutures interrupted *doxa*, and a heterodoxy, a discourse or practice that exposes and/or subverts doxa. However, claiming that a national doxa exists is laden with disagreement over the definition and use of the term.

Generally defined as "mere opinion," *doxa* leads to questions as to "whose opinion?" and what is the role of *doxa* in rhetoric and discourse?[28] The word *doxa* was problematic in ancient Greece because it attempted to facilitate the transition between a notion of truth built upon religious beliefs (*aletheia*) and truth built upon scientific reasoning (*episteme*). Isocrates, for example, understood *doxa* as reasonable opinion built upon past precedent from which one could make a wise decision.[29] Unlike Isocrates, Plato found decision making based on *doxa* like shooting in the dark; nonetheless he accepted that *doxa* was an important rhetorical strategy for decision-making.[30] In Platonic dialogues, however, *doxa* is still assigned a derogatory status since it only approximates truth and could lead to falsehood and deception.[31] Like Plato, Aristotle found *doxa* to be an inferior form from which to build knowledge. However, he could not reconcile the fact that some *doxa* of the polis were well reasoned and, therefore, needed to be accounted for in a rhetorical situation. To resolve this tension, in *Nicomachean Ethics*, Aristotle used the term *endoxa* to denote elder statesmen's opinions based on perceptions of phenomenon.[32] Like Isocrates' view of *doxa*, *endoxa* accounted for the shared values and opinions between the rhetor—in Aristotle's case, the rhetor was an elder statesman—and his audience.[33]

Victor Vitanza synthesizes this ancient debate through Heidegger's work concerning the connections between *logos* and *doxa*. He argues that Heidegger's work reveals the linkages between *logos* and *doxa*, which complicates the commonplace definition of the latter as "mere opinion."[34] Vitanza explains that because Heidegger emphasized that knowledge and truth are constantly in a transition between concealing and revealing/appearing, *logos* is the way to make that which is concealed or revealed appear in *doxa*:

Doxa in *logos* and *logos* in *doxa* are concealed and unconcealed to us. In other words, *logos* speaks *doxa* which is an unconcealment and simultaneously a concealment of some aspect of episteme/truth, which can never be completely gathered, or unconcealed. Unless rudely forced! [35]

Vitanza argues against Plato's dismissal of *doxa* as an inferior philosophical ("mere opinion") tool because *doxa* can reveal hidden (albeit transitory) truths that lead to knowledge production. While *doxa* might be an opinion that is not based on an ultimate truth, *doxa* nonetheless expresses a truth about the logic and values of a given time or group of people.

To illustrate Vitanza's point, consider the nearly universal doxa of contemporary nation-states. Almost every nation-state functions under the belief that it is an eternal and necessary construct; [36] Anderson highlights this when he mentions that the nation evolved out of the demise of the empire in order to provide a "limitless future" to those who identified as members of the nation. [37] Likewise, Yuval-Davis points out that the nation uses narratives of "common destiny" to perpetuate itself. [38] By its very definition, a nation-state uses what Louis Althusser calls State Apparatuses, for example, bureaucratic systems, to give the appearance of eternal self-preservation. [39] However, when one looks at the larger scope of history, the nation-state has been a relatively recent addition to a long line of sovereignties. Since the emergence of the nation-state as a form of sovereignty in the eighteenth century, various nation-states have emerged, evolved, and dissolved; notable examples include: Israel established in 1948, Bangladesh established in 1971, former East and West Germany 1949–1990, former Zaire 1972–1997, and the former Union of Soviet Socialist Republics (USSR) 1922–1991. Despite the observable historical evidence that the nation-state is not a static or eternal entity, a nation-state functions under the doxa of eternality, or as Kaplan, Alarcón, and Moallem write in their introduction, the nation-state must be "an interminable project of production and reproduction." [40]

What is especially noteworthy in the above definition, though, is that this doxa of interminability goes unstated in the various State Apparatuses while playing a crucial part in nation-building. Rarely, if ever, will a politician, citizen, or governmental official state explicitly the belief that a given nation-state is an eternal or limitless project. For example, in the U.S. context, one might hear a politician talk about "endurance" during time of crisis, but such discourse relies on generic platitudes, for example, "We will endure!," that bring into question who constitutes a "we" and what *exactly* will endure. [41] Instead, this national doxa functions as the unspoken component of an enthymeme, normalizing the assumption as a common value between a rhetor and his or her audience.

Furthermore, the national doxa also functions like an ideological fantasy that is reinforced by the interpellation of the citizens who gain recognition from its perpetuation. Althusser's theory of ideology and Žižek's concept of ideological fantasy are at work in this doxa of the nation-state as a limitless project. Althusser argues that ideology structures an imaginary relationship (*illusion*) between individuals and their lived material condition.[42] In the case of the nation-state, the doxa functions as the ideology that allows citizens to imagine themselves as part of a stable and eternal entity (the nation-state), thus providing them a stable individualized national identity. However, such a stable sense of self is in direct conflict to the observable phenomenon of the nation-state as a liminal construct (e.g., East and West Germany).

Nevertheless, the ideological illusion still holds some relationship (*allusion*) to the lived reality of the individual. It is this tension between the ideological illusion and allusion that Žižek calls ideological fantasy. Žižek relies on the Marxian formula of "they do not know it, but they are doing it" to frame such a relationship, but he alters the phrase to denote the ambivalence involved in ideological fantasy, writing, "they know very well how things really are, but they are still doing it as if they did not know."[43] Žižek's altered phrasing of the Marxian formula encapsulates how the doxa of the nation-state as a limitless project remains an unspoken assumption despite the lived reality that such a doxa functions as an ideological fantasy. What I mean is that many of the people who are recognized as national citizens accept the fantasy—in this case the doxa—of the nation-state as an interminable project because it gives the appearance of a seemingly stable and continuous social ordering through national identities, which in turn provides citizens with a seemingly stable sense of self.

Instead of being contested based on lived realities, this doxa becomes naturalized and accepted as implicit ideological fantasy of the nation-state. Bourdieu finds that all established social ordering, such as the nation-state and national identities, "tend to produce . . . the naturalization of its own arbitrariness."[44] In the case of the national doxa as an interminable project, the lack of language to support such doxa is exactly what creates a sense that this, in fact, *is* the natural ordering of the social world. One does not have to argue for the nation-state to be an eternal sovereignty because it is the presumed natural ordering of people and places. It goes without saying that the nation-state will exist forever. For Bourdieu, "what is essential *goes without saying because it comes without saying*: the tradition is silent, not least about itself as a tradition."[45] Therefore the essential doxa of the nation-state would be one that is least likely to be said or the least likely to identify itself as a national tradition. I argue that the belief in its own infinite destiny is *the* central doxa of the contemporary nation-state. For clarity purposes, the belief in an infinite national destiny (doxa) will not be italicized to differentiate it from the classical rhetorical term, *doxa*.

In order for this implicit doxa to continue, social orders and traditions emerge to secure the semblance of continuity and stability. Using socially constructed identities such as race, gender, sexuality, and class to structure labor and democratic participation is one way to ensure that the nation-state achieves a sense of stability. This means that individuals who are disempowered by given social structures will fall in line with the logic of the structure—even when it is against the individual's best interest. Bourdieu explains that individuals of a social organization, for example, a nation-state, who become disenfranchised through its perpetuation must still engage in the social roles assigned to them by the dominant social structure.[46]

As detailed earlier in the chapter, women belong to one such collective that falls into this problematic social space as they play vital, even if simultaneously oppressed, roles in the biological and ideological reproduction of nation-states. Gendered divisions of labor are one way to secure the nation-state's stability and reinforce the national doxa. As outlined in *Between Women and Nation*, each nation-state creates gendered constructions of citizenship and labor in order to create national stability. Men and women alike fill tacit and active social roles that appear self-evident in the continuation of the nation-state.

One masculinized social role in many nation-states is that of leadership, but one must not mistake contemporary male national leadership as the "patriarchy" held up in many feminist critiques. Instead, male leadership of nation-states forms a fraternity. According to the work of Carole Pateman, social contract theory informs the contemporary nation-state—a theoretical tradition that fought against the patriarchy of monarchies. But Pateman argues that it is not patriarchy, per se, that structures contemporary national leadership since patriarchy is the rule of *fathers*.[47] Pateman calls the contemporary structure of the nation-state a fraternity, or more precisely, "fraternal patriarchy," to indicate the part of the social contract that subjugates women to "men *as men*" first and foremost, meaning that men do not have to be a father to assume power, but that they have the power inherently as male bodies.[48] Fraternal patriarchy creates another unspoken doxa for nation-states, emerging during the eighteenth and nineteenth centuries as men automatically became the leaders of a nation-state since most women did not hold the right to vote nor the right to stand for national elections until the twentieth century, with very few exceptions of women's suffrage in the very late nineteenth century.[49] The doxa of fraternal patriarchy perpetuated in spite of suffrage because social structures adhere "to relations of order which, because they structure inseparably both the real world and the thought world, are accepted as self-evident."[50] There was no reason to contest fraternal patriarchy and male leadership because it was assumed to be the natural order of human relations.

However, since the first administration of Sirimavo Bandaranaike (Sri Lanka) in 1960, which is generally recognized as the first administration to be led by a woman as a head of state for a modern nation, the fraternal patriarchy of male leadership has seen its power challenged by women gaining access to executive leadership positions.[51] This challenge, thus, brings the doxa of the nation-state into language, meaning that the tacit becomes visible in the potential rupture of tradition. Each nation-state, however, responds differently to women's participation in executive national leadership. While putting the national doxa in crisis, women who hold or pursue national executive office can come to represent either a force that reinforces the doxa or one that continues to challenge it.

The word "leader" has been normalized as a masculine term, partially based on the historical practices of male leadership covered briefly in the previous section. A leader is also assumed to be male because the characteristics associated with leadership are stereotypically ascribed to men: strong, aggressive, confident, and powerful. In occupational and organizational studies, management or leadership roles have been built around "masculine modes" of hierarchical and autocratic behavior such as assertiveness.[52] While I do not agree that assertiveness is an inherently masculine mode of communication, this brand of gendered stereotyping emerges in many discursive spaces, especially business and political settings. Political scientist and lawyer Jane A. Jensen argues that men are seen as being competitive and decisive, characteristics of effective national leaders.[53] This logic means that there is never a need to additionally gender the term "leader" when a male holds a leadership position—as in indicating that he is a "man leader." In English, "leader" is always already a gendered term to denote a "man." In claiming this tautology (leader = man), I borrow the logic of Monique Wittig's argument that the category of "man" was created as the dominant social, political, and economic category: "'woman' as well as the category 'man' are political and economic categories not eternal ones."[54] In other words, Wittig is drawing attention to the fact that both "man" and "woman" comprise an ideological and false dichotomy that is not built upon a natural or eternal truth, but instead predicated upon established power relations. Understood in this manner, the category of "man" functions as a master to lead or to dominate "woman," which is why the word "leader" connotes a masculine person.[55]

Since the word "leader" is already gendered as male, when a person who is recognized as a woman in a nation-state context, she is often labeled a "woman leader."[56] Take for example Jensen's book, *Women Political Leaders*; or even Michelle Norris' NPR report that opened this chapter, "Are U.S. Voters Ready to Elect a Woman President?" It is highly likely that when one refers to a political leader who is a woman, she will be called some variation of a "woman leader." But what is the rhetorical implication of such a label? Does inserting the word "woman" before "leader" mean that this person will lead differently or provide a revolutionary model of leadership? Does "woman leader" mitigate some of the negative connotations that one might associate with women or with leaders? And most importantly, what does a "woman leader" mean for the doxa of the nation state?[57]

The category of "woman leaders" rhetorically bridges the disconnect between the logic of leader = man and the appearance of women in national politics, which is an interruption to the doxa of the nation-state. For a "woman leader" is not a "woman" since "woman" is a category created around the historically and material social relationship of servitude she has to "man."[58] If a body that is identified as "woman" is leading the nation-state, she can no longer be classified as woman because, in theory, she is no longer the heteronormative servant to "man." However, a "woman leader" cannot entirely be a "leader" because she is not "man;" furthermore, her position of power is modified by her gendered identity.

The discourse of "woman leader" and the presence of women as heads of state conflicts with unspoken doxa of masculinized leadership. This confrontation challenges the larger, unarticulated national doxa of the nation-state as an interminable project in that a tradition of male leadership provided the appearance of continuity and stability. In other words, this challenge holds the potential to become what Bourdieu calls heterodoxy to national doxa because her appearance in national government challenges the seemingly stable, identical, and continuous governing of the nation-state. Heterodoxy is the "existence of *competing possibles*" that are often viewed as blasphemous or heresy.[59] As a *doxa* moves from being unspoken to articulated through heterodoxy, in this case the appearance of women as national leaders, those invested in the maintenance of the national doxa will construct an orthodoxy, in this case "women leaders," which is language meant to reaffirm the structure of the previously unarticulated doxa.

Both orthodoxy and heterodoxy exist through language, and both are rhetorical arguments for the way the social world is understood and structured. What is interesting about the discourse surrounding "woman leaders" is that it can simultaneously represent both heterodoxy and orthodoxy. A political woman's existence offers a competing possibility (heterodoxy) to the doxa of the nation-state as an eternal and stable entity because she visibly represents a change or a shift in traditional gendered roles. However, the name "woman leader" is a means of securing through language (orthodoxy) that leader = man still holds true. Therefore, women as national leaders can simultaneously reaffirm national doxa while putting it in crisis. Such a crisis is important because it is "a necessary condition for a questioning of doxa" but as Bourdieu points out, crisis is not "a sufficient condition for the production of critical discourse."[60] The discourse surrounding women in positions of leadership does manifest the tacit doxa of the nation-state in that "woman leader" challenges the social structure of male leadership that ensured that the doxa did not need to be articulated. However, "woman leader" does not forcibly mean that the discourse that emerges around her administration will be able to change existing, sexist social hierarchies, nor will it forcibly undo the *doxa* of stability and continuity.

For example, as I have written elsewhere, the discourse of "Iron Lady," beginning ostensibly with Margaret Thatcher and circulating to other national leaders' administrations (e.g., Benazir Bhutto, Ellen Johnson Sirleaf, Indira Gandhi, Angela Merkel) provides a concrete instance of where a differently gendered performance of executive national leadership can both expose the fiction of national doxa and suture that rupture so that the doxa can continue undisrupted.[61] By creating an imaginary tradition of Iron Ladies in positions of leadership, one can imagine a woman world leader as part of a stable, even if emerging, tradition, which then aligns women as heads of state into collusion with the hegemonic structures and values of the nation-state.

But something has *happened* when a differently identified body enters a traditionally limited, exclusive space of leadership, even if a rhetorical bridge attempts to suture the disruption. Figuring out what a woman world leader *does* to the rhetorical constructedness of the nation-state means delineating the potential actions that she *could do*. This can only be identified with the understanding of how the agency of a woman world leader allows for specific actions, which means venturing into the murky waters of agency, action, and the interrelation of the two. In "Shifting Agency: Agency, *Kairos*, and the Possibilities of Social Action," Carl Herndl and Adela Licona argue, in line with Foucauldian understandings of power, that agency does not exist since it is not a thing that can receive any action.[62] In light of this understanding, Herndl and Licona employ the term *constrained agency* for evaluating potential actions; they do so in order to move away from individualized notions of agency and to be attentive to the interplay between agency and authority. Constrained agency implies an understanding that: 1) agency is situational, and 2) authority controls action. Therefore in constrained agency, authority functions to serve both as a limit to and facilitator of agency. In their own words: "Agency speaks, then, to the possibilities for a subject to enter into a discourse and effect change—even change that might serve to further entrench a dominant social order."[63] Even in a position of national leadership, women who are world leaders experience constrained agency since authority in the form State Apparatuses (including Ideological State Apparatuses)—works with and against each leader's potential for action. This means that a political woman, regardless of her geopolitical position, will not receive *carte blanche* for the actions available to her because the various State Apparatuses she is subject to will limit her.

It is difficult, if not impossible and undesirable, to make a generalization about the collective, constrained agency of political women who are world leaders. This group of leaders experiences the (in)ability to perform certain actions since constrained agency is highly situational. But the range of actions available to them will be what Bourdieu calls interested actions. An agent, such as a political leader, cannot engage in a "gratuitous" action, meaning that any action a leader takes will not be without some reasonable interest in the outcomes. And by "reasonable," Bourdieu does not mean to imply that these actions are necessarily rational, conscious, or logo-centric. [64] Instead, the world leader is positioned in a political "game," to use Bourdieu's metaphor, and she will only choose actions that correspond to the game she is playing. If she is a good player, she will choose an action in anticipation of the game play; if she is a poor player, she will choose ones that appear to be "off tempo." [65] Differently stated, a woman who is head of state will select only actions that have ends that correspond to her reasonable objectives—the efficacy of her actions depends on her feel for the political game she is playing.

One example of a woman world leader's feel for the game is Margaret Thatcher's response to her nickname, the Iron Lady. Calling Thatcher an Iron Lady was originally thought of as a strategy to degrade Thatcher's administration; however subsequent interviews of Yury Gavrilov reported in *The Daily Telegraph* show that he had a more nuanced intent for the nickname. [66] In her response to the name, Thatcher highlights her performance of traditionally female clothing and style in citing her makeup, jewelry, hairstyle, and clothing:

> I stand before you tonight in my red chiffon evening gown, my face softly made up, my fair hair gently waved . . . the Iron Lady of the Western World! Me? A cold war warrior? Well, yes—if that is how they wish to interpret my defense of the values and freedoms fundamental to our way of life. [67]

In this response, Thatcher discursively moves nimbly among gendered expectations, neither accepting nor denying such expectations, showing a "feel for the game" of being read as a woman in a traditionally male position.

Since they play a transparently political, social game, political women have avenues for social/political action. This deliberate drive toward political and social actions is evident in Bhutto's desire to bring democracy to Pakistan, as written in her autobiography. She writes, "I am a female political leader fighting to bring modernity, communication, education, and technology to Pakistan" [68] and that in spite of losing loved ones for her convictions, "grief will not drive [me] from the political field or from our pursuit of democracy." [69] These passages, and others like them, leave no doubt that Bhutto saw herself as playing a political game.

Another clear statement of the political, social game can be found in the Council of Women World Leaders' (CWWL) mission statement—an initiative of the Aspen Institute to make visible women in positions of global leadership. It is the goal of the CWWL to "promote good governance and enhance the experience of democracy globally by increasing the number, effectiveness, and visibility of women who lead at the highest levels in their countries."[70] Both of these examples, the CWWL's collective or Bhutto's individualized statements, show how political women play an inherently political game. But the game is also, if perhaps less transparently, a rhetorical one. By rhetorical action, I meant that the game is predicated around rules to engage a given audience to reaffirm and/or subvert audience expectations. For political women, the rhetorical aspects of their agency work to affirm/contradict the doxa of the nation-state. However, rhetorical and political actions are not discrete events; I see political and rhetorical action interacting in a mutually interdependent relationship. One is not the opposite of the other; rhetorical and political action bleed into each other.

With the tradition of male leadership underlining the doxa of the nation-state, the entrance of a differently understood body places such doxa in crisis because it highlights the fluid and rhetorical nature of the imagined national community. And, as stated through the language of Bourdieu, a crisis is the necessary condition to question *doxa*, but it does not guarantee an action, a change, or even a critical space to begin an ethical rhetorical action. A crisis means that the participants of a system or structure are confronted with the inconsistencies of that entity—but it does not mean that they will advance means to alter the way in which the system or structure functions.

The discourses surrounding women world leaders do put the doxa of the nation-state in crisis, which is evidenced by asking questions as to whether or not a nation-state is ready for a political woman as a leader. The sense of discontinuity demands multiple rhetorical responses; discontinuity, according to Gerard Hauser and Riedner and Mahoney, is where the pedagogy of rhetorical action takes place: "'the need for discourse arises most pointedly at times when disruptions or gaps occur in the normal course of events'—we would add, when political action *creates* such disruptions or gaps."[71] In the act of electing (or considering) a woman as the president, prime minister, or head of state, rhetorical actions emerge to either suture the discontinuity or to break it open even further.

The election of Barack Obama to the U.S. presidency is an excellent example of how a political action creates a disruption or gap, and thus creates exigency for discourse. As overviewed through the work of Campbell and Jamieson, as well as Dana Nelson, the U.S. presidency is a rhetorical construct that functions around a fraternity of white male leadership. As the first black man elected U.S. President, Obama serves as a visual disruption to this racialized tradition. This disruption, beginning before his election, has given rise to competing discourses about what Obama's presence represents in terms of the crisis it creates for the U.S. Presidency; some of those conversations include: Obama signifying a post-ethnic America, Obama being or not being "black enough," and contention over Obama's religious affiliation.[72] Regardless of the logic or political slant behind each argument, conversations like these take for granted that Obama's embodied difference inherently signifies some sort of change in the concrete; this assumption was not ignored by the Obama campaign strategists who used the rhetoric of change as the foundation of the campaign, even going so far as to make the official president-elect web address: www.change.gov. But assuming change through a visual, embodied disruption to national leadership is not merely a rhetorical strategy of one political philosophy. The symptoms of this assumption surface in both conservative and liberal spaces. Conservatives remark that Obama marks a change that has gone too far, at times linking U.S. icons with those of the USSR to imply a shift to Soviet Communism, and liberals express impatience with the lack of global remedy of all social injustices, which is found, for example, in critiques of the Obama administration's lack of social justice agenda for the Lesbian, Gay, Bisexual, Transgender, and Queer (LGBTQ) community. Both perspectives demonstrate that critics assumed that the crisis Obama's election placed on the U.S. presidency meant that change—broadly writ—would occur, even though they disagree over the political direction (an implementation) of such change.

Despite the different political maneuvering, multiple rhetorical actions have emerged from the crisis Obama represents on the doxa of the nation-state; some of these actions are ethical, seeking to open up the potentials of action and to break open hegemonic social structures, and some of them are unethical in that they limit the potentials of action, sometimes by trying to bridge over and obscure the disruption with discourse.

I see women elected into world leadership positions in a similar position to that of President Obama in the U.S. context, in that they provide an exigency for discourse in their interruption of doxa of the nation-state. But unlike Obama, the interruptions to national social structures caused by women as world leaders are understood not only as a unique localized geopolitical experience but also as participation in a global collective through the discourse of "women world leaders." Because the construct ("women world leaders") functions as a complex discourse that both refers to actual, existential women as leaders in local and immediate geopolitical spaces as well as symbolically representing these existential agents in what Spivak calls a "strategic essentialism" of an imagined collective, "women world leaders" can frame a pedagogy of social action in either ethical or unethical rhetorical actions.[73] Or, differently stated, "women world leaders" is a discursive space of rhetorical action that both limits and expands the potentials for social action.

For example, the crisis brought on by the introduction of women as leaders of the nation-state in Scandinavian countries has been an action that led to changes in policies that have traditionally been framed as feminist issues. Norway, Finland, and Iceland have all been represented by women in the executive office, and as of 2007, 41.8 percent of Scandinavian parliamentary seats and 55.1 percent of cabinet seats were held by women—numbers that represent an exceptionally high level of women's participation in national leadership compared to global counterparts.[74] Jensen reports that there are several factors that have led to the success of women as world leaders in Scandinavia. First, she cites the Viking tradition of egalitarianism and the inclusion of women in some civic activities. Next Jensen outlines how the traditional economy of Scandinavia was structured around sailors being away from home thus leaving women to fill the gaps the men left behind. But perhaps most importantly have been the success of women's organizations in the 1960s and 1970s, as well as the unsuccessful attempt to adopt a quota system for parliamentary representation in the 1980s.[75] This complex nexus of rhetorical actions toward egalitarian participation in leadership has led to women as world leaders as agents toward ethical social action; these political women have, in turn, used their administration to advance some of the most progressive legislation on parental leave and sex work.[76] Scandinavian women as world leaders are part of a sustained ethical rhetorical action for equity and advancement of social justice issues.

Another example of a political woman as world leader who participated in ethical rhetorical action would be Janet Jagan, the first woman as Prime Minister and, eventually, President of Guyana. Alongside her husband, Cheddi Jagan, Janet led worker revolutions in the 1940s and 1950s in the former British colony by organizing domestics and rubber plant workers into unions.[77] She co-founded the People's Progressive Party (PPP) and the Women's Progressive Organization (WPO). She and Cheddi fought for Guyanese independence from the British in the 1960s and 1970s and led the PPP until the first official election in 1992, when Cheddi was elected president. After Cheddi's death in 1997, Janet was elected President of Guyana. While this is but a snippet of Janet Jagan's political and activist career, it shows that her election was, again, a part of an ethical rhetorical action to increase the social possibilities for women, workers, and the Guyanese. Of course neither Jagan nor Scandinavian political women are beyond reproach since their leadership appears to be part of ethical rhetorical action. It is a not a zero-sum game that political women play. Instead, these two brief examples are meant to show how some political women find the space to challenge the status quo of patriarchal laws and hierarchy.

What is of equal importance, though, in these past two examples, is that these women are hardly household names outside of their nation-state or regional position. Of Jagan, Finnbogadóttir and Sigurðardóttir (Iceland), Halonen and Jaatteenmaki (Finland), and Brundtland (Norway), all but Sigurðardóttir are official members of the Council of Women World Leaders and Brundtland held the position of the Director General of the World Health Organization, indicating some level of global recognition of their positions. And yet these women occupy marginal spaces in the discussions of women who are world leaders or "women presidents," outside their specific, local political space or in academic discourses of political science and gender studies. These women as world leaders can be understood as taking part in ethical rhetorical action because they occupy the marginal symbolic space in the discourse surrounding women world leaders.

However, women world leaders denote not just a collective of political women but also an ideological discourse practice surrounding political women, as represented by phrases like "woman president" or "female politician." I argue that "women world leaders" is a rhetorical construction that participates in unethical rhetorical action that responds to the nation-state's crisis upon the introduction and visibility of women holding positions of global leadership.[78] Instead of allowing for more possibilities or new ways of reading the nation-state, this discursive practice attempts to reinforce the doxa of the nation-state, which is brought into question with the visible appearance a traditionally minoritized body in a position of the highest national power. It averts the crisis of the nation-state by creating a false tradition of women as world leaders in order to assuage the citizens that the nation-state is a static entity, instead of engaging the fact that the national fabric is always shifting. Recalling the beginning of this chapter, NPR featured an unnamed man who expressed he would only vote for a woman as president if the other, presumably male candidates were "horrible maybe" or if "the country was going downhill." In this participant's view, there is no need to unsettle the *continuity* of the nation-state unless it has already been unsettled. Much like Thatcher's often repeated slogan of "There is no alternative," "women world leaders," as an unethical rhetorical action, attempts to limit the imagination on what the nation-state could be and what it could evolve into.

The false tradition created by the discourses of women world leaders discourses function in a similar manner to the U.S. presidency, as outlined in the work of Campbell and Jamieson. In their latest edition of *Presidents Creating the Presidency: Deeds Done in Words*, Campbell and Jamieson argue that the presidency functions like a "corporate entity . . . encompass[ing] more than a single person."[79] By re-interpreting current and former U.S. Presidents in relation to one another based on their rhetorical performances of various presidential genres, "presidents increase or decrease their powers as individuals, and even of more importance, affect the powers available to their successors."[80] Based on the research into political women, "women world leaders" is emerging to become the "presidency" of transnational politics where women as world leaders can be accounted for and placed into a tradition that reaffirms the global hegemony of the nation-state. Because women as world leaders are not unified by the same institutional affiliation, like U.S. Presidents, women as world leaders become a part of the collective of women world leaders through discursive and visual practices.[81]

Unlike Campbell and Jamieson, I could not rely on institutionalized genres of political performance. Nor could I rely on a specific, commonly accepted language, such as the "presidency," to frame this discursive space. It is important to note that the construct, women world leaders, is not always phrased with that specific language. By using the phrase, women world leaders, I implicate those rhetorical strategies that put women as world leaders into a transnational tradition of leadership in order to reread their performances of power. While I acknowledge that, unlike the U.S. presidency, the language of "women world leaders" is hardly ever framed verbatim in those explicit terms, I argue that the lack of transparency of language is what makes this unethical rhetorical action all the more insidious. The lack of transparency allows the discourse to shift shape and style to avoid detecting and easy critique.

This means that the more that women as world leaders participate in the discursive and visual practices of "women world leaders," the less likely they will be able to affect progressive social action. Instead, those women as world leaders who find themselves interpreted as "women world leaders" become a likely exigency of orthodoxy that reaffirms the doxa of the nation-state; instead of taking part in an ethical rhetorical action, these female politicians' work will be used to reassure people that the nation-state is an enduring entity. Perpetuating the same discussions about "women presidents" sutures the potential disruption that political women might bring to a nation-state. This is why reports focus on the same issues of "readiness," "women presidents," and political women in other parts of the globe. "Women world leaders," as a rhetorical construct, bridges over the crisis of the nation-state, obscuring the fissures of its hegemony, restricting the ability to revolutionize or reorganize the social relations upon which it was built, and reframing the embodied woman as world leader—and the crisis she can signify to the nation-state—into a politics of representation.

NOTES

1. Michelle Norris, "Are U.S. Voters Ready to Elect a Woman President?" 12:21, audio file from *National Public Radio* on December 19, 2006, www.npr.org/templates/story/story.php?storyId=6648890.
2. Ibid.
3. Ibid.
4. Ibid.
5. Samantha Bee, "Ready for a Woman President?," *The Daily Show* video, 5:05, from a television show by Comedy Central on September 17, 2007, www.thedailyshow.com/watch/tue-september-18-2007/ready-for-a-woman-president-.
6. Ibid.
7. Ibid.
8. Ibid.
9. Sarah Palin, "Sarah Palin Michele Bachmann in Minneapolis," 4:47, video from You-tube.com on April 7, 2010, www.youtube.com/watch?v=oMnaRFZNn7I.

10. Ibid.

11. Ibid.

12. Sarah Palin, "Michele Bachmann Rally in Minneapolis: Part 2," 5:01, video from Youtube.com on April 7, 2010, www.youtube.com/watch?v=O0YeydDCWIQ.

13. In order to differentiate between *doxa* as a general, rhetorical concept and national doxa of the nation-state as eternal and inevitable, I will italicize the former and not the latter.

14. See Pierre Bourdieu, "Conclusion: Classes and Classifications," *Outline of a Theory of Practice*; and *Practical Reason*, trans. Richard Nice (Cambridge, UK: Cambridge University Press, 1977).

15. Carole Pateman, *The Sexual Contract* (Cambridge, U.K: Polity Press, 1988).

16. Inderpal Grewal, *Transnational America: Feminisms, Diasporas, Neoliberalisms* (Durham, NC: Duke University Press, 2005).

17. Suad Joseph, "Women Between Nation and State in Lebanon," in *Between Woman and Nation: Nationalisms, Transnational Feminisms, and the State*, ed. Caren Kaplan et al. (Durham, NC: Duke University Press, 1999), 162–181.

18. Benedict Anderson, *Imagined Communities: Reflections on the Origin and Spread of Nationalism* (London: Verso, 2006), 37.

19. Ibid., 6.

20. I borrow the term "fictive ethnicity" from French political scientist Etienne Balibar's work because he is attentive to how "no nation possesses an ethic base naturally" and that in creating a fictive ethnicity, the nation obscures its own dubiousness. Or as he argues, "without it, the nation would appear precisely only as an idea or an arbitrary abstraction" (224).

21. Anderson, *Imagined Communities*, 7.

22. Arjun Appadurai, *Modernity at Large: Cultural Dimensions of Globalization* (Minneapolis: University of Minnesota Press, 1993), 32.

23. Chandra Mohanty's book about Third World Feminisms enacts such a model of scholarship that allows for recognizing both functions of the nation-state: the imagined and material consequences. "Third World Feminisms" is Mohanty's term, not mine. She critiques this phrase "third world" but uses it nonetheless.

24. Elspeth Probyn, "Bloody Metaphors and Other Allegories of the Ordinary," in *Between Woman and Nation: Nationalisms, Transnational Feminisms, and the State*, ed. Caren Kaplan et al. (Durham, N. C.: Duke University Press, 1999), 49–50.

25. Inderpal Grewal et al., eds., *Scattered Hegemonies: Postmodernity and Transnational Feminist Practices* (Minneapolis: University of Minnesota Press, 1994).

26. Caren Kaplan et al., eds., *Between Woman and Nation: Nationalisms, Transnational Feminisms, and the State.* (Durham, NC: Duke University Press, 1999).

27. Nira Yuval-Davis, *Gender and Nation* (London: Sage Publications, 1997), 37.

28. It should be noted that the term *doxa* became widely used in a Judeo-Christian tradition after the creation of the Septuagint between the third and first centuries BCE. With the translation of the Hebrew Bible into Greek, the word *doxa* became linked to various Hebrew definitions such as "glory," "honor," and "power." Practitioners of Judeo-Christian religious traditions commonly understand these definitions of *doxa*. However, I am not invoking these definitions in my use of the term.

29. Takis Poulakos, "Isocrates' Use of Doxa," *Philosophy and Rhetoric* 34, no. 1 (2001): 73.

30. WKC Gutherie, *A History of Greek Philosophy*. Vol. 4, Plato, the man and his dialogues, earlier period (Cambridge, UK: Cambridge University Press, 1975), 503–47.

31. Ibid.

32. Ekaterina Haskins, "Endoxa, Epistemological Optimism, and Aristotle's Rhetorical Project," *Philosophy and Rhetoric* 37, no. 1 (2004): 4.

33. I am using the masculine pronoun in this unique occasion since rhetors, in ancient Greece, were explicitly conceived of as male. However, I acknowledge that women engaged in rhetorical activities during this time period. For more information on this topic, see Cheryl Glenn, *Rhetoric Retold: Regendering the Tradition from Antiquity Through the Renaissance*.

34. Victor J. Vitanza, *Negation, Subjectivity, and the History of Rhetoric* (Albany: State University of New York Press, 1997).

35. Ibid., 78.

36. I use the modifiers "nearly every" and "almost" to acknowledge the various nation-states that might be more attentive to their liminal historical nature. I have found evidence that some nation-states function without the doxa of eternal stability. One such example that does not always rely on this doxa is Israel, as evidenced in the autobiography of Golda Meir. However, Israel is a paradoxical case in that much of the nation-state's logic relies on Zionism, which inherently reproduces the national doxa of a natural, eternal project. However, Israeli leaders, such as Meir, acknowledge the liminal nature of the nation-state of Israel.

37. Anderson, *Imagined Communities*, 12.

38. Yuval-Davis, *Gender and Nation*, 19.

39. Louis Althusser, "Ideology and Ideological State Apparatuses," in *Lenin and Philosophy: and Other Essays* (New York: Monthly Review Press, 2001), 85–126.

40. Kaplan et al., *Between Woman and Nation*, 8.

41. Such statements are akin to the statement "We are all in this together," which Rosi Braidotti critiques as a move of transnational feminist ethics of "common humanity" (35). Rosi Braidotti's work does an excellent job of explaining how this statement is at once a contingent truth about human existence *and* a fantasy of pan-humanity. In the same vein, the statement "we will endure" holds a contingent truth about national experience and identity while it also creates an ideological, national doxa.

42. Althusser, "Ideology and Ideological State Apparatuses," 110.

43. Slavov Žižek, *The Sublime Object of Ideology* (London: Verso, 1989), 32.

44. Pierre Bourdieu, *Outline of a Theory of Practice*, trans. Richard Nice (Cambridge, UK: Cambridge University Press, 1977), 164.

45. Ibid., 167.

46. Ibid., 164–65.

47. Pateman, *The Sexual Contract.*

48. Ibid., 3.

49. New Zealand appears to be the first country to allow some women to vote in elections in 1893, though the country was still a British colony at the time. Australia was the first sovereign nation-state to grant women the right to vote in 1902. I use the timeline of the late nineteenth and twentieth centuries for women's suffrage because, as Ramirez, Soysal, and Shanahan report, "between 1890 and 1994, women in 96 percent of all nation-states acquired the right to vote and seek public office" (735).

50. Pierre Bourdieu, "Conclusion: Classes and Classifications," in *Distinction: A Social Critique of the Judgment of Taste*, trans. Richard Nice (Cambridge, MA: Harvard University Press, 1984), 471.

51. Jane S. Jensen, *Women Political Leaders* (New York: Palgrave Macmillan, 2008), 15.

52. Marlos L. Van Engen et al., "Gender, Context and Leadership Styles: A Field Study," *Journal of Occupational and Organizational Psychology*, 74 (2001), 581.

53. Jane A. Jensen, *Women Political Leaders: Breaking the Highest Glass Ceiling* (New York: Palgrave Macmillan, 2008), 9.

54. Monique Wittig, *The Straight Mind* (Boston: Beacon Press, 1992), 15.

55. Ibid., 14–16.

56. The term "woman leader" is a specifically English rhetorical gesture. Research is needed in other languages, examining how this trope gets picked up or modified in different linguistic contexts. For example, how are *politiciennes* framed in francophone discussions of women in positions of power? How often is the gendered noun used, and in which countries?

57. I use quotation marks around the phrase "woman leader" to indicate two rhetorical moves: 1) to gesture to how this phrase represents subcategories of "woman president," "female politician," and "woman head of state" 2) to continually remind readers of the fictitious and problematic nature of this labeling.

58. Monique Wittig, *The Straight Mind*, 20.

59. Bourdieu, *Outline of a Theory of Practice*, 169.

60. Ibid., 169.

61. Rebecca S. Richards, "Cyborgs on the World Stage," *Feminist Formations* 23, no. 1 (2011): 19–20.

62. Carl G. Herndl et al., "Shifting Agency" in *The Cultural Turn: Perspectives on Commu-nicative Practices in Workplaces and Professions*, ed. Mark Zachery and Charlotte Thralls (New York: Baywood Publishing, 2007), 137.

63. Ibid., 135.

64. Pierre Bourdieu, *Practical Reason* (Stanford: Stanford University Press, 1998), 76.

65. Ibid., 80.

66. "Real Story Behind the Iron Lady," *The Daily Telegraph*, February 26, 2006, 26.

67. Margaret Thatcher, quoted in Andrew Delahunty, *Goldenballs and the Iron Lady: A Little Book of Nicknames* (New York: Oxford University Press, 2004), 114.

68. Benazir Bhutto, *Daughter of Destiny* (New York: HarperPerennial, 2007), xii.

69. Ibid., 307.

70. The Council of Women World Leaders. October 22, 2012, www.cwwl.org.

71. Gerard Hauser, quoted in Rachel Riedner et al., *Democracies to Come* (Lanham, MD: Lexington Books, 2008), 32.

72. See David Hollinger, "Obama, the Instability of Color Lines, and the Promise of a Postethnic Future," *Callaloo* 31, (2008): 1033–1037; Ta-Nehisi Coates "Is Obama Black Enough?" *Time*, February 1, 2007, www.time.com/time/nation/article/0,8559,1584736,00.html (accessed February 8, 2013); Sheryl Gay and Stolberg, "In Defining Obama, Misperceptions Stick," The New York Times, August 18, 2010, www.nytimes.com/2010/08/19/us/politics/19memo.html (accessed February 8, 2013).

73. Spivak argues that an essentializing position can be a useful strategy for minoritized groups of people. However, "strategic essentialism" should only be used scrupulously as a means of gathering power or position. Chela Sandoval's method of "differential consciousness" argues that, in order to oppose dominant ideologies, minoritized groups must continually move between different positionings.

74. Jensen, *Women Political Leaders*, 10.

75. Ibid., 11.

76. See Julie Bindel "Iceland: The World's Most Feminist Country," *The Guardian*, 25 March 25, 2010, www.guardian.co.uk/lifeandstyle/2010/mar/25/iceland-most-feminist-country (accessed February 8, 2013); Katrin Bennhold "In Sweden, Men Can Have It All," *The New York Times*, June 9, 2010, www.nytimes.com/2010/06/10/world/europe/10ihtsweden.html?pagewanted=all& r0 (accessed February 8, 2013); and Dean Clark "Getting Paid for Parenting," *U.S. News and World Report*, March 18, 2007, wwwusnews.com/usnews/news/article/070318/26childcare.htm (accessed February 8, 2013).

77. Nadira Jagan-Brancier, *Cheddi Jagan Research Centre*, www.jagan.org (accessed February 8, 2013).

78. Quotation marks around "women world leaders" indicate the rhetorical construct of a tradition of political women, as opposed to the embodied women who serve in national leadership.

79. Campbell et al., *Presidents Creating the Presidency* (Chicago: University of Chicago Press, 2008), 18.

80. Ibid., 27.

81. See Rebecca Richards, *From Daughters of Destiny to Iron Ladies* (manuscript forthcoming).

Chapter Five

Leadership and the [Vice] Presidency

The Nomination Acceptance Speeches of Geraldine Ferraro and Sarah Palin

Michele Lockhart

> *To the women who should have been [vice] president;*
> *To the women who tried to be [vice] president;*
> *To the women who will be [vice] president.*
> —Karlyn Kohrs Campbell and Kathleen Hall Jamieson
> *Presidents Creating the Presidency: Deeds Done in Words*

This chapter focuses on two case studies, specifically, the two women nominated to run for vice president of the United States on a major party ticket, Democrat or Republican, specifically, Democrat Geraldine Ferraro and Republican Sarah Palin.[1] The purpose of this chapter is to determine the extent to which women's political rhetoric has changed, and to gain a better understanding of women's use of political rhetoric while determining its strengths and weaknesses; consequently, one can deduce what a woman in the national political arena must, or should, say in order to be more effective and successful with her audience. The political discourse analysis of both vice-presidential nomination acceptance speeches shows how and why certain language women use in politics is considered effective or ineffective. The credibility (*ethos*) of each individual and the context of the speech (*kairos*) are woven into the analysis. This interdisciplinary study incorporates areas such as rhetoric, women in politics, political rhetoric, and leadership and the presidency in order to investigate the language women use in politics. There are implications for the vice-presidential nominee running alongside a presidential nominee with or without evident or potential leadership qualities because the unity of the team is affected. The potential leadership qualities of Ferraro,

71

Palin, and their respective presidential counterparts are examined within each vice-presidential nominee's speech. Specifically, I analyze the use of the following three topics.[2] (See Table 5.1).

Table 5.1.   Topic and Description

Topic	Description
"individual experience"	Within the speech, "individual experience" includes instances when an "I" and either an infinitive or statement concerning prior work or educational experience appeared.
"presidential running mate"	Within the speech, the term "running mate" or the actual name of the running mate appeared.
"party opponent"	Within the speech, "party opponent" includes instances when the opponent is addressed by name, title, "administration," or "opponent."

Material generated by author

LEADERSHIP AND THE PRESIDENCY

When it comes to leadership and the presidency, there are many factors to consider; some argue that particular factors are more important than others: "It is one thing for potential voters to think a woman nominee is a good idea, or an idea whose time has come. It is another thing to vote a particular way because of a vice-presidential candidate."[3] I argue, however, that the vice-presidential nominee and the language used to better identify the presidential nominee (implicitly and explicitly) affects and influences the audience. Ultimately, Frankovic concludes:

> What is important to note is that in most elections the vice-presidential candidates are ancillary to the campaign; in most circumstances they are liked, respected, and they matter almost not at all in voters' presidential choices. The vice-presidential candidates in 1984, linked in public assessment with their running mates, mattered only marginally in the public's final voting decision.[4]

I disagree that the vice-presidential running mates "mattered only marginally." It is within this leadership component that I attempt to prove otherwise. The leadership component takes into consideration the vice-presidential nominee herself and her contribution to increasing either the strengths of her presidential nominee counterpart or herself.

Throughout the analysis, Greenstein's six leadership qualities as defined in *The Presidential Difference: Leadership Style from FDR to George W. Bush* will be drawn upon.[5] The six leadership styles are derived from Greenstein's work, and include the following: public communication; organizational capacity; political skill; vision; cognitive style; emotional intelligence.

For clarification purposes, the following definitions will be used: public communication, "the outer face of leadership" and the "proficiency as a public communicator;"[6] organizational capacity, "the inner workings of the presidency"[7] and "his ability to rally his colleagues and structure their activities effectively;"[8] the third and fourth, political skill and vision, "political operator"[9]—"his *political skill* and the extent to which it is harnessed to a *vision* of public policy,"[10] cognitive style, "the president processes the Niagara of advice and information that comes his way,"[11] and emotional intelligence,[12] "the president's ability to manage his emotions and turn them to constructive purposes, rather than being dominated by them and allowing them to diminish his leadership" [*emphasis in original*].[13]

The strengths and weaknesses of both the vice-presidential nominee and the presidential nominee each play a role in the success or failure of the ticket. The leadership analysis will include examples of when Ferraro and Palin used one of the six leadership qualities to highlight either their strengths or their counterparts' strengths.

Leadership and the presidency explore the partnership between the presidential and vice-presidential nominees as well as the nature of power transformation. The partnership has implications for the vice-presidential nominee and the language she uses. The amount of literature dedicated to U.S. vice presidents serving as a counterpart to the president as well as the research available on Ferraro and Palin is not rich. Greenstein corroborates my findings by noting in the interview I conducted with him: "There are many analysts of presidential leadership—Neustadt, Barber, and Hargrove, for example. I know of none who focus on vice presidents, however."[14]

THE NOMINATION ACCEPTANCE SPEECHES[15]

This analysis focuses on the rhetorical strategies evident in the U.S. vice-presidential nomination acceptance speech delivered by 1984 Democratic candidate Geraldine Ferraro,[16] which she delivered on July 19, 1984 in San Francisco, California, and 2008 Republican candidate Sarah Palin,[17] which she delivered on September 3, 2008 in Minneapolis—St. Paul, Minnesota. The content analysis reveals trends and rhetorical techniques within each acceptance speech.[18]

The analysis presents the quantitative data within Ferraro's acceptance speech. The analysis draws connections between *ethos* and *kairos* employed within the speech, revealing significant realities and expectations concerning both the individual candidate and our society as a whole. Leadership qualities based upon the language used are included in the analysis. The analysis, as well as the length of each speech, is based upon the delivered speech, not the speech drafted by the speechwriter. Within the nomination acceptance speeches and among the previously selected analysis parameters, Ferraro and Palin address the following topics: "individual experience," "presidential running mate," and "party opponent." These topics and terms within the speech, as presented in the various graphs below, are explicated. Quantified-qualitative research methods fulfill the purposes of this analysis while illustrating patterns among the categories within the speech.

Analysis: Individual Experience

In the "individual experience" category, Ferraro first addressed the topic at the 16th percent of the speech while Palin first addressed it at the 26th percent of the speech. (See Figure 5.1).

Neither Ferraro nor Palin had extensive leadership experience. Voters consider the fact that the vice president has the potential to become president in certain situations. In other words, some people look at the vice-presidential nominee as the potential president. Both women address their "individual experience." Ferraro began addressing the topic earlier than Palin, five times in the first fifth of the speech, and Ferraro did not address her "individual experience" again. Palin, on the other hand, noted her experience fourteen times in total—six times in the second fifth of the speech and eight times in the third fifth of the speech.

Ferraro incorporates her "individual experience" chronologically, and all five instances occur within the first fifth of the speech. In her first instance, she asserted, "If you work hard and play by the rules, you can earn your share of America's blessings. Those are the beliefs I learned from my parents. And those are the values I taught my students as a teacher in the public schools of New York City."[19] Ferraro first attempts to connect with a particular group

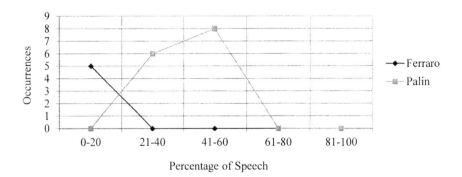

Figure 5.1.   Note: Within the speech, "individual experience" includes instances when an "I" and either an infinitive or statement concerning prior work or educational experience appears.

within the audience—hard-working teachers.[20] She reaches out to the every-day working Americans and presents herself as such.

She continues to promote her strong work ethic by pointing to her continued education: "At night, I went to law school. I became an assistant district attorney, and I put my share of criminals behind bars."[21] Most important here is her rationale and endgame for attending law school. Note that Ferraro made clear that she worked to put "criminals behind bars"—she did not practice other kinds of law that would, perhaps, have been more lucrative financially. Additionally, Ferraro made it clear that she—a Democrat and a woman—was tough on crime.

Finally, Ferraro reveals her success as a political figure against all odds. She stated, "When I first ran for Congress, all the political experts said a Democrat could not win my home district in Queens. I put my faith in the people and the values that we shared. Together, we proved the political experts wrong."[22] Ferraro stated that because of her strong work ethic, good intentions, and faith, she has been able to come this far. She does not question how much further she and the American people can go. Ferraro illustrates her own cognitive style—her ability to process advice and information.[23]

Within this same category, the focus of the analysis shifts to Palin—she describes and points to her "individual experience" fourteen times within the second and third fifths of the speech. "I was just your average hockey mom, and signed up for the PTA."[24] From involvement with her children's education to her early career in politics, Palin ensures she reaches out to particular groups within the audience. "And when I ran for city council, I didn't need focus groups and voter profiles because I knew those voters, and I knew their families, too."[25] Palin then describes her responsibilities in local and state politics, in general.

> Before I became governor of the great state of Alaska, I was mayor of my hometown. And since our opponents in this presidential election seem to look down on that experience, let me explain to them what the job involves. I guess—I guess a small-town mayor is sort of like a "community organizer," except that you have actual responsibilities.[26]

Palin points to her motivation to continue in the political arena at the state level. "And I pledge to all Americans that I will carry myself in this spirit as Vice President of the United States. This was the spirit that brought me to the governor's office, when I took on the old politics as usual in Juneau, when I stood up to the special interests, and the lobbyists, and the big oil companies, and the good-ol' [*sic*] boys."[27] Those four areas that Palin noted are things she is inherently and adamantly against—all of which she points to explicitly and implicitly throughout the speech. By pointing out her assertiveness and ability to process information from various sources, she highlights her cognitive style.

Palin continues to point to her "individual experience" as Governor of Alaska while pointing to specific examples that have resulted in change. "I came to office promising major ethics reform, to end the culture of self-dealing. And today, that ethics reform is the law."[28] Palin continues to point to changes she has made (that affect her directly) that have resulted in saving taxpayers money:

> While I was at it, I got rid of a few things in the governor's office that I didn't believe our citizens should have to pay for. That luxury jet was over the top. I put it on eBay. I love to drive myself to work. And I thought we could muddle through without the governor's personal chef, although I've got to admit that sometimes my kids sure miss her. [. . .] I told the Congress "thanks, but no thanks," on that Bridge to Nowhere. If our state wanted to build a bridge, we were going to build it ourselves.[29]

Within the previously defined leadership style components, Palin effectively demonstrates her organizational capacity, political skill, and vision. Within the political skill and vision categories, Palin explains how she stood up to certain groups who agreed with "politics-as-usual" and fought to bring needed changes to public policy. Palin also pointed to ethics reform that became law while she was in office. Within "organizational capacity," Palin cited what she removed from the budget—the jet and the chef—and declined the "Bridge to Nowhere."

Analysis: Presidential Running Mate

Ferraro addressed her "presidential running mate" five times while Palin addressed him seventeen times. (See Figure 5.2).

Even though Ferraro does address her "presidential running mate," she does not explicitly point to any of his qualities or leadership attributes within the speech. In total, she addresses him five times—once in the first fifth, three times in the second fifth, and the final occurrence in the last fifth of the speech.

Ferraro first addresses the fact that they are running on the same ticket. "And I am proud to run with a man who will be one of the great Presidents of this century, Walter F. Mondale."[30] Ferraro first identified her presidential running mate as "Walter F. Mondale" as opposed to "Walter Frederick Mondale." It is within the second occurrence that Ferraro calls Mondale "Fritz" and asserted their imminent victory. "In this campaign, Fritz Mondale and I have put our faith in the people. And we are going to prove the experts wrong again. We are going to win. We are going to win because Americans across this country believe in the same basic dream."[31] By addressing her presiden-

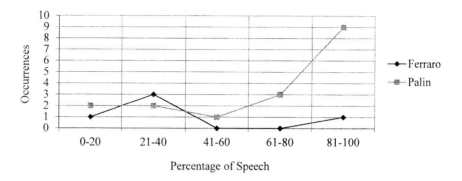

tial nominee with a casual nickname, "Fritz," Ferraro builds the notion of their everyday, personable interaction with one another. The nickname also draws the audience in closer as opposed to if Ferraro constantly used Mondale's formal title within the speech. Mondale did give the appearance of a stern, quite serious individual. The nickname, even though seemingly insignificant, may have improved or lightened Mondale's image. Their relationship is reiterated with the third and fourth instance. "Last week, I visited Elmore, Minnesota, the small town where Fritz Mondale was raised. And soon Fritz and Joan will visit our family in Queens."[32] Pointing to the locations where each nominee is from opens the discussion to two Americans coming from different walks-of-life yet coming together with one common goal. Ferraro noted, "I wanted to point out that although nine hundred people live in Mondale's hometown of Elmore, Minnesota, whereas in Queens there are two thousand people on some blocks, we all have the same values, the same hopes for our children."[33] Ferraro deliberately incorporates particular facts into her speech with a purpose in mind. She is cognizant of the message she wants to send to her audience.

Finally, Ferraro stated, "I know in my heart that Walter Mondale will be that President."[34] Even though her assertion is unsubstantiated and based solely on her "heart," one must also take into consideration *pathos*. Within political discourse, *pathos* can be quite effective. Similar to Ferraro's use of Mondale's nickname and lightening his image, Ferraro's use of "heart" may have been an attempt to do the same for her image. In addition to her claim, Ferraro's emotional feeling holds little weight due to the fact that Mondale's *ethos* was not addressed. Ferraro is relying on his established credibility as a former vice president. However, Ferraro is explicit when addressing Mondale's credibility in her book, "In the six years I had known Fritz Mondale, I had come to admire him greatly as an intelligent, thoughtful man, capable of outstanding leadership."[35] Ferraro did not dedicate any of her acceptance speech to addressing Mondale's "outstanding leadership" qualities, such as public communication, organizational capacity, political skill, vision, cognitive style, or his emotional intelligence. The rationale as to why Mondale's leadership qualities were not addressed in her nomination acceptance speech is not explained in Ferraro's memoir. This fact, in conjunction with similar instances throughout much of the campaign, has effects on the election results.

Within this same category, the focus of the analysis shifts to Palin—she dedicated a substantial amount of her speech to her "presidential running mate," Senator John McCain. In total, Palin mentioned the presidential contender seventeen times while the most occurrences were in the last fifth of her speech—there she pointed to his qualities nine times. She consistently mentioned McCain throughout the speech. In fact, Palin uses her most assertive language within this topic. Additionally, within the leadership style qualities, Palin does an effective job of presenting her "presidential running mate" and highlighting his leadership qualities.

Palin uses different titles to refer to her running mate. For example, she calls McCain "John S. McCain," "Senator John McCain," "John McCain," and "Senator McCain." By using the word "Senator," Palin points to his already established credibility as a leader, and by calling him "John McCain," she points to him as a person.

Palin begins by not only "accepting" a call to serve but also by describing the challenges her running mate has overcome:

> I accept the call to help our nominee for President to serve and defend America and I accept the challenge of a tough fight in this election, against confident opponents, at a crucial hour for our country. And I accept the privilege of serving with a man who has come through much harder missions, and met far graver challenges, and knows how tough fights are won—the next President of the United States, John S. McCain.[36]

Palin also uses *ploche* when she stated, "I accept." She takes the active role and accepts the offer and responsibility of serving. Such repetition, *ploche*, is defined as "referring to anything plaited or woven, a single word reappearing like a single strand in a braid or fabric."[37] Palin asserted her confidence in her running mate by stating the title of what she believes he will soon be called—President of the United States. Palin then dismisses certain claims when she asserted, "But the pollsters—the pollsters and the pundits they overlooked just one thing when they wrote him off. They overlooked the caliber of the man himself—the determination, and resolve, and the sheer guts of Senator John McCain."[38] In her memoir, Palin explains, "I reminded Americans that it hadn't been so long ago that the polls and pundits had written John off."[39] Those polls and pundits also affect the beliefs of the audience—Palin explicitly decreased the credibility of those sources.

Palin asserted McCain's straightforwardness and consistency with various audiences when she noted, "As for my running mate, you can be certain that wherever he goes, and whoever is listening, John McCain is the same man."[40] In addition to his consistency, Palin also points to the confidence that voters can have in his word: "Senator McCain, also, he promises to use the power of veto in defense of the public interest, and as a chief executive, I can assure you it works."[41] When Palin stated that Senator John McCain "promises to use the power of veto in defense of the public interest,"[42] she demonstrates McCain's political skill and vision, two of Greenstein's six leadership qualities. She also effectively pairs herself within the same categories (as well as with her running mate) by confirming that vetoes work.

In addition to the confidence voters can have in McCain, Palin expresses her confidence in the ticket when she stated, "Starting in January, in a McCain-Palin Administration, we're going to lay more pipelines, and build more nuclear plants, and create jobs with clean coal, and move forward on solar, wind, geothermal, and other alternative sources."[43] By noting that the McCain-Palin ticket is not only possible, but also probable, she noted what action they plan to take.

The motivation behind the actions of an individual is telling. Palin points to McCain's selflessness: "And then there are those, like John McCain, who use their careers to promote change."[44] She continues by pointing to results and action taken as opposed to simply talking.

> And then there is the idealism of those leaders, like John McCain, who actually do great things. They're the ones who are good for more than talk, the ones that we've always been able to count on to serve and to defend America. Senator McCain's record of actual achievements and reform helps explain why so many special interests, and lobbyists, and comfortable committee chairmen in Congress have fought the prospect of a McCain presidency—from the primary election of 2000 to this very day.[45]

Analysis: Party Opponent

Within the "party opponent" category, Ferraro addresses the category six times while Palin addresses it eleven times. The manner in which each nominee addressed the "party opponent" category holds great weight. Both Ferraro and Palin address the presidential candidate of the opposing party; however, Palin also addressed her opposing vice-presidential candidate. Ferraro used terms such as "administration," "Ronald Reagan," and "Mr. President" to address her "party opponent." Palin, on the other hand, used terms such as "opponent(s)," "a man," "Democratic nominee for President," and "Senator Obama and Senator Biden." (See Figure 5.3).

Throughout this study, I remained cognizant as to whom the opponent might be. Additionally, I considered whether the vice-presidential nominee was only to spar directly with the opposing vice-presidential nominee, or if the opposing presidential nominee was fair game, too. Ultimately, the "party opponent" parameters (as described in Table 5.1) were the most accurate representation.

Ferraro addresses her "party opponent" six times—twice in the second fifth, twice in the third fifth, once in the fourth fifth, and once in the last fifth. In fact, addressing her "party opponent" is the most assertive language used by Ferraro in the nomination acceptance speech, and from a rhetorical stand-point, this topic is the most effective among the other topics. Ferraro's asser-tiveness further diminishes the credibility of her opponent. "Americans want to live by the same set of rules. But under this administration, the rules are rigged against too many of our people."[46] Essentially, Ferraro explains that with the administration in place, there is no hope for the majority of the American people. Ferraro continues by stating, "It isn't right that this year Ronald Reagan will hand the American people a bill for interest on the national debt larger than the entire cost of the federal government under John F. Kennedy."[47] Ferraro makes a rhetorically effective move: she compares her opponent to one of her Party's former presidents, John F. Kennedy. Ferraro calls her opponent out by name and points to a concrete flaw. Ferraro elevates her language by becoming more assertive in the third instance, "It is time Ronald Reagan stopped scaring our senior citizens."[48] The repetition of Ronald Reagan's name in a negative light can be a rhetorically effective move; such repetition is described as *ploche*. The precise repetition of a term within or across several sentences is effective. Ferraro is successful in these two instances because she cites a particular example and reaches out to a certain demographic within her audience.

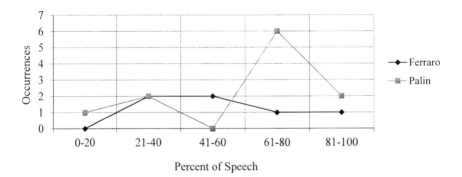

Figure 5.3.   Note: Within the speech, "party opponent" includes instances when the opponent is addressed by name, title, "administration," or "opponent.

It is toward the end of the speech that Ferraro addresses "the Administration." Ferraro incorporates loaded issues while addressing her party opponent as well as providing her own response—a dialogue of sorts: "To an Administration that would have us debate all over again whether the Voting Rights Act should be renewed and whether segregated schools should be tax exempt, we say, Mr. President: Those debates are over."[49] Because Ronald Reagan was the incumbent, Ferraro referred to him as "Mr. President" while in all other instances, she referred to him as "Ronald Reagan." Using Reagan's title as opposed to his first and last name is a much more direct and bold move. Ferraro's use of Reagan's title presses upon the audience that he—the president—is the one at fault while Ferraro implicitly noted that the Mondale-Ferraro ticket would in fact end those debates.

The organization of addressing "the Administration" continues into the last fifth of the speech: "To an Administration that would savage student loans and education at the dawn of a new technological age, we say: You fit the classic definition of a cynic; you know the price of everything, but the value of nothing."[50] Ferraro explains that the "You fit the classic definition of a cynic" statement was, "ostensibly to the Administration but [was] aiming at Reagan himself."[51] She explains, "In the dawn of a new technological age, when we needed educated young people more than ever, the Republicans wanted to savage student loans, cut support that would broaden educational opportunities, and grant tax exemptions to segregated schools."[52] Ferraro's definition of her opponent as a "cynic" is indeed the most assertive language used by Ferraro in the speech. Ferraro incorporates her lessons learned from Carol Gilligan's book, *In a Different Voice*. Those lessons include the inherent differences of how women and men think, how they develop solutions, and how they engage with one another.[53] By pressing upon her audience the importance of education, Ferraro sets their sights on the bigger picture. Ferraro noted, "Instead of thinking in win-lose terms, women were more apt to consider the gray areas in between."[54] Clearly, Ferraro was thinking of the future and using aggressive language to give weight to her assertion. Additionally, when Ferraro says, "the price of everything, but the value of nothing," she is using the figure *antithesis*, the "conjoining contrasting ideas."[55] Ferraro is able to address particular aspects of the administration that she, her party, and her supporters are against while speaking on the behalf of the American people.

In another example of *antithesis*, Ferraro engages in a sort of conversation style, which is elevated in the second and final example. There she points to the "administration's confusion" and then answers once again on the behalf of the audience. "To those who have watched this administration's confusion in the Middle East, as it has tilted first toward one and then another of Israel's long-time enemies and wonder: 'Will America stand by her friends and sister democracy?' [W]e say: America knows who her friends are in the

Middle East and around the world."[56] Such a technique draws the audience in as they wait for the answer: "[T]he dialogue often bears no relation to any actual prior utterance but rather frames a current utterance as dialogue in order to dramatize the speaker's evaluation of it and to create a recognizable scene as well as captivating rhythm."[57] From a rhetorical standpoint, the "party opponent" topic is the most effective among the other topics.

Interestingly, a direct feud between Ferraro and the opposing vice-presidential nominee, George Herbert Walker Bush, is non-existent in this speech. Ferraro addresses the opponent (the administration and Ronald Reagan himself). Even though Ferraro does not address her rationale as to why she did not address her opposing vice-presidential nominee in her memoir, I assert that Reagan was indeed the "opponent" in the mind of the audience. Such an assertion follows the belief that the vice-presidential nominees cannot make-or-break a ticket, and second, that the presidential nominees are above those attacks—the attacks are left for the vice-presidential nominees. Additionally, Ferraro's credibility as a leader positions her to confront Reagan. Furthermore, both the campaign and Ferraro are well aware that she will have her opportunity to address her opposing vice-presidential nominee during the debate. The manner in which Ferraro addressed her opponents during the nomination acceptance speech and pointed to concrete examples, lends itself to fit within the political skill and vision leadership categories.

Within this same category, the focus of the analysis shifts to Palin. The parameters within "party opponent" include many things, and Palin covered all of her bases. She addressed her "party opponent" eleven times, with six instances occurring in the fourth fifth of her speech.

Palin first describes her opponents as "confident" when she stated, "I accept the call to help our nominee for President to serve and defend America and I accept the challenge of a tough fight in this election, against confident opponents, at a crucial hour for our country."[58] Palin's acknowledgment of her opponents is effective—she knows what the ticket is up against and she knows what it will take to win. She then diminishes her opponent's credibility:

> Before I became governor of the great state of Alaska, I was mayor of my hometown. And since our opponents in this presidential election seem to look down on that experience, let me explain to them what the job involves. I guess—I guess a small-town mayor is sort of like a "community organizer," except that you have actual responsibilities. I might add—I might add that in small towns, we don't quite know what to make of a candidate who lavishes praise on working people when they're listening, and then talks about how bitterly they cling to their religion and guns when those people aren't listening. No, we tend to prefer candidates who don't talk about us one way in Scranton and another way in San Francisco.[59]

When Palin acknowledges her opponent's self-described status as a "community organizer," she sets herself up for a more powerful attack. The rhetorical figure is *concessio*: "The speaker concedes a point, either to hurt the adversary directly or to prepare for a more important argument."[60] Palin attacks her opponent through her use of sarcasm. There is a fine balance a female politician must keep while showing her audience she is tough but not harsh. Additionally, Palin must also weigh the risk as to whether the audience will keep her "community organizer" statement within context of her "party opponent," or if some in the audience might generalize and consider the comment as an attack on *all* community organizers. Nevertheless, Palin set the statement up, and I assert that the comment was effective as presented based upon the audience's response.

By discrediting her opponent's solutions in a sarcastic tone, she strategically diminishes his credibility without negatively affecting her own: "Our opponents say, again and again, that drilling will not solve all of America's energy problems—as if we didn't know that already. But the fact—the fact that drilling, though, won't solve every problem is no excuse to do nothing at all."[61] The language is effective based upon the response from her audience; the audience supported drilling as a solution to some of America's energy problems. Palin remembers the crowd cheering which she describes as "a shout-out to independent-minded Americans who didn't look to government for all the answers."[62] Later in her speech, Palin remembers the audience chanting, "Drill, baby, drill! Drill, baby, drill!"[63] In 2008, a substantial point of contention between the Republicans and Democrats surrounded energy sources; one was for drilling while the other was against it, respectively. Additionally, Palin's connection to the Alaska natural gas pipeline as well as her record of "fighting the oil company monopoly" was a clear indicator of her intentions concerning energy sources should she (and McCain) be elected.[64]

Palin points to her opponent's language next when she observes, "And now I've noticed a pattern with our opponent. And maybe you have, too. We've all heard his dramatic speeches before devoted followers."[65] Palin effectively addresses the language and style of her opponent's speeches, something that his supporters will consider. Moreover, Palin describes his supporters as "devoted followers," which has a negative connotation. Palin is addressing two audiences—her supporters cheering for her and her opponents "devoted followers," and she is effectively drawing attention to her opponent's flaws.

While walking the fine-line of addressing her "party opponent," Palin sets up a powerful point: "And there is much to like and admire about our opponent. But listening to him speak, it's easy to forget that this is a man who has authored two memoirs but not a single major law or even a reform, not even in the state senate."[66] Palin draws on her earlier statement concerning her opponent's language and then adds his inaction to the statement.

The focus on her opponent's language continues.

> This is a man who can give an entire speech about the wars America is fighting, and never use the word "victory" except when he's talking about his own campaign. But when the cloud of rhetoric has passed, when the roar of the crowd fades away, when the stadium lights go out, and those Styrofoam Greek columns are hauled back to some studio lot—when that happens, what exactly is our opponent's plan? What does he actually seek to accomplish, after he's done turning back the waters and healing the planet? The answer—The answer is to make government bigger, and take more of your money, and give you more orders from Washington, and to reduce the strength of America in a dangerous world. America needs more energy; our opponent is against producing it.[67]

Palin employs a rhetorical technique when she stated, "When the cloud . . . when the roar . . . when the stadium lights."[68] The rhetorical figure used is *incrementum*:[69] "words or clauses placed in climactic order."[70] The building of the sentence leads the audience to a question, one for which Palin supplies the answer. The dialogue pattern is effective when drawing the audience closer to the speaker. Additionally, when Palin stated, "take more . . . give you more,"[71] she is using the rhetorical technique, *antithesis* (with one cola).

She continues with the next instance, within the parameters of this study, and addresses the party itself when she asserted, "The Democratic nominee for President supports plans to raise income taxes, and raise payroll taxes, and raise investment income taxes, and raise the death tax, and raise business taxes, and increase the tax burden on the American people by hundreds of billions of dollars."[72] Palin effectively uses the rhetorical technique, *ploche*, when she emphasizes the words "raise" and "taxes." She couples the emphasis on "taxes" with a rhetorical question to the audience. "How are you—how are you going to be better off if our opponent adds a massive tax burden to the American economy?"[73] Finally, by Palin stating "our opponent," she positions herself on the side of her supporters in the audience and a sense of unity is further established.

The final occurrence within the parameters of this analysis explicitly stated the names of her opponents. "And though both Senator Obama and Senator Biden have been going on lately about how they are always, quote, 'fighting for you,' let us face the matter squarely."[74] Palin was certain to address the opposing vice-presidential nominee and presidential nominee directly and diminish their statement of "fighting for you."

POST-ELECTION

The Reagan-Bush ticket won with "over fifty-two million" votes while the Mondale-Ferraro ticket had "thirty-six million" votes.[75] The end to the campaign marked the end of an historic journey for Ferraro. Her nomination to run as the first woman vice-presidential candidate marked a moment in time for women in the United States. Ferraro described Election Day, and noted that she had been working on her concession speech[76] that afternoon.[77]

Having been the first woman nominated to run for vice president in the United States, Ferraro's success or failure was projected upon the female gender. Even though Ferraro made history and did make progress in women's equality, she asserted that the fight was not over. She asserted, "The country is never going to be ready for anything new until people are put in the position of experiencing it."[78] Experiencing history is exactly what the country did. Ferraro stated in her memoir, *Ferraro: My Story*, "The real test of my candidacy will come when the next woman runs for national office. Only then will we know if she, too, is going to be judged by a standard different from that used for her male opponents; if she, too, is going to have to be better in order to be judged equal."[79] Twenty-four years later, the test came.

The McCain-Palin ticket did not win, and the cohesiveness within the campaign and communication among key players did not improve. Palin and her speechwriters prepared two speeches depending on the results of the election. Palin did not deliver a concession speech[80] on November 4, 2008.[81]

CONCLUSION

The conclusions of this chapter suggest that the language women use in U.S. politics at the national level is becoming more assertive and direct. The language female political figures use to address particular topics has changed substantially, as evidenced by the case studies of Geraldine Ferraro and Sarah Palin. Managing emotional intelligence while remaining cognizant of the aforementioned variables is of greatest importance. The leadership qualities of the vice-presidential nominee and her contribution to increase either the strengths of her presidential nominee counterpart or herself greatly affect the success of the party ticket. The women who mark a trail for future generations of political women to build upon are speaking the language of politics in an ever-changing discourse community. This discourse community must be taken into consideration as the language of politics continues to evolve for women. Currently, women have joined the U.S. vice-presidential discourse community, but only as candidates. Women have not yet made it fully into the elected vice-presidential or presidential discourse community.

Moreover, in so attempting to join the vice-presidential and/or presidential discourse community, women are changing the discourse of politics. By analyzing the discourse that makes women in politics *possible*, it is natural for one to point to specific recommendations, which would make a woman in a U.S. vice-presidential or presidential position *probable*. Therefore, for the political woman to be effective and electable, she must first continue to use the language she used prior to her national nomination. A consistent tone in her message not only reflects the character of the person but also her *persona*. In other words, her consistent rhetoric creates her credible *persona*.

NOTES

1. There has been a dichotomy between the two parties—Democrat and Republican—since the parties were formed. Each party caters to a particular discourse community, which holds its own ideologies. For purposes of clarification, definitions of ideologies for the Democratic Party will generally fall within liberal ideals while the Republican Party will generally fall within conservative ideals. Consequently, the language a candidate uses within each party to address their supporters is markedly different. Any additional analysis regarding specifics within the ideologies are beyond the scope of this analysis. The complexity when taking into consideration the differences in party, Democrat and Republican, time differences, 1984 and 2008, are great, and it becomes clear that there are too many variables to present a complete and accurate overview.

2. A unique methodological design for statistical representation of qualitative data was created in order to illustrate graphically when particular terms were used within Ferraro's and Palin's speeches. In order to present the qualitative data quantitatively, I developed three categories with well-defined parameters applicable to each of the delivered speeches. In order to accurately represent and compare two speeches, each of which had a different word count, the calculation was based upon the percentage of the word within the speech as opposed to word count. The word location of when a particular word occurred was divided into the total number of words within that speech. Graphs represent the percentage when particular words were used. Each graph was divided into fifths in order to ensure a well-defined middle section of the speech. I conducted an interview with Fred I. Greenstein. Emeritus Professor of Political Science at Princeton University; Director of the Research Program in Leadership Studies at the Woodrow Wilson School of Public Affairs and International Affairs. Interview conducted February 2010. Greenstein's analysis of the six leadership dimensions explicated in his text, *The Presidential Difference: Leadership Style from FDR to George W. Bush*, plays a substantial role in my analysis.

3. Kathleen Frankovic, "The 1984 Election: The Irrelevance of the Campaign," *American Political Science Association* 18.1, 1985, accessed February 6, 2010, www.apsanet.org.

4. Ibid., 47.

5. Greenstein acknowledges his influence by Richard E. Neustadt, *Presidential Power*, and James David Barber, Fred Greenstein, *The Presidential Difference: Leadership Style From FDR to George W. Bush* (New Jersey: Princeton University Press, 2004), 283.

6. Fred Greenstein, *The Presidential Difference: Leadership Style From FDR to George W. Bush*, 5.

7. Greenstein stated, "I use the masculine pronoun throughout to avoid gender-free locutions in discussing an office that has had only male incumbents at the time of writing [first edition published in 2000]. It is highly unlikely, however, that the presidency will remain a male bastion," ibid., 3.

8. Ibid.

9. Ibid.

10. Ibid., 5–6.

11. Ibid., 6.

12. Greenstein acknowledges Max Weber, German sociologist, as describing the notion of emotional intelligence as "the firm taming of the soul," ibid., 6; Daniel Goleman, *Emotional Intelligence* (New York: Bantam Books, 1995), 265.

13. Ibid.

14. Fred Greenstein, *Re: Interview* (Message to the author, February 17, 2010).

15. Politicians have relied on and consulted with speechwriters at various levels. The occasion and audience certainly play a factor in the level of involvement with the speechwriter(s). In either case, once the political figure speaks the words within the speech and delivers the message to the audience, the political figure gains authorship.

Ferraro appears to have relied less on speechwriters as opposed to more. Within her memoir, Ferraro is clear to point out that she contributed to the writing of various speeches and revised her speaking points in consultation with her speechwriter(s). There are no instances in her memoir of Ferraro being handed a speech and simply reading its contents to an audience. Ferraro does acknowledge individuals who helped her write various speeches. For example, Ferraro relied on the assistance of Jan Kalicki, and David Koshgarian, the legislative director of Ferraro's Washington office who was also serving as a speechwriter, when preparing to address the World Affairs Council Geraldine Ferraro, *Ferraro: My Story* (Evanston: Northwestern University Press, 2004), 109. Ferraro addresses her "speechwriter" during the campaign as Fred Martin, ibid., 220.

As a vice-presidential nominee, Palin utilized the expertise of speechwriters throughout the campaign while making a concerted effort to contribute to the text when possible. Palin's lead speechwriter for her nomination acceptance speech was Matthew Scully. He had worked for McCain previously and was already on board the campaign. Palin describes writing the convention speech as a "team effort" and acknowledges the leader of the team was "an ace speechwriter," Sarah Palin, *Going Rogue: An American Life* (New York: HarperCollins, 2009), 239.

16. Michael Eidenmuller, "Geraldine Ferraro," *American Rhetoric*, n.d., accessed October 28, 2008, www.americanrhetoric.com.

17. Michael Eidenmuller, "Sarah Palin," *American Rhetoric*, n.d., accessed December 2, 2008, www.americanrhetoric.com.

18. Number of words delivered in vice-presidential acceptance speeches: Ferraro: 1,757; Palin: 3,155.

19. Michael Eidenmuller, "Geraldine Ferraro," *American Rhetoric*, n.d., accessed October 28, 2008, www.americanrhetoric.com.

20. In addition, Ferraro was able to address implicitly a group of teachers, such as the National Education Association (NEA), who were watching the speech on television throughout the country.

21. Ibid.

22. Ibid.

23. Greenstein, *The Presidential Difference*, 6.

24. Michael Eidenmuller, "Sarah Palin," *American Rhetoric*, n.d., accessed December 2, 2008, www.americanrhetoric.com.

25. Ibid.

26. Ibid.

27. Ibid.

28. Ibid.

29. Ibid.

30. Eidenmuller, "Geraldine Ferraro."

31. Ibid.

32. Ibid.

33. Geraldine Ferraro, *Ferraro: My Story* (Evanston: Northwestern University Press, 2004), 19.

34. Eidenmuller, "Geraldine Ferraro."

35. Ferraro, *Ferraro*, 33.

36. Eidenmuller, "Geraldine Ferraro."

37. Jeanne Fahnestock, *Rhetorical Figures in Science* (New York: Oxford University Press, 1999), 158.

38. Eidenmuller, "Sarah Palin."

39. Sarah Palin, *Going Rogue: An American Life*, 241.

40. Eidenmuller, "Sarah Palin."

41. Ibid.

42. Ibid.

43. Ibid.

44. Ibid.

45. Ibid.

46. Eidenmuller, "Geraldine Ferraro."

47. Ibid.

48. Ibid.

49. Ibid.

50. Ibid.

51. Ferraro, *Ferraro*, 19.

52. Ibid.

53. Ibid., 57.

54. Ibid.

55. Richard Lanham, *A Handlist of Rhetorical Terms* (Los Angeles: University of California Press, 1991), 16.

56. Eidenmuller, "Geraldine Ferraro."

57. Deborah Tannen, *Talking Voices: Repetition, Dialogue, and Imagery in Conversational Discourse*, 2nd ed. (New York: Cambridge University Press, 2007), 9.

58. Eidenmuller, "Sarah Palin."

59. Ibid.

60. Lanham, *A Handlist*, 38.

61. Eidenmuller, "Sarah Palin."

62. Palin, *Going Rogue*, 242.

63. Ibid., 243.

64. Ibid.

65. Eidenmuller, "Sarah Palin."

66. Ibid.

67. Ibid.

68. Ibid.

69. *Incrementum* is found within the definition of *auxesis*.

70. Lanham, *A Handlist*, 26.

71. Eidenmuller, "Sarah Palin."

72. Ibid.

73. Ibid.

74. Ibid.

75. Ferraro, *Ferraro*, 311.

76. Text of speech as prepared for delivery is unavailable. An audio CD, *Geraldine Ferraro Concession Speech following the 1984 Presidential Election*, is available through inter-library loan from Michigan State University, courtesy of the G. Robert Vincent Voice Library at the Michigan State University Libraries. I transcribed the speech on November 22, 2009.

77. After her defeat in the 1984 campaign, Ferraro served four years as the Ambassador to the United Nations Human Rights Commission, practiced law, co-hosted CNN's *Crossfire*, and later went on to run unsuccessfully for the U.S. Senate in 1992. Geraldine Ferraro. *Changing History: Women, Power, and Politics*, 2nd ed. (Kingston: Moyer Bell Ltd., 1998) and in 1998. Ferraro consistently brought attention to the issues she cared about, such as the economy and human rights, whether through politics or her books. Ferraro wrote two texts after the election: *Ferraro: My Story* and *Changing History: Women, Power, and Politics*. Ferraro appeared on various news channels as a guest political commentator and contributor. Ferraro played a role in Senator Hillary Rodham Clinton's U.S. presidential campaign in 2008. Ferraro served as a member on Clinton's finance committee, but later resigned after a comment she made regard-

ing Senator Barack Obama. Ferraro suggested that Obama "is where he is politically because he is black." Perry Bacon, "Ferraro Leaves Clinton Camp Over Remarks About Obama," *Washington Post*, March 13, 2008. Access date July 31, 2010. www.washingtonpost.com. In response to Ferraro's comments, Obama stated that her comments were "ridiculous," "wrongheaded," and "divisive," ibid. Ferraro did not apologize for her comment. On March 26, 2011, Ferraro died at the age of seventy-five.

78. Ferraro, Geraldine. *Ferraro: My Story*, (Evanston: Northwestern University Press, 2004), 322.

79. Ibid.

80. It appears there is not a steadfast rule in the books when it comes to concession speeches. Typically, the conceding party decides whether the vice-presidential nominee will address the nation.

81. After her defeat in 2008, Palin returned to her post as Governor of Alaska. Her run at the national level brought its share of turmoil when she returned to the state level—she and her office became the targets of what Palin describes as, "frivolous ethics complaints." Sarah Palin, 342. Eventually, Palin's attorney fees totaled over $500,000, Ibid., 363. On July 3, 2009, Palin announced her resignation, ibid., 377. Eventually, the ethics charges against Palin and her staff were dropped and one charge was "settled with a finding of no wrongdoing," ibid., 364.

After the 2008 election and her resignation as Governor of Alaska, Palin published her first book, *Going Rogue: An American Life*; her second book, *America By Heart: Reflections on Family, Faith and Flag* (New York: HarperCollins Publishers), was released in November 2010. Palin has made a concerted effort to explain her experience as a vice-presidential nominee and her decision to resign as Governor of Alaska. Palin has since appeared on various news channels as a guest political commentator and contributor. Palin remains active with the Republican Party in terms of endorsing candidates for office.

Chapter Six

No Laughing Matter

Saturday Night Live*'s Portrayal of Geraldine Ferraro
and Sarah Palin*

Kathleen Mollick

In any lead up to a general election, the excitement generated by a vice-presidential candidate's selection is something akin to any kind of entertainment event that requires voting, whether it be the Oscars or the Heisman Trophy. But selecting a vice president isn't that trivial; it's a presidential candidate's indication of what he is looking for in his second-in-command. Jody Baumgartner, in the article "The Veepstakes: Forecasting Vice Presidential Selection in 2008," thinks that the reason we should care about who the candidate's running mate is because "beyond being the constitutional successor to the president in the event of a presidential vacancy, vice presidents play an increasingly important role, formally or otherwise, in their presidents' administrations."[1] Baumgartner also believes that "few would argue that a lack of experience makes one more competent. Therefore, it is reasonable to assume that presidential candidates factor the issue of experience into their selection calculus."[2] Franklin Roosevelt's choice of Harry Truman as a vice president, John F. Kennedy's choice of Lyndon Johnson, and George McGovern's ill-fated choice of Thomas Eagleton as his running mate indicates that these decisions do have an impact on American history, if not only on the outcome of a presidential election.

One cannot overlook the role of the media in influencing political campaigns, either. As Baumgartner notes, proximity to the highest office in the land, as well as competence, plays a key role in determining a presidential candidate's choice for vice president. Judith Stein believes that after the changes to both major parties' primary systems in the early 1970s, "the media played a much more important role than it had under the old system," which boded well for a more educated American public.[3] In the 1970s, with access to candidates via newspapers, radio, and television, voters could learn more about their political leaders. But Karen Stein believes that "the media reflect traditional American concepts of women's proper roles and perpetuate a discomfort with powerful women."[4] And nowhere would the more pragmatic political needs collide with the increased role of the media in political campaigns than in the campaigns of former Vice President Walter Mondale and Senator John McCain. Their choices of Representative Geraldine Ferraro and Governor Sarah Palin, respectively, gave Americans a sense of their ability as leaders. But what also became clear was that one area of the American public's reaction to these changes could be viewed in the entertainment wing of the media, specifically on the variety show *Saturday Night Live*. In this chapter, I will discuss how the satirical portraits of both Ferraro and Palin on *Saturday Night Live* showed that while some views of women in positions of political leadership had changed in the nearly twenty-five-year gap between both campaigns, some views did not.

THE CONTEXT: WALTER MONDALE AND GERALDINE FERRARO

Before he was chosen to be former Governor Jimmy Carter's vice president in 1976, Walter Mondale had been a United States senator from Minnesota. He was well-versed in national and international politics, so he would have had an understanding of what Judith Stein described when she said that as the political primary system changed in the Democratic and Republican parties, "appropriate racial and gender representation were becoming mandatory in many areas of national life."[5] After Mondale selected Geraldine Ferraro as his running mate, the editorial board of *Time* magazine crowed, "Seven weeks ago, *Time* posed a question on its cover: 'And for Vice President . . . Why Not a Woman?' Last week the Democrats answered it resoundingly. It was obviously a question the nation was prepared to address."[6] Not only that, but the editors at *Time* believed a woman vice presidential would bring excitement to the race and that such an event could come as early as the 1984 election.[7] Needing a boost for the upcoming run against President Ronald Reagan, Mondale made a choice that attempted to show the political savvy to choose a woman vice-presidential candidate to possibly pull in more women voters, with the historical appeal of a first-time woman vice-presidential candidate. Roger Rosenblatt, covering the event for *Time*, described Mondale's exuberance at the campaign rally that introduced Geraldine Ferraro to the nation; according to Rosenblatt, Mondale characterized his choice of Ferraro as "exciting choice. 'Let me say that again,' says the delighted Mondale. 'This is an exciting choice!' The crowd goes wild. Mondale is clapping, too. Does he know yet what he has done?"[8] Rosenblatt's question was one that would be answered throughout the remainder of the election, and in many different ways. Yet at the time of the decision, there was no clearly defined answer.

The answer to Rosenblatt's question of whether or not Mondale knew the consequences of the choice he had made was both yes and no. Of course Mondale knew what he was doing. As a longtime politician, he knew that his campaign needed jolt of energy, and that the increase of women in the House indicated that Americans were growing more comfortable with the idea of women leaders in public office. Mondale's choice also reflected an aware-ness of a vice-presidential candidate whose political views were similar to his own. The surprising choice also would inject an element of political theater into the campaign as well. In December of 1983, Jane Perlez of the *New York Times* believed that Representative Ferraro either had a vice presi-dential spot or a cabinet position in her future should Mondale beat Reagan in the general election.[9] Elisabeth Bumiller stated in the *Washington Post* in April 1984 that Ferraro "is one of the Democratic women most often men-tioned as a vice presidential candidate."[10] So the tide of history was headed in Mondale's direction, and he did seriously consider a woman vice-presiden-tial candidate. As Judith Stein noted, Mondale took that idea much more seriously once "the lead that Reagan enjoyed lengthened to 14 percent."[11] And Ellen Goodman believed that the boost Ferraro provided was just what the ticket needed, again, because of Mondale's more reserved campaign style: "She plays daring to his cautious. She is camera-warm and he is camera-cold."[12] The idea of a woman vice-president was not that far-fetched by the time Mondale and his advisors began vetting potential candidates.

Along with the surge of excitement at the historic choice of a woman vice president came a surge of issues that took the emphasis off of the campaign and placed it on social etiquette. Rosenblatt acknowledged that discussions involving the complexities and challenges of a woman vice-presidential can-didate would be a messy yet welcome addition to American political discourse: "There should be wonderful national bull sessions, too: heated, sophomoric sessions."[13] And there were. One dealt with the way that the candidates interacted with each other. Ellen Goodman pointed out that "Fer-raro doesn't look up at Mondale when he's speaking in the requisite pose for wives. She looks directly into the audience . . . If the Democratic ticket is a partnership, then the vice president is the junior partner."[14] Alex Brummer reported in the London *Guardian* that the two candidates had to negotiate physical space, proximity, and how they walked together.[15] There was a serious discussion in the *Washington Post* about what Ferraro wore and how she wore her hair, with no less than Alison Lurie weighing in that "We don't know much about her, so how she looks will be important, particularly to women." Lurie says while men get sexual messages from women's clothes, women use them to judge another woman's character and personality."[16] And one final lament came from *New York Times* editorialist William Safire, who declared that, "It breaks my heart to suggest this, but the time has come for Ms. We are no longer faced with a theory, but a condition. It is unacceptable for journalists to dictate to a candidate that she call herself Ms. Or else use her married name."[17] Of course there were other discussions, too, about the roles of women in politics. But one place where the discussion could have played out, but didn't, was on the sound stage of *Saturday Night Live*.

THE SKETCHES: GERALDINE FERRARO

There were only three sketches aired on *Saturday Night Live* (*SNL*) that involved Mary Gross as Geraldine Ferraro. One sketch that highlights Gross's characterization of Ferraro can be viewed in "Saturday Night News," which eventually became the more familiar "Weekend Update." According to the *SNL Archives*, Mary Gross appeared as Geraldine Ferraro three times, and all of her appearances were in the fall of 1984: October 6, October 13, and November 3.[18] For the purposes of this chapter, I selected two sketches to illustrate how Ferraro's candidacy was satirized by *SNL*: the "Saturday Night News" sketch and "Bait and Tackle," in which Ferraro is discussed, but Gross does not appear. The visible woman candidate and the invisible woman candidate created by male voices seemed appropriate for this time period.

The first example of Geraldine Ferraro's satirical turn on *Saturday Night Live* occurred in a "Saturday Night News" segment, in which she appeared as Representative Ferraro, responding to a comment made by Barbara Bush after the vice-presidential debate: "Barbara Bush weighed in, too, calling Rep. Ferraro a 'four million-dollar . . . I can't say it, but it rhymes with rich.'"[19]

In the clip, Gross's physical appearance is a forerunner of the Tina Fey school of an almost uncanny recreation of the candidate. She bears a good physical likeness to Ferraro and her voice is quite close to the original, but her material doesn't allow her to get under the skin of Ferraro as much as some other political impersonators on *SNL*. Gross's Ferraro delivers her monologue by repeating what Mrs. Bush said, and then says:

> What do you think Little Miss Prep School was calling me? A ditch? A witch? A hitch? No, I think Babsie had something else in mind and I'm fuming mad about it. How dare she accuse me of being a snitch? I've never squealed on anyone in my life. And if you don't believe me, just ask my husband. Or the auditors in the Internal Revenue Service. That bitch has no right calling me a snitch.[20]

Ferraro (as portrayed by Gross) goes on to say that Mrs. Bush was able to cheat the Internal Revenue Service out of even more money than the Ferraros did, and that Mrs. Bush had no right to count her money, since she (Ferraro) didn't even know how much she had, and she had help from high-priced accountants. Finally, Gross's Ferraro wraps up her editorial by saying to Mrs. Bush, "You're a real witch. Or something that rhymes with that."[21]

Three months after the 1984 election, Ferraro is invoked in a telling way in the sketch "Bait and Tackle." Gary Kroeger and Julia Louis-Dreyfus portray Walter and Joan Mondale, recuperating from the campaign in a cabin in northern Minnesota. The plaintive crying of a moose can be heard as the Mondales situate themselves in their cabin. As he castigates himself for the choices he's made, Mondale cries out, "Geraldine Ferraro . . . what was I thinking?!"[22] When some lost hunters come to his cabin, they ask him, "Did you really think you could win with a woman?" and the hapless Mondale replies, "I thought it was a good idea at the time."[23] Toward the end of the sketch, it is revealed that the hunters came to the cabin because the sound of Mondale's crying sounds like a mating call of a moose to them, but the sound is more like that of a female moose in heat rather than the call of a male moose.[24]

Why the short shrift delivered to this historic candidacy? At the time of the 1984 election, *SNL* had fallen on hard times. Lorne Michaels, the original producer of the show, had left the show, and Dick Ebersol, originally in the sports division at NBC, was producing the show. *People* magazine's Jeff Jarvis criticized the show's tenth season, saying, "political humor, once *SNL*'s mainstay, is now stale and tasteless . . . [Billy] Crystal imagines Geraldine Ferraro's past New York boyfriends saying, 'I slept wid her' . . . The new *SNL* does not try to find humor in the times, in Reagan, Yuppies, computers or MTV. Instead . . . it is the voice of no era at all."[25] John Matviko believed that, for *SNL*, "attacking the Reagan presidency proved difficult . . . It could also be argued that the Reagan years coincided with what most critics consider a decline in the show's quality . . . the show declined because a weekly target of its satire, the presidency, was now held by a man whose immense popularity, even with *SNL*'s core audience, made satire difficult."[26] Brad Hall, a cast member of *SNL* during that time period, indirectly blamed Ebersol, for the lack of political satire: "There was stuff we could have been parodying. I don't think [Dick] Ebersol wanted that. I don't think NBC did. Someone's taste did not run toward satire. And so the very thing that originally made the show popular was really resisted . . . You look back, it's kind of bizarre, the election in 1984, there's almost no political humor during an entire political election. Nothing."[27]

In both sketches involving Ferraro as a vice-presidential candidate, the writing is thin, even for a sketch comedy show which can't fully flesh out characterizations because of time limitations. Gross only had two months in which to develop her portrayal of Ferraro, and the view of her developed in "Saturday Night News" doesn't go much beyond a quick, stereotypical portrayal of Ferraro, based on her appearance and voice. In the sketch, the Geraldine Ferraro character takes on Barbara Bush's criticism of her (and Barbara Bush's veiled reference to Representative Ferraro as a bitch) by saying Mrs. Bush is wrong, that she (Rep. Ferraro) is not a snitch (being something that rhymes with "witch"). The humor in this situation is supposed to be that Ferraro wouldn't understand that she was being referred to as a bitch, but that seems incredibly naïve, particularly for a politician from New York who had been in the national spotlight for several months. To then wrap up the first part of the Ferraro monologue by having the Ferraro character call Bush a bitch out loud sounds crude more than anything. The humor may have been in having one woman calling another woman a bitch directly, but in the context of the sketch, it's jarring.

And in "Bait and Tackle," Ferraro is an invisible character, not seen and not heard. She's made invisible by the writers, and the blame for Mondale's loss is doled out largely to her. The sketch singles out Ferraro as the reason why Mondale lost, particularly with the three visiting hunters asking Mondale, with a smug air, if he actually thought choosing a woman running mate would make him more popular with voters. The Mondale character's half-hearted response plays to stereotypical gender ideas of men being weakened by women, and that Mondale's choice of Ferraro as a running mate indicates a weakness in intelligence and a weakness in estimating the emotional tenor of the voters. Even the reference at the end of the sketch to Mondale's cries sounding like female moose mating cries that draw the cries of the male moose in the area contributes to the crowning insult of the sketch, which is finding humor in Mondale's cries being feminine enough to attract male moose looking to mate. Whether Geraldine Ferraro was actually present in a sketch relating to her or not, the writers seemed not to know exactly how to write her, just as the country seemed to view her candidacy with skepticism. Fortunately, by the time Sarah Palin came on the political radar, that attitude had been muted itself. Or had it?

THE CONTEXT: JOHN MCCAIN AND SARAH PALIN

Many Americans in 2008 were surprised by John McCain's choice of the governor of Alaska as his running mate, and not only because she would be the first woman vice-presidential candidate in the history of the Republican Party. Brox and Cassels state that "McCain's campaign for the White House was an uphill battle from the beginning . . . an unpopular incumbent and a failing economy made it obvious that the only road to a Republican victory involved 'throwing a football through a tire at fifty yards; it's doable theoretically, but it is very difficult and it needs a bit of luck.'"[28] But at least one person considered it a real possibility that McCain might run with a woman. Baumgartner presented a predictive model that he believed could narrow the list of conceivable choices for McCain's vice presidential pick among a list of reasonable, potential male and female candidates. On the short list for women were Kay Bailey Hutchinson and Condoleezza Rice.[29] Interestingly enough, Rice made the short list of ultimate candidates that Baumgartner created, and she was the top choice.[30] The editors at *PS: Political Science and Politics* allowed him to add a postscript to his article, and he added that "John McCain, who announced his pick on August 20, was reportedly considering Sen. Joe Lieberman (CT), Gov. Sarah Palin (AK) . . . Sarah Palin was not even included in the original model . . . Regardless, she was predicted with a 7.2 percent probability."[31] There has been some discussion as to just how seriously the McCain camp took the search for a vice president, and despite some theories posited to the contrary, it's difficult to believe that the McCain campaign did not take the search for a vice-presidential candidate seriously. Brox and Cassels say that McCain's strategists had very specific credentials in mind and that the best choice for the spot would need to "restore McCain's 'maverick' credentials . . . help the campaign attract women voters . . . increase the distance of the campaign from unpopular President [G.W.] Bush . . . and the nominee had to excite the base of the Republican Party."[32]

But this campaign, also headed by a veteran politician, made a crucial misstep in keeping Palin away from the press initially. As Young noted, Fey's appearance at this point in the campaign "came after the press had been following the tight-lipped McCain camp for two weeks . . . Those early refusals to talk to the press likely left journalists simultaneously frustrated and in need of story content."[33] Young also believe that "Fey's Palin allowed journalists to channel those concerns . . . journalists were able to use Fey's performance as a lens through which they could consider issues of Palin's competence and reticence . . . while appealing to entertainment value in news."[34] Although this wouldn't have been the only reason that the press would have then focused more scrutiny on Fey's performance as Palin, it didn't help that the cold open is the first sketch that opens any show, and helps to set the mood for the rest of the show. It may also have had some bearing on setting the mood for the rest of the campaign, too.

THE SKETCHES: SARAH PALIN

Unlike Mary Gross's Geraldine Ferraro character, according to the *SNL Archives*, Tina Fey was able to play Sarah Palin six times during the 2008 election cycle, and then on two other occasions after the election.[35] Lorne

Michaels was back at the helm of *SNL* as well, and upon his return, *SNL* hit the ground running again with its political satire in 1988. That was the year that Dana Carvey debuted his George H. W. Bush impression, and Jon Lovitz contributed a rather believable Michael Dukakis. After that, political satire became a regular staple of *SNL*.

Fey gives Lorne Michaels credit for launching her career as the first woman comedy writer at *SNL*, and in 2008, as Darrell Hammond was portraying John McCain and Fred Arminsen was portraying Barack Obama, Fey had departed *SNL* for her own show, *30 Rock*. So she was no longer a regular on the show when she played Sarah Palin for the first time in the cold open for the September 13, 2008 show.[36] Also, the sketch didn't just spotlight Fey as Palin; Amy Poehler, who was a regular on the show and Fey's frequent collaborator, portrayed Hillary Clinton. Poehler had already played Clinton on the show, and with the audience familiarity with both Poehler and Fey, the audience was as familiar with them as with the women political figures they were portraying.

The premise of the "joint political announcement" that was the focus of the cold open that first featured Tina Fey and Amy Poehler was that Palin and Clinton were getting together to tell the media to quit making sexist remarks about both of them during the campaign. Poehler's portrayal of Clinton focused on the more stereotypical aspects of Clinton's public persona as tightly controlled and aggressive. Palin, however, was not as well established in the public mind as Clinton, which brought more focus to Fey's portrayal of Palin; it allowed Fey and the *SNL* writers to create more of a narrative for Palin. Fey's Palin emphasizes the real-life Palin's political naiveté with such lines as "I can see Russia from my house!" and admitting that "I don't know what that is" in regards to the Bush doctrine.[37] The Palin of *SNL* also is comfortable discussing her more traditional feminine appeal (particularly in contrast to Poehler's Clinton) when she asks the media, "Reporters and commentators, stop using words that diminish us, like pretty. Attractive. Beautiful."[38] Young's earlier statement that Palin's arrival to the McCain campaign and that campaign's shielding her from the press played against the campaign's best interests because in the absence of a strong narrative introducing her to the public, a narrative in essence was created for her. *SNL* capitalized on that in this cold open; much like Will Ferrell's portrayal of George W. Bush emphasized his frat boy persona and arrogance, Tina Fey emphasizes Sarah Palin's awkwardness at being thrust in the national spotlight so quickly with her artless responses and she also plays up the media's focus on her appearance.

The "McCain/QVC Cold Open" sketch shows a more relaxed Fey stepping into her Palin heels and putting on her "Tina Fey glasses" one last time before Election Day. Aired three days before the election, the reality of the financial and political misfortune that had come to the McCain campaign dampens the comedic spirit of this sketch. Watching in hindsight, Fey seems slightly less comfortable playing Palin, particularly when she's standing right next to John McCain. He is the main focus of the sketch, selling political products to fund his campaign until the November general election. Fey stays in the background for most of the sketch until near the end of it, when she delivers a *tour de force* monologue that reminds the audience who the real political force of this political campaign is. Fey's Palin suddenly breaks away from the candidate, and delivers the following pitch *sotto voce*:

> Listen up, everybody, I'm goin' rogue right now, so keep your voices down. [Palin picks up a "Palin 2012" t-shirt.] Available now we got a bunch of these 2012 t-shirts. Just try and wait until after Tuesday to wear 'em, okay? Because I am not goin' anywhere. And I'm certainly not goin' back to Alaska. If I'm not goin' to the White House, I'm either gonna be runnin' in four years or I'm gonna be a white Oprah. So I'm good either way.[39]

This part of the sketch highlights the perception cultivated in the media which portrayed Palin as a more overtly ambitious political figure than previously thought. Enormously popular among many conservatives, men and women alike, Fey emphasizes the more grasping side of how parts of the public viewed Palin. In this sketch, Fey's wardrobe is less vibrant and her hairstyle is more subdued than in the initial cold open that introduced her portrayal of Palin; in this sketch, the emphasis is on how well Palin has adapted to presidential politics, and is much more open to stating her political ambitions and is less focused on her appearance. Well after the 2008 campaign was over, Young coined the term "Feylin phenomenon," believing that Fey's portrayal of Palin led to Fey having an incredibly strong presence in the discourse that occurred in the campaign after Palin's selection as vice president.[40] Although this sketch is humorous, its humor is rooted in a deep discomfort. Unlike the "Bait and Tackle" sketch almost twenty-five years earlier, the premise is that the only reason John McCain is hosting *SNL* is because his campaign is in trouble, and Fey's characterization of Palin as not being phased at all by a possible defeat, but instead seeing real potential for a political future for herself, highlights a perception of the real-life Palin as being politically opportunistic at the expense of her political benefactor. Although these end-of-the-campaign sketches vary in their treatment of each vice-presidential candidate, the message appears to be the same: each male presidential candidate who chose a woman to run with him can find fault with the woman who agreed to run with him.

SATIRE AND WOMEN IN POLITICS

There are definitely clearly defined differences in regard to how both Geraldine Ferraro and Sarah Palin were satirized in *Saturday Night Live*. One can't ignore that Geraldine Ferraro came first, and thus bore the brunt of the uncertainty of how to address women in politics, both in the field and in the press. By the time Palin came on the scene, women in politics were much more prevalent. The difference in eras may have also played a role; whether Dick Ebersol bears responsibility for the content of the writing during the 1984 election, critics appear to agree that the show was not at the top of its game in 1984. Thus, Mary Gross, more of a performer than a writer, had less opportunity to perfect her portrayal of Ferraro. And when one looks at the time frame in which Gross had to develop her portrayal of Ferraro (less than one month) as opposed to Fey (who had two months), it's clear that the Ferraro character had the distinct disadvantage.

Somewhat surprisingly, though there were some similarities between the portrayals of each woman, there was an almost twenty-five-year gap between the two women vice-presidential candidates. Karen Stein noted that "in patriarchal culture men are the standard, the universal, the neutral, the unmarked gender . . . Women are the other, the marked gender; they have come to be linked with the body, and with the domestic, private space."[41] In both sketches, the figures of Ferraro and Palin are definitely marked, although the ways in which they are marked differ slightly. In Mary Gross's appearance as Geraldine Ferraro in the "Saturday Night News" sketch, her characterization of Ferraro shows the conflict that actually did come to the forefront of the real-life Ferraro's bid for higher office. That conflict was to what a degree a candidate's spouse could damage a political candidate's career. In this sketch, Ferraro is seen as having limited influence in her family's finances. The sketch also addresses the how aggressive women are defined in society. Barbara Bush's comment that Ferraro behaved like a bitch in the debate she had with Vice-President George H. W. Bush, as well as the Bush operative's comment that Ferraro was "bitchy . . . arrogant . . . [and] crabby,"[42] fit conveniently with Ferraro's background as a tough district attorney from Queens, New York. Gross's Ferraro illustrates the conflicting ways in which the public viewed her, condensed in the confines of her brief appearance in this sketch: the woman whose husband controlled the finances and the woman who had the audacity to challenge the vice president in a debate. She had to be tough, but not too tough.

What the sketch couldn't capitalize on was Ferraro's reaction to the characterizations of her behavior. There is no way that Geraldine Ferraro wouldn't know that Barbara Bush was calling her a bitch, so Gross's Ferraro saying that Bush was calling her a snitch, and then trying to play off of her Italian-American husband's trouble with the Internal Revenue Service fell flat with the audience. And then to compound the problem, the Ferraro character calls Bush a "bitch" anyway, which seems out of place even now. Ferraro was tough, but she wasn't crude, and the crudity of the line further weakens an already weak sketch. Even the last line about Bush being "a witch. Or something like it" does nothing to save the sketch. The writers fundamentally did not understand Ferraro's character or the appeal of her candidacy, which was, in part, due to the fact that a woman was a vice presidential candidate on a major party ticket. The writers also didn't understand that the very conflict that was going on at that time (from what Ferraro wore to how she was addressed) was serious for many women. Their tin ear for what was funny weakened what was a fairly good characterization by Ferraro.

In the "Bait and Tackle" sketch, Ferraro is not present physically, but she's denigrated by Gary Kroeger's Walter Mondale, who questions his judgment in selecting her and blaming her husband for being a "crook." His manhood is also questioned at the end of the sketch, as the hunters who come by to harass him for losing the election say that his crying sounds like the mating call of a moose. So Ferraro is marginalized completely, and the lion's share of the blame for Mondale's defeat is placed on her as well as him (for not being manly enough). The sketch isn't good satire and, the biggest crime of all, not funny.

In the Sarah Palin/Hillary Clinton cold open, the writing and the satire are funny, but there's a darkness to the sketch. Poehler's Clinton seems on the verge of a complete nervous breakdown; she is Ferraro's legacy, a tough-talking, ball-busting former candidate who, in the sketch, is on the short end of the stick in the sexism debate that has arisen since Palin's candidacy. Fey's Palin is the third-wave feminist, secure in her good political fortune and good looks, oblivious to the wrath of the former first lady. Stein's earlier description of the woman in politics being marked by her body is what differentiates her portrayal from Ferraro to some extent. She appears in the sketch as Heflick and Goldenberg identified as the media narrative of her, which was focused on her appearance.[43] In the last appearance Fey makes as Palin before the election, the candidate, the writers target her as the reason the McCain campaign is foundering. Although her political ambition is what she articulates most passionately in the sketch, Heflick and Goldenberg suggest that the American public may have decided that the biggest negative factor working against the real-life Sarah Palin was her appearance: "We suggest that it [her appearance] hurt the Republican ticket. In short, we suggest that it led people to perceive Palin as less competent, warm, and moral and may have even undermined the competency of her own performances . . ."[44] They further posited that when "research demonstrating that voting choices are highly contingent on candidates' perceived competence and character, this suggests that the objectification of Palin may have exerted a causal role in objections to Palin, and ultimately, the Republican defeat in 2008."[45] And her plug for her "Palin in 2012" t-shirt and her statement that "I'm not goin' anywhere," while getting appreciative howls from the audience, indicates that Palin was perceived as more focused on her own career at this point, and that she had no loyalty to McCain. So in the end, she, too, shares the fate of the trailblazer before her: the woman gets the blame for defeat.

CONCLUSION

Ironically, although both women were chosen in part because of the belief that each could pull in women voters, neither Geraldine Ferraro nor Sarah Palin could significantly deliver the women's vote for their candidates.[46] While their portrayal on *Saturday Night Live* probably didn't have a significant impact on the outcome of either election, what the *Saturday Night Live* sketches show is the ways which sensibilities about women in politics both changed and did not change in regard to American popular culture. Mary Gross's portrayal of Geraldine Ferraro wasn't developed soon enough or was portrayed enough to be as memorable as Tina Fey's portrayal of Sarah Palin. Both Walter Mondale and John McCain wanted to appeal to women voters because they wanted to boost their chances of getting elected, and both men thought they had chosen women candidates that would complement their ticket, rather than overwhelm it in a negative manner. Yet the views that the writers at *SNL* apparently had of Ferraro were not that sharp or sophisticated, either; all one gets when seeing her portrayed on these shows is not at all revealing of what made her such a compelling figure when she walked on to the international stage in regard to her strengths and weaknesses. In that regard, Palin is a much more nuanced character; having strong writers and allowing Palin to play off other characters made Fey's characterization of Palin rank with Will Ferrell's portrayal of George W. Bush in terms of capturing the essence of the political figure. Yet both women are obliquely tagged as being key contributors to the loss of their candidate. Ferraro is blamed outright in the "Bait and Tackle" sketch, but she's not physically present in the sketch, while Fey's Palin is present in the sketch but her covert offer of "Palin in 2012" t-shirts indicates she is so venal that she'll run for president once she's rid of McCain.

    With the advent of Hillary Clinton's presidential candidacy for the Democrats in 2008, and the 2012 presidential candidacy of Michele Bachmann in 2012, it is quite possible that the in the twenty-five years that will follow the vice-presidential candidacy of Sarah Palin, the United States might not have another woman vice presidential candidate at all, but instead nominate a woman as a presidential candidate for either or both major political parties. It may also be possible that less than twenty-five years will pass before the next woman vice presidential candidate is named for a major presidential ticket. No matter what the outcome, and no matter if it's *Saturday Night Live* or another television show with a satiric lens, the role of women in positions of serious political leadership will always be subject to critique through the lens of humor. That sharpened humor can reveal the weaknesses of the candidate, and it can also reveal the ways in which the culture views its women in non-traditional roles. What will fuel future research in this area will be how satire can be used to create a narrative for the women who serve as major political candidates, whether they will be seen as dynamic figures with their own strengths and weaknesses, or if they will be seen as scapegoats, or as filling more stereotypical political roles (the shrew or the glamour girl). No matter how they are portrayed, shows like *Saturday Night Live* will be commenting on the men choosing the women to stand by their sides as presidential running mates until a woman tries again to run for her party's nomination for the presidency.

NOTES

1. Jody C. Baumgartner, "The Veepstakes: Forecasting Vice Presidential Selection in 2008," *PS: Political Science and Politics* 41, no. 1 (October 2008), 765, accessed January 3, 2012, doi:10.1017/S1049096508081043.

2. Ibid., 766.

3. Judith Stein, *Pivotal Decade: How the United States Traded Factories for Finance in the Seventies* (New Haven: Yale University Press, 2010), 57.

4. Karen F. Stein, "The Cleavage Commotion: How the Press Covered Senator Clinton's Campaign," in *Cracked but Not Shattered: Hillary Rodham Clinton's Unsuccessful Campaign for the Presidency*, ed. Theodore F. Heckles (Lanham, MD: Lexington Books, 2009), 137.

5. Stein, *Pivotal Decade*, 56.

6. "Untitled," *Time* 124, no. 4 (July 23 1984), 1, accessed on March 5, 2012, ehis.ebscohost.com.zeus.tarleton.edu:81/ehost/search/advanced?sid.

7. Ibid., 1.

8. Roger Rosenblatt, "Mondale: This is an Exciting Choice," *Time* 124, no. 4 (July 23, 1984), 1, accessed March 7, 2012, doi: 57880387.

9. Jane Perlez, "Mrs. Ferraro for Vice President," *New York Times* (Dec. 23 1983), A14, accessed January 5, 2012, www.lexisnexis.com.zeus.tarleton.edu:81/hottopics/lnacademic, A14.

10. Elisabeth Bumiller, "The Rise of Geraldine Ferraro, Mastering the Process of Politics With a Careful Eye Ahead," *Washington Post* (April 29 1984), K2, accessed 30 December 2011, lexisnexis.com.zeus.tarleton.edu:81/hottopics/lnacademic/.

11. Stein, *Pivotal Decade*, 272.

12. Ellen Goodman, "Ferraro's First," *Washington Post*, (July 19, 1984), A21, accessed December 11, 2011, www.lexisnexis.com.zeus.tarleton.edu:81/hottopics/lnacademic/.

13. Rosenblatt, "Mondale," 1.

14. Goodman, "Ferraro's First," A21.

15. Alex Brummer, "Ferraro Struggles with the 'Etiquette Gap,' Advisors," *The Guardian* (London), (July 26, 1984), 1, accessed March 12, 2012. www.lexisnexis.com. zeus.tarleton.edu:81/hottopics/lnacademic/.

16. Donnie Radcliffe, "Fashioning a 'Ferraro Look;' The New Conventions, Credibility, and the Candidate's Clothes," *Washington Post* (July 23 1984), C1, accessed March 12, 2012, www.lexisnexis.com.zeus.tarleton.edu:81/hottopics/lnacademic/.

17. William Safire, "On Language: Goodbye Sex, Hello, Gender," *New York Times* (Aug.5 1984), 8, accessed February 5, 2012, www.lexisnexis.com.zeus.tarleton.edu:81/hottopics/lnacademic.

18. "Geraldine Ferraro," *SNL Archives*, 2012, accessed on April 4, 2012, snl.jt.org/listimp.php?i=G.

19. Mary Leonard, "Saturday Diary: Storming the Barricades with Gerry Ferraro," *Pittsburgh Post-Gazette*, 2, accessed April 2, 2011, www.post-gazette.com.

20. "Saturday Night Live: Gerry Ferraro," *Zimbio*, accessed March 12 2012, www.zimbio.com/watch/eORaDBf0WkP/Gerry+Ferraro/Saturday+Night+Live.

21. Ibid.

22. "Bait and Tackle," *Saturday Night Live*, National Broadcasting Company, accessed March 11, 2012, www.nbc.com/saturday-night-live/digital-shorts/video/bait-and-tackle/1357838/.

23. Ibid.

24. Ibid.

25. Jeff Jarvis, "Picks and Pans Review: Saturday Night Live," *People*, 22, no. 17 (Oct. 22, 1984): 1, accessed December 12, 2012, www.people.com, 1.

26. John Matviko, "Television Satire and the Presidency: The Case of Saturday Night Live," *Hollywood's White House: The American Presidency in Film and History*, eds. Peter C. Rollins and John E. O'Connor (Lexington, KY: University Press of Kentucky. 2003), 340.

27. Tom Shales and James Andrew Miller. *Live from New York: An Uncensored History of Saturday Night Live* (Boston: Little, Brown and Co. 2002), 274.

28. Brian Brox and Madison Cassels, "The Contemporary Effects of Vice Presidential Nominees: Sarah Palin and the 2008 Presidential Campaign," *Journal of Political Marketing*, 8 (2009): 349–363, accessed March 17, 2012, 350, ehis.ebscohost.com.zeus.tarleton.edu:81/ehost/search/advanced?sid=9a1261b5-f0ae-491f-8aa7-9d4440aabaf6%40sessionmgr115&vid=1&hid=107.

29. Baumgartner, "The Veepstakes," 769.

30. Ibid.

31. Ibid., 770.

32. Brox and Cassels, "The Contemporary Effects," 352.

33. Dannogal Young, "Political Entertainment and the Press's Construction of Sarah Feylin,"*Popular Communication* 9, no. 4 (October-December 2011), 262, accessed March 1, 2012, ehis.ebscohost.com.zeus.tarleton.edu:81/ehost/search/advanced?sid=9a1261b5-f0ae-491f-8aa7-9d4440aabaf6%40sessionmgr115&vid=1&hid=107.

34. Ibid.

35. "Sarah Palin," *SNL Archives*, 2012, accessed on March 14, 2012.

36. Ibid.

37. "Clinton/Palin Cold Open," *Hulu*, 2012, accessed March 31, 2012, www.hulu.com.

38. Ibid.

39. "QVC Cold Open," *Hulu*, 2012, www.hulu.com.

40. Young, "Political Entertainment," 252–54.

41. Stein, "The Cleavage Commotion," 173.

42. "Saturday Night Live: Gerry Ferraro," *Zimbio*.

43. Nathan Heffelick and Jamie L. Goldenberg, "Sarah Palin, a Nation Object(ifie)s: The Role of Appearance Focus in the 2008 U. S. Presidential Election," *Sex Roles,* 65, 2011, 149, accessed on April 1, 2012, ehis.ebscohost.com.zeus.tarleton.edu:81/ehost/search/advanced?sid=9a1261b5-f0ae-491f-8aa7-9d4440aabaf6%40sessionmgr115&vid=1&hid=107.

44. Ibid., 149–50.

45. Ibid., 150.

46. Box and Cassels, "The Contemporary Effects," 357.

Chapter Seven

Meghan McCain is GOP Proud

A Rhetorical Analysis of the Political Discourse Surrounding Feminist Leadership in the Republican Party

Nichelle D. McNabb and Rachel B. Friedman

When one thinks of contemporary feminist leaders, it is likely that senators and presidential and vice-presidential candidates come to mind. It is less likely that an outspoken twenty-eight year-old daughter of a failed presidential candidate would be considered a leading feminist voice. However, during her father's 2008 bid for the presidency, Meghan McCain began writing a blog called McCain Blogette, designed to appeal to younger voters. Following the election, she continued to speak her mind in a blog that has evolved into a column for *The Daily Beast*. Since the 2008 election, Meghan McCain has published two books: *Dirty Sexy Politics* and *America, You Sexy Bitch*. McCain has appeared on television shows such as: *The View*, *Larry King*, *The Colbert Report*, *The Rachel Maddow Show*, *Fox and Friends*, *The Tonight Show*, and *The O'Reilly Factor*. As of January 16, 2013, she had 221,304 twitter followers.

Meghan McCain's message is surprising because although she is a self-proclaimed Republican who supported the war in Iraq, is a member of the National Rifle Association, and is pro-life, she takes some less conservative positions on social issues. McCain supports the legalization of marijuana and gay marriage, she does not believe in abstinence only education and favors greater access to birth control, and she openly admits to being a feminist. Libit reported that when Meghan McCain sat down with Larry King in March of 2009, she "made headlines by confirming her 'support' for Presi-

105

dent Barack Obama."[1] Thus, her appeal extends to people beyond traditional Republican voters, such as young voters, feminists, and independents.

What makes Meghan McCain's voice as a feminist interesting is a mass appeal that transcends party allegiances. However, McCain is even more intriguing because she largely speaks out about the mistakes Republicans are making in their attempts to reach out to younger voters. She is not restricted by the party line and she is less vocal about the Democrats. Meghan McCain astutely identified the rifts in the Republican Party by arguing at the Log Cabin Republican Convention in 2009, "I think we're seeing a war brewing in the Republican party, but it is not between us and Democrats. It is not between us and liberals. It is between the future and the past."[2] McCain sees the Republican party as too dogmatic in their conservatism and she urges them to move to the center: "If Republicans are going to gain power again, and more importantly, remain in power, we must recognize the value of centrism—instead of turning to extreme right-wing members of the party like Rush Limbaugh (which I have made clear I think is a dangerous thing for the party to do)."[3] Her plea for centrism has landed her in a host of conflicts with the likes of Glenn Beck, Bill O'Reilly, Michelle Malkin, Sarah Palin, and Laura Ingraham. This chapter will explore McCain's political rhetoric, the conflicts she has had with her fellow Republicans and how those conflicts reflect upon contemporary feminism.

MCCAIN'S RHETORIC

In addition to sometimes disagreeing with more conservative Republicans on issues, Meghan McCain also speaks hard truths to party power. In her April 6, 2012 column, for example, she gave her honest assessment of the Republican presidential candidates for the 2012 election:

> Santorum, who is a lunatic, right-wing fringe candidate that is hanging on to his candidacy for no other reason than, once this election cycle is over, he knows no one will ever listen to him again. I half expect Santorum to start throwing a tantrum on stage after he loses yet another primary and scream: "If I'm not going to be the nominee, no one is!"
>
> Then, there is Newt Gingrich, the over-blown relic of the 90s, with so much baggage and anger that he really should move to a country where he can be dictator.
>
> Finally, there's my boy Mitt—whom, yes, I support and no matter what, will vote for but . . . as his wife has even admitted "needs to unzip."[4]

One can imagine why calling one candidate a "lunatic right-wing fringe candidate" capable of public tantrums and another candidate a dictator wannabe might be offensive to leading Republican prognosticators. Many have compared her to her maverick father. McCain claims not to embrace the comparison, but she evoked it herself in her 2009 speech to the Log Cabin Republicans: "I have my Dad's 'heartburn-inducing' ability to say what he thinks almost whenever he wants. The person who stands before you is not confined within the mold of what a daughter of a Republican Presidential candidate 'should' be for some."[5]

Though Meghan McCain appears to be more critical of Republicans than Democrats, she explains that she critiques the party because she loves it and wants to make it stronger. McCain wrote in her column "In recent weeks, I've been critical of some of the most hard-core ideological elements of the GOP. As a consequence, some have requested I leave the party altogether, and say that I am now an unwelcome member. Let me be clear: No one wants the Republican Party to succeed more than I do."[6] As noted earlier, she embraces traditional Republican values on issues like abortion and she is a self-described supporter of the Second Amendment right to bear arms. Indeed, she is critical of Obama's "star" power and the fact that he appeared on *Ellen* and danced. In issuing advice to potential Republican candidates, McCain wrote, "You should instead take on the role of the smart candidate, the serious candidate, the one who isn't concerned about how well you dance on *Ellen*. You should want to fix the economy and stop the bleeding that is going on in Washington. We are living in some of the most serious times this country has ever faced, and the next election can't turn into a popularity contest."[7] Americans observing the party from afar might wonder about McCain's conflicts with members of her own party who are frequently telling her that she is not conservative enough or that she is not a real Republican. After all, her father was the 2008 Republican Presidential nominee, she takes conservative positions on issues, and she publicly proclaims her love for the party.

Arguments with the likes of Rush Limbaugh, Laura Ingraham, and Glenn Beck are further complicated by the fact that they are known for their extreme statements and at its base, McCain's political rhetoric is quite reasonable in a number of ways. For example, her dominant overwhelming message is that Republicans should come together and appeal to voters in the middle, who are neither Republicans nor Democrats. McCain wrote: "here's a little reality check. We will need moderate Republicans, we will need independents, and we will need blue-dog Democrats to win 2012 and unseat Obama. There is no media strategist anywhere who would debate that fact."[8] It has long been conventional wisdom in any election that candidates who appeal to the middle prevail. Thus, her message seems reasonable. As noted above, even though she is not an Obama fan and certainly wanted her father to beat him in the 2008 presidential election, she wished Obama well, for the good of America.

When Meghan McCain urged Newt Gingrich to drop out of the presidential primary in her column she provided sound reasons for doing so, "If Gingrich continues to stay in the race until the convention, the result will be an embarrassing bloodbath that will split the Republican Party in two. He will be giving Democrats time and ammunition. President Obama will only have to continue to reference Gingrich in his attacks against Romney."[9] Newt Gingrich responded: "How would she have a clue?"[10] Interestingly, he seemed to be the lone person in the party who was willing to dismiss McCain's comments without engaging her in argument. However, McCain's comment that Gingrich should not give the Democrats ideas for arguments against Romney seems to indicate that she has the party's best interests in mind. Though she can be extremely frank and use harsh language at times, at her core, McCain appears to have reasons to support her views.

When writing about the fact that the Occupy Wall Street movement lacked a coherent message, McCain wrote:

> The anger from Occupy Wall Street is coming from this simple fact: America no longer seems to be a place where you can work your way up, from rags to riches, from lower class to middle class to upper class. If people aren't given a fair shot, how can they work to achieve their dreams? This should be the message of Occupy Wall Street: We just want a chance; our government needs to give us a chance. But through all the pot smoke and distracting costumes, I'm not sure if that message is getting out.[11]

In a party determined to support the continuation of tax breaks for the richest 1 percent of the American people while the nation struggles to recover from the greatest economic crisis since the Great Depression and the ranks of the middle class continue to shrink while the rich get wealthier, McCain seems to identify with the average American. She wrote, "I have been given every opportunity that anyone could possibly dream of. I was given those opportunities as a result of the hard work from both sides of my family. What struck me more than anything is that for the first time possibly in history, people aren't being given the same opportunities that my parents and grandparents had."[12] Again, Meghan McCain seems informed, capable of empathy, and well meaning. She seems infinitely reasonable.

REPUBLICAN FRAY

Coulter/Ingraham vs. McCain

Two specific Republicans that Meghan McCain engaged in public conflict with are Ann Coulter and Laura Ingraham. Ann Coulter said on CNBC's television program *The Big Idea*, that America would be better if all

Americans were Christians and that Jews needed to be "perfected" by converting to Christianity. Coulter also referred to Al Gore as a "total fag."[13] McCain criticized Ann Coulter in her March 9, 2009 column, arguing that Coulter perpetuates "negative images about Republicans" and that McCain finds her "offensive, radical, insulting, and confusing all at the same time."[14] McCain explained:

> Coulter could be the poster woman for the most extreme side of the Republican Party. And in some ways I could be the poster woman for the opposite. I consider myself a progressive Republican, but here is what I don't get about Coulter: Is she for real or not? Are some of her statements just gimmicks to gain publicity for her books or does she actually believe the things she says? Does she really believe all Jewish people should be "perfected" and become Christians? And what was she thinking when she said Hillary Clinton was more conservative than my father during the last election?[15]

The reason she gave for critiquing Ann Coulter was, for McCain, part of a larger attempt to generate discourse about why Republicans had trouble appealing to young and moderate voters. McCain explained, "if figureheads like Ann Coulter are turning me off, then they are definitely turning off other members of my generation as well"[16] with the extreme statements she makes.

Her critique of Ann Coulter provoked Laura Ingraham to defend far right members of the party. Ingraham said, "Ok, Meghan. Do you think that anyone would be talking to you if you weren't kind of cute and you weren't the daughter of John McCain? Or do you just think that they would just think that you were just another Valley Girl gone awry?"[17] The implication here is that Meghan McCain is a young kid, who is cute, but not worthy of serious respect. Corley reported, "On her radio show today, Laura Ingraham responded to McCain's critique of far right conservatives, saying that she is 'just another Valley Girl gone awry.' In a mocking faux-Valley Girl voice, Ingraham made fun of McCain's body, joking that she didn't get a 'role in the Real World' because 'they don't like plus-sized models.'"[18] McCain responded, "Instead of intellectually debating our ideological differences about the future of the Republican Party, Ingraham resorted to making fun of my age and weight, in the fashion of the mean girls in high school."[19] We feel this is significant because Laura Ingraham is twenty years older than Meghan McCain and more established as a commentator. Yet, she resorted to attacking McCain's appearance. Moreover, rather than getting upset that Ingraham attacked her appearance, Meghan McCain merely pointed out that Ingraham's reply lacked any real substance.

Glenn Beck

In 2011, Meghan McCain did a public service announcement called "Naked," for skin cancer. In the ad, "naked," was a metaphor for going out without wearing sunscreen. She and other celebrities appeared naked, though viewers really did not see much, and the ad said that in order to avoid being a skin cancer statistic, we should all wear sunscreen. Glenn Beck seized this opportunity to comment on McCain's nakedness. O'Reilly provides a transcript of what took place:

> (BEGIN VIDEO CLIP)
> BECK: Watching this Meghan McCain video where she's naked.
> (SOUND EFFECT: THROWING UP)
> UNIDENTIFIED MALE: I'm having multiple . . .
> BECK: Are you still looking at the Meghan McCain?
> (SOUND EFFECT: THROWING UP)
> (END VIDEO CLIP)[20]

The implication was that someone who looks at Meghan McCain naked will vomit because her appearance is somewhat hideous. In the interview with Bill O'Reilly, Beck goes on to proclaim, "I have had enough of Meghan McCain, as much as she has had of me."[21] Meghan McCain responded by writing an open letter to Glenn Beck in her *Daily Beast* column. In the letter, McCain says that she was trying to draw attention to a disease that both of her parents had suffered from. The letter is masterfully constructed and much longer than we are able to share here. However, in the letter, she writes:

> You're a full-grown man with teenage daughters who are probably dealing with the sexist body-obsessed media environment that is difficult for all women. Is this really the legacy you want to be leaving for yourself?
>
> As a person known for his hot body, you must find it easy to judge the weight fluctuations of others, especially young women. If any of your daughters are ever faced with some kind of criticism of their physical appearance or weight, they should call me, because women's body image is another issue I feel passionate about, and have become accustomed to dealing with and speaking with young women about on my college tours.
>
> So, thanks for spreading the word Glenn. And, next time, instead of jumping straight to the "Meghan McCain fat jokes," maybe try out some new material. Because the fat-joke thing, it's been done so many times, I know a creative intellect such as yourself can do better than that.
>
> Love,
>
> Meghan[22]

Meghan McCain is generating dialogue on a number of serious social issues in addition to objecting to her party's trek to the right. Far right Republicans have challenged her and responded with attacks on her physical appearance. In these exchanges, we argue, McCain clearly triumphs. From a rhetorical perspective, several observations must be made. First, her responses indicate that she is not intimidated by these inherently intimidating people. Meghan McCain told Rachel Maddow on her show that, ". . . if it was too hot in the kitchen, I'd get out. I know what I'm doing."[23] So, McCain does seem tough. Second, she appears above the fray. She is attempting to begin a critical dialogue within her party, designed to make it stronger, and people who are supposed to love the party as much as she does are circumventing informed debate with name calling. McCain calmly acknowledges and answers their attacks with both humor (she told Glenn Beck she knew he was known for his body) and rational arguments (she called Ingraham out for refusing to engage in intellectual argument). This is made worse by attacks such as Ingraham on her age. If she really is too young and inexperienced to know what she is talking about, then why lose a debate of ideas to her by name calling? Third, McCain uses humor in her responses. Her letter to Glenn Beck is a fine example. Instead of attacking Glenn Beck, McCain chose to write a humorous letter to him. This letter, however, also raised some serious points. She noted that he is a full-grown man with teenage daughters. She suggested that if Beck's daughters have body image issues she would be willing to help them. This implies that he should not be treating McCain this way because it is childish (not acceptable conduct for a "full-grown man") and because he would not want someone to treat his own daughter that way. She also pointed out that the fat jokes are "overdone." We think this is her way of reiterating that this behavior is not very grown up and that he is apparently unable to offer a serious political response to McCain. The letter is humorous or ironic. We doubt that she is really feeling friendly toward Beck, yet she said that he is known for his hot body and she signed the letter with "love." We think that this response is preferable to a counter attack on Beck or to an emotional rant. Her humor makes her more likeable. It also helps to reinforce the fact that she is not threatened enough to become emotional or to cry. Her response to these personal attacks also may make viewers feel sorry for her or identify with her because many women face insecurity over body image. Attacking a woman's physical appearance is perhaps the most personal attack one can wield.

Thus, McCain's rhetoric undermines her critics' *ethos*. One final factor that plays a role in her ability to disarm her critics is Meghan McCain's age. Her youth works against her critics for at least three reasons. Her blog column is written to people her own age. She is also writing about how the party can better appeal to the youth voter. Her age uniquely positions her to lead this discussion. Older, more experienced media figures have little advantage here. Moreover, McCain began with a little known independent blog. She was having these "debates" with media figures who had their own radio and television shows. By engaging her, they made *her* views known. Ingraham and Beck would have been better off ignoring McCain rather than attacking her physical appearance because they brought even more attention and media coverage to her. Finally, Meghan McCain's age makes her critics childish. She wrote to Glenn Beck, "You're a full-grown man with teenage daughters." She also noted that Laura Ingraham was like a "mean girl" from high school. If her critics are so powerful, why engage in calling a child names?

REFLECTION ON FEMINISM

The double bind, as described by Kathleen Hall Jamieson, suggests that women who exercise power in public life are inevitably perceived in ways that undermine their ability to assert power. Characteristics that traditionally make male political candidates appealing do not tend to draw voters to female politicians. For example, people prefer physically attractive candidates in the media age. That is, we elect politicians who look like George W. Bush and Bill Clinton instead of William Howard Taft or the physically disabled Franklin Delano Roosevelt. Looks definitely play a role in terms of electability. Yet, we often fail to take good looking women, such as Sarah Palin, seriously. Moreover, Jamieson has suggested that while we prefer that male leaders be confident, assertive, and decisive, a woman, such as Janet Reno or Hillary Clinton, is considered unnatural (not feminine) or "bitchy" if she displays these same qualities. The point is that female leaders are criticized no matter what choices they make. Some women are criticized for not having any children and some are criticized for having too many. Hillary Clinton has constantly suffered from gendered criticism, suggesting that she is too feminine or too masculine at times. There is also criticism that she is too opportunistic or not tough enough. When ABC's *Good Morning America* asked her what she would do if Iran attacked Israel, she said we would "totally obliterate them." She was compared to George Bush and his harsh, direct style of communicating. Molly Watson (2008) argued, "Far from reassuring the U.S. electorate that ambition has not turned her into an insensitive bitch after all, the thought that she may be far too feminine to hold high office will terrify them."[24] Thus, Watson is suggesting Clinton's tears could represent the femininity so many Americans find problematic. Thus, either way, she cannot win. The list of too much or not enough goes on when it comes to how women assert their power. Jamieson (1995) suggests the double bind "den[ies] women access to power and, if individuals manage to slip past their constraints, the double bind serves to undermine their exercise of whatever power they achieve. The strategy defines something "fundamental" to women as incompatible with something the woman seeks—be it education, the ballot, or access to the workplace."[25] Thus, women are always caught in this place where they are subject to criticism should they choose to assert their leadership skills outside of the home. Though this phenomenon applies to women in politics, it is not unique to political leadership. Women may also face these constraints in attempting to exercise leadership in corporate America, at the Parent Teacher association, or anywhere else they attempt to lead.

Since Americans remain resistant to strong, assertive females in part because of this bind, we will lay out the framework of Jamieson's theory and see how it applies to Meghan McCain. Below are categories of the double bind that Jamieson identifies in her work—*Beyond the Double Bind: Women and Leadership*:

> Women can exercise their wombs or their brains, but not both.
> Women who speak out are immodest and will be shamed, while women who are silent will be ignored or dismissed.
> Women are subordinate whether they claim to be different from men or the same.
> Women who are considered feminine will be judged incompetent and women who are competent unfeminine.
> As men age, they gain wisdom and power; as women age, they wrinkle and become superfluous.[26]

The double binds Jamieson identified limit women's success and power are sometimes deliberate and sometimes unconscious because they are ingrained in the culture, but they are always working against women who seek power. Jamieson further suggests that each bind has an implication. The first bind gives the woman the choice between using her womb or her brain but not both. This creates a "no-choice choice."[27] The second bind—silence/shame is exemplified by the self-fulfilling prophecy which is explained as "a false definition of the situation evoking a new behavior which makes the original false conception true."[28] In simpler terms, women are not permitted to speak and are also condemned for not speaking. So, women's inability to speak is a self-fulfilling prophecy where they are judged for speaking out and ignored for not speaking at all. The third bind, sameness/difference, suggests women will lose whether they claim to be similar or different from a man because the standard or "norm" is male-defined and centered. Thus, Jamieson says the way to break this bind is to create "a form of equality not solely based on a male norm."[29] The fourth bind is termed femininity/competence, which suggests if a woman is feminine, she cannot be competent and vice versa. Thus, a woman must be both feminine and competent to be successful. Jamieson says "by this standard, women are bound to fail"[30] because it allows men to define what is feminine or femininity. Finally, the last double bind, the double standard, is defined by aging/invisibility. This is directly related to the fourth bind on femininity/competence. The bind suggests that as a woman ages, she becomes invisible. And we see this reinforced in our society since we are often taught that men get more attractive as they age and women just get old(er).

So, while society has made progress toward the empowerment of women, there are still hurdles to overcome. "Gender is probably the most restricting force in American life," Steinem wrote, "whether the question is who must be in the kitchen or who could be in the White House. This country is way down the list of countries electing women and, according to one study, it polarizes gender roles more than the average democracy."[31] One need only look back to the 2008 election and the controversy over Sarah Palin's wardrobe or anecdotal comments about Hillary Clinton looking old, tired, or wearing too many pantsuits as evidence that the way society views women is still strongly associated with looks. The question then becomes, is beauty a source of power? We will now examine how Meghan McCain tries to shatter the double bind.

"Women can exercise their wombs or their brains, but not both"

McCain is twenty-eight years old. She is not married and has no children, but does recognize that women are critiqued if they try to have both a career and be a parent. Meghan McCain commented on the treatment of her father's 2008 running mate, Sarah Palin, as someone who tried to be both the Republican Vice Presidential nominee and parent. McCain wrote,

> The brutal criticism of Sarah Palin—which will only increase when her memoir comes out—is yet another example of the double standard and cruel treatment of women in politics. Sarah has been attacked for everything from her hair to her clothes to the number of children she gave birth to. Maureen Dowd even nicknamed her "Caribou Barbie." I can't even begin to think of what that kind of judgment—criticizing parts of your life that have nothing to do with what you stand for or want to accomplish politically—feels like.[32]

Thus, McCain is aware of how the media criticized Palin's actions as a mother. Certainly, men are much less likely to have the media critique their effectiveness as parents. It is generally not considered to be relevant to their roles as public servants. In other words, our argument is that McCain is drawing attention to Jamieson's "no-choice choice" double bind because male politicians, such as Bill Clinton or George W. Bush, are not judged for their treatment of their children or their children's actions. They are viewed as public servants who happen to have children. Women, however, are evaluated by the media and the public as moms who happen to be public servants. McCain worries that this double bind will keep future female leaders from trying to have a career in politics. She wrote:

> It seems to me the male-dominated media suffers from a Goldilocks Syndrome
> that keeps women from shattering the glass ceiling. Worse, I fear it will pre-
> vent tomorrow's female leaders from even seeking office. This one is too hard.
> This one is too soft. Who will ever be just right?[33]

As research shows, women have a harder time shattering this glass ceiling in
part because they choose to have children during their careers. Furthermore,
women working in male dominated environments struggle with the glass
ceiling in addition to judgment from others regarding their choices of career
and family. This creates the effect that society criticizes women like Hillary
Clinton and Sarah Palin for possessing similar flaws (for example, in their
appearance, or in how personable they are) even though they are very different women.

"Women who speak out are immodest and will be shamed, while women who are silent will be ignored or dismissed"

Meghan McCain knows a great deal about being publicly shamed for making
her beliefs known. We have mentioned that bloggers and political talk show
hosts have called McCain fat and ugly in response to her ideas and thoughts
about making the Republican Party better. She has publicly denounced the
extremism of her party as this is her primary issue. She is also fully aware of
the consequences of speaking out against the people with those fundamentally conservative views. McCain stated:

> Whether or not the media wants to face this, I believe some women are less
> likely to speak out publicly about their political beliefs because they see the
> way I am talked about. Why would any woman want to speak out on television
> when the inevitable result will be a merciless critique of her physical appear-
> ance?[34]

We believe the Republican women are criticized differently than their Democratic counterparts. For example, we cannot imagine Rachel Maddow, Lawrence O' Donell, or Al Sharpton responding to political commentary by
Chelsea Clinton with an argument that she's fat, ugly, or should just wear a
burka as Glenn Beck told Meghan McCain. Why is it that conservative
pundits feel more comfortable criticizing a woman's appearance? Could it be
that conservatives favor more traditional views of women in all respects,
including appearance, while progressives value education and breaking free
from gender and career stereotypes?

While we are pointing out a difference between the rhetorical responses
on the left and the right, others have also noticed differences in physical
appearance. Colleen M. Carpinella, a UCLA graduate student in psychology
and lead author, reported the findings of her study on UCLA's webpage:

"Female politicians with stereotypically feminine facial features are more likely to be Republican than Democrat, and the correlation increases the more conservative the lawmaker's voting record." We believe this may be related to differences in party members' values. For example, we are unaware of a corresponding rhetoric among Democrats, where journalists like Rachel Maddow, Chris Matthews, or a similar pundit might respond to criticism of the Democratic Party by attacking the critic's physical appearance. Republican values focus more on traditional family structures with a stay-at-home mother and working father, thus there is the expectation of the stay-at-home mother which seems to include cooking, cleaning, and looking a certain way. In fact, Naomi Wolf said, ". . . Strong men battle for beautiful women, and beautiful women are more reproductively successful. Women's beauty must correlate to their fertility, and since this system is based on sexual selection, it is inevitable and changeless."[35] Thus, it would make sense that those embracing traditional views on family might also embrace the notion of the beautiful wife, the strong husband and protector. Furthermore, if we compare the conservative woman with the liberal woman, it is possible that the liberal woman gets a greater sense of self from her education or her career. This might make criticism of one's beauty less damaging to one's sense of self. In any case it appears that conservative women may face a greater requirement to be traditionally or stereotypically feminine and beautiful.

Meghan McCain is both a feminist and a traditional woman in the way she has constructed her image and lived her life thus far. But certainly, she has spoken out against prominent people in her party, which has resulted in others trying to shame her by calling her fat, ugly, indecent, and an embarrassment to the Republican Party. In fact, many other Republicans who have had confrontations with people like Limbaugh have apologized afterward. This includes: Congressman Eric Cantor, Congressman Todd Tiarht (through 2011), 2009 Congressional Candidate Jim Tedisco, previous Republican Chairman Michael Steele, Congressman Phil Gingrey, Ex-South Carolina Governor Mark Sanford, and Congressman Darrell Issa just to name a few. McCain spoke up to Rush Limbaugh (and other leaders of the Republican Party) without apologies.

"Women are subordinate whether they claim to be different from men or the same"

This part of the double bind suggests women are judged up against a male standard and they cannot win because they are not men and cannot be defined as such. This bind is a bit tricky as McCain has not run for office herself. However, she is accused of not being conservative enough by many in her party. Since this notion of conservativeness is largely male-defined, we think this bind applies. She writes,

> I'm often criticized for not being a "real" Republican, and I have been called a RINO—Republican In Name Only—in the past. Many say I am not "conservative enough," which is something that I am proud of. It is no secret that I disagree with many of the old-school Republican ways of thinking. One of the biggest issues from which I seem to drift from the party base is in my support of gay marriage. I am often criticized for previously voting for John Kerry and my support of stem-cell research. For the record, I am also extremely pro-military and a big supporter of the surge and the Iraq war. [36]

Here we see McCain trying to align herself with the party while also arguing why she believes differently than others in her party. Thus, her views on ideological issues like this cause rifts with people like Ann Coulter who more broadly support the conservative male values of the party. McCain has said: "I am sure most extreme conservatives and extreme liberals would find me a confusing, walking contradiction. But I assure you, there are many people out there just like me who represent a new, younger generation of Republicans." [37] McCain tries to bridge her feminist orientation and her Republican value system together but struggles to get approval from the Republican base because she is seen as too moderate. We believe this compares to a woman trying to argue she is both similar and different from the male counterpart in that it works sometimes, but one really has to be an insider for it to work and many conservatives do not really consider her an insider. In fact, some conservatives have suggested people would not know or care who she was if she were not John McCain's daughter.

"Women who are considered feminine will be judged incompetent and women who are competent unfeminine"

On June 21, 2012, Meghan McCain interviewed Michele Bachmann about her experiences running for office, as well as her opinions on Romney and Obama. McCain posited the question: "But was it ever hard for you? I see what women are going through in politics right now, and I do think politics is sexist, especially when I see what you [went] through along with Ann Romney, Sarah Palin, and Hillary Clinton. Would you want your daughters to grow up and run for office?" [38] Bachmann's answer was lengthier than we will share here, but this was the crux of her response: "If you're a conservative woman, you have a tougher time because we have a hair and makeup standard and a clothing standard that we have to pass through at very different gauntlets. We can't be shrill, but yet we have to be tough." [39] This is perhaps the biggest challenge of the feminine/incompetent double bind— How can a woman be both tough and feminine? According to Foust, "Per-

haps the idea that a tough woman may have political agency in policy making is too frightening for mainstream culture, even if her toughness is supported by feminine public virtue and the neo-conservative scene."[40]

In 2009, McCain wrote about Sarah Palin and Hillary Clinton's commo-
nalities explaining, "So yes, Sarah Palin is a woman with five children and
her physical appearance is deemed 'too beautiful for politics.' And on the
other end, Hillary Clinton is criticized for not being beautiful enough, for
being 'too tough' in the man's world that she resides."[41] McCain is well
aware of the struggles women in politics experience in trying to exert their
power while also remaining feminine. McCain further explains, "Must we, as
Republican women, clone ourselves in every way as Sarahbot's to have a
serious chance of running for office? And if so, what kind of dangerous
message is this sending young women?"[42]

McCain herself is subject to this same scrutiny. When she blogs or talks
about how the Republican Party could improve by veering away from the
extremism, she is heckled, called fat, ugly, and is criticized for only being
heard because she is John McCain's daughter. By calling her fat and ugly,
McCain's critics elevate Meghan McCain, or they magnify the significance
of what she is saying. Initially, it was her critics, and not McCain, who were
famous and thus likely to receive wide media coverage for their comments.
As we discussed earlier, if she really is too young and inexperienced, why
resort to name calling? Why not challenge her ideas instead of her looks?

Thus, we believe McCain is doing a fine job of trying to manage this
double bind. She is feminine and tough. Many blog comments suggested
support for McCain after she was attacked by Beck and Ingraham. People
said she was attractive and many moderate Republicans agreed with her that
the extremism is a problem in the Republican Party. Perhaps one day McCain
will be dubbed something strong and feminine such as "steel magnolia" like
Roslyn Carter or "The Iron Maiden" like Margaret Thatcher. Again, this
double bind seems to pose a larger challenge to the Republican women
perhaps because their standard is a bit "tougher" as Michele Bachmann
said—more of the "Sarahbot" is perhaps expected.

"As men age, they gain wisdom and power; as women age, they wrinkle and become superfluous"

Jamieson writes, "Powerful men are sexy, sexy women are powerful, and
these propositions are not at all the same."[43] If men get more attractive as
they age, this suggests women have less power as they age because they are
seen as less attractive. Meghan McCain is only twenty-eight years old, so this
is not much of an issue for her at this time. Perhaps people do pay more
attention to her because she is young and attractive (despite being told otherwise), but certainly there is much more to come for her.

IMPLICATIONS/FUTURE RESEARCH

Meghan McCain is interesting and exciting because she is challenging her own party to move to the center and appeal to more voters and in doing so she is weakening several of these double binds. She is very aware of how women in power and politics are treated. The way some conservatives react to her is part of a larger issue involving women's roles and societal expectations. McCain is responding to this and criticizing the no-win situations created by the Republican Party's values, and this, at the very least, is causing some much needed discourse. McCain is actively reframing the values, which according to Jamieson, "invites an audience to view a set of options from a different perspective and confront the fact that the options offered are false."[44] McCain is also recounting what happened to her through narratives, which for her are blogs. Rather than reciprocating by calling her critics names, she is demonstrating that she is intelligent and that her critics are engaged in ad hominem attacks instead of responding to her arguments. In doing so, she is undermining the double binds. For example, she is both attractive and intelligent and she is both assertive and likeable. Rather than serving as a polarizing figure, people seem to like Meghan McCain and they seem to have sympathy for her. Jamieson says women "can use the narrative—more effectively than other available means of persuasion—to explain who she is, why she belongs there, and what principles define her."[45] McCain is doing so through her blogging.

We believe future research should focus not only on the Hillary Clintons, Elizabeth Doles, and the Sarah Palins, but the up and coming women like Meghan McCain as well. All of the female political leaders have been put up against these double binds and all of them have succumbed to them in some way because the notions of beauty and success are so male-centered. We are hopeful, that as the presence of women in the public sphere become normalized, the ways to navigate the double binds will become more numerous. The task of future research is to explore these new avenues of political expression.

NOTES

1. Daniel Libit, "Crashing the Republican Party," *Politico*, April 11, 2009. www.politico.com.

2. Meghan McCain, "Republican in Name Only? Try the future of the GOP. The following is Meghan McCain's address to the Log Cabin Republicans Convention—a group that promotes gay issues within the GOP," *The Daily Beast*, April 18, 2009. www.thedailybeast.com.

3. Meghan McCain, "What I Learned From the Democrats: The mistakes liberals like Harry Reid and Nancy Pelosi are making can teach Republicans how to regain power—and how to hold onto it," *The Daily Beast*, April 7, 2009. www.thedailybeast.com.

4. Meghan McCain, "Meghan McCain: Is It Too Late for Mitt Romney and Republicans?" *The Daily Beast*, April 6, 2012. www.thedailybeast.com.

5. Meghan McCain, "Revenge of the RINOs," *The Daily Beast*, April 18, 2009. www.thedailybeast.com.

6. Ibid.

7. Meghan McCain, "Meghan McCain's 7 Tips for Republican Hopefuls: 2012 election," *The Daily Beast*, June 20, 2011. www.thedailybeast.com.

8. Meghan McCain, "Shut Up About My Body Glenn Beck," *The Daily Beast*, May 12, 2011. www.thedailybeast.com.

9. Meghan McCain, "Meghan McCain on Why Newt Gingrich Should Quit After Florida Primary," *The Daily Beast*, January 31, 2012. www.thedailybeast.com.

10. Karin Tanabe, "Newt Disses Meghan McCain," *Politico*, October 27, 2011. www.politico.com.

11. McCain, "Meghan McCain on Why Newt Gingrich," *The Daily Beast*, December 8, 2011. thedailybeast.com.

12. Ibid.

13. Kathleen Parker, "Another McCain Throws Down a Challenge," *The Washington Post*, March 25, 2009. www.washingtonpost.com.

14. Meghan McCain, "My Beef With Ann Coulter," *The Daily Beast*, March 9, 2009. thedailybeast.com.

15. Ibid.

16. Meghan McCain, "Quit Talking About My Weight, Laura Ingraham," *The Daily Beast*, March 14, 2009. www.thedailybeast.com.

17. Matt Corley, "Laura Ingraham Mocks Meghan McCain as Being 'Plus-Sized,'" *Think Progress*, March 12, 2009. thinkprogress.org.

18. Ibid.

19. McCain, "Quit Talking About My Weight, Laura Ingraham."

20. Bill O'Reilly, "Beck Responds to Meghan McCain's Criticism," *The O'Reilly Show Transcript, Lexis-Nexis*, May 13, 2011. www.lexisnexis.com.

21. Ibid.

22. McCain, "Shut Up About My Body Glenn Beck."

23. Rachel Maddow, "The Rachel Maddow Show, Transcript," *Lexis-Nexis*, March 11, 2009. www.lexisnexis.com.

24. Molly Watson, "It's My Political Party and I'll Cry if I Want to," *The Times*, (2008): 2. journalisted.com.

25. Kathleen Jamieson, "Beyond the Double Bind: Women and Leadership" (USA: Oxford University Press, 1995), 13–14.

26. Ibid., 16.

27. Ibid., 17.

28. Robert Merton, "The Self-Fulfilling Prophecy," *Antioch Review* (1948): 195. www.jstor.org.

29. Jamieson, "Beyond the Double Bind," 18.

30. Ibid., 18.

31. Gloria Steinem, "Women Are Never Front-Runners," *New York Times*, January 8, 2008. www.nytimes.com.

32. Meghan McCain, "Hillary and Sarah's Common Theme," *The Daily Beast*, November 8, 2009. www.thedailybeast.com.

33. Ibid.

34. Meghan McCain, "Stop the Fat Jokes," *The Daily Beast*, October 14, 2009. www.thedailybeast.com.

35. Naomi Wolf, *The Beauty Myth* (New York: Doubleday, 1991): 239–40.

36. McCain, "My Beef With Ann Coulter."

37. Ibid.

38. Meghan McCain, "Meghan McCain Interviews Michele Bachmann on Obama, Romney and More," *The Daily Beast*, June 21, 2012. www.thedailybeast.com.

39. Ibid.

40. Christina Foust, "A Return to Feminine Public Virtue: Judge Judy and the Myth of the Tough Mother," *Women's Studies in Communication* (September 2004), 287. www.questia.com.

41. Meghan McCain, M. "Hillary and Sarah's Common Theme," *The Daily Beast*, November 8, 2009. www.thedailybeast.com.

42. Meghan McCain, "My Palin Problem," *The Daily Beast*, October 5, 2010. www.thedailybeast.com.

43. Jamieson, "Beyond the Double Bind: Women and Leadership," 151.

44. Ibid., 190.

45. Ibid., 195.

III

Women and Politics:
2012 and the Future of Women Leaders
in America

Chapter Eight

The Female Email

*Examining the Leadership and Rhetoric of Female
Representations of the 2012 Obama Campaign*

Alison Novak and Janet Johnson

Since President Barack Obama's announcement on April 4, 2011, of his intention to run for reelection in 2012, his campaign sent 1670 emails to voters and constituents.[1] Each email came from the same "no reply" email address (info@BarackObama.com); however, the ascribed authors of each email varied according to the topic and content of the message. Among the authors exists a group of women who send emails on behalf of the campaign, including First Lady Michelle Obama, Dr. Jill Biden, and Deputy Campaign Manager Julianna Smoot.

This chapter presents research investigating the topics addressed by these women as well as the style and language that assert leadership in online campaigning. Previous research by Winograd and Hais identified political emails as a resource that can be used to explore the strategies of a campaign.[2] Emails are a good source for studying gender and politics because the segmentation of topics and rhetoric used by each gender is showcased in the email channel and reveals the contemporary set of gendered political norms, roles, and language used to enact leadership in campaigning. Drawing from previous research on women in campaigning and the role of email in contemporary campaigns, this chapter looks at the topics and rhetoric of the women involved in the 2012 Obama campaign. This mixed methods study of the 1670 emails includes a content analysis of topics and a rhetorical analysis of messages. The findings of this these analyses contribute to the conversation on the current role of women in online presidential campaigning because as we study the gender of those who send emails we expand our understanding of how the campaign both is and wants to be understood.

BACKGROUND

Women in Presidential Campaigning

Historically, women did not participate in presidential campaigns. They did not travel with their spouses, siblings, or parents, and other relationships with candidates were formal and distanced. However, the role of women in presidential campaigns has increased since 1920. In the 1920 campaign, Eleanor Roosevelt, wife of Franklin D. Roosevelt, changed that trend and manifested as an important part of husband's campaign. As Candidate Roosevelt traveled across the country to campaign, Mrs. Roosevelt was the only woman in his entourage.[3] Roosevelt's campaign manager and former newspaperman Louis Howe taught Eleanor about national politics and the press and involved her in planning and preparation.[4] For example, Howe would ask Mrs. Roosevelt to review speeches and to help him to plan press conferences.[5]

The shift toward incorporating women in the actual campaign process continued during the women's movement in the 1960s and 1970s as women's roles in politics and in world events continued to expand. Kellerman's 1978 article, "The Political Functions of the Presidential Family," explains, "The women's movement has lent a new import to the wife of the president (as well as to other female relatives)."[6] While women were not stepping into the U.S. Presidency, their presence in the political arena grew. Although Jacqueline Kennedy's role was "virtually nonexistent" in her husband's campaign—her role would expand as the first lady—former President Jimmy Carter wanted his wife Rosalynn on the campaign trail to illustrate to the electorate that he and his wife had a true partnership.[7]

Since Carter's campaign, candidates have more frequently involved the candidates' spouse, and as time as gone on, the vice-presidential candidate's wife has also taken a part in the campaign. In fact, the candidates' wives are now part of the candidates' strategies, and "it is clear that a great deal of thought went into the use of the presidential and vice presidential candidates' wives as surrogates in the 2004 campaign."[8] In fact, the 2004 U.S. Presidential campaign was a turning point. MacManus and Quecan explain, "The sheer number of candidates on both sides of the aisle and the heavily front loaded campaign season have made using the wives and of the candidates a 'must.'"[9] Women who campaign for a presidential candidate—the candidates' wives but also now highly qualified female campaign staff members—are becoming leaders in campaigns, and campaigns are using these women to attract more women voters as well as hone their own political ambitions.

To explore the shift of gender roles—or at least the recent inclusion of accomplished women—in the campaign process, we must examine women's roles in presidential campaigns. Lazar's edited collection on *Feminist ritical Discourse Analysis* argues that we need to understand the "complex and subtle ways in which taken-for-granted social assumptions and hegemonic power relations are discursively produced, perpetuated, negotiated, and challenged."[10] This is true as we consider what roles these women take and how their involvement influences the populace. Therefore, we must analyze the discourse surrounding these women and their roles in the campaigns so we can discover contemporary power relations and understand their effects.[11] Fairclough and Wodak adopt gender as an ideological structure that can then be identified within text, and we use that structure as the framework of our analyses.[12] And, through the narrative and rhetoric of a text, we can identify gendered language, leadership, rules, and norms, all of which are positioned within the culture around gender.[13] Remlinger, in her chapter "Feminist Critical Discourse Analysis: Gender, Power, and Ideology in Discourse," focuses on this approach in works, identifying gendered structures within various forms of discourse such as newspapers, classroom discussions, and advertisements.[14] Lazar also proposes the study of female discourse as necessary to discover women's roles and evaluate developments in the ongoing debates of gendered leadership, equality, and citizenship.[15]

Gender issues remain complex, and thus, to comprehend these issues, we must break down discourses. Thus, by studying the role of women in contemporary presidential campaigns, researchers can develop an understanding of the place of women on the national election stage as understood and constructed by society. As we seek to understand these issues in the political realm, rhetoric becomes increasingly important; the rhetoric related to political campaigns reflects the vocalized intentions and efforts of a campaign to connect with potential voters and also reflects the ontological assumptions by campaign organizers about the leadership potential of campaigners, specifically female campaigners.[16] The rhetoric becomes the mechanism by which the campaign forms an identity and stance on an issue, especially for a target audience such as women.

Through the language and rhetoric of a message on a topic, a reader is able to build an understanding of the stance of the campaign. Therefore, the selection of representatives of a campaign has become increasingly important. Choosing the right voice for a topic can make or break a campaign's image and relationship with voters. As a result, the sender considers a campaign's message as it becomes the voice by which the sender delivers the rhetoric to the reader. Lazar suggests that the author of a text helps to form the identity of those who the rhetoric represents,[17] and the authors who participated in Lazar's text (Remlinger, Wodak, and Gouveia) identified different features of women's campaign strategies and the topics that women most successfully approach.[18] Specifically, women are often relegated to talk about "big picture" topics—family, morality, military, and the economy—while male campaigners spend more time talking about small issues, such as current issues and local challenges.[19] This difference is one source of power relationships in politics that relate to the discourses surrounding contemporary campaigning.

Women are now spokespersons in specific sectors that their husbands cannot easily reach and that traditionally concern women. During the 2000 U.S. Presidential campaign, President George Bush's wife Laura Bush spoke about literacy programs. Then Senator Hillary Clinton—who twice helped her husband President Bill Clinton to successfully campaign—promoted children and education. And, even though Senator Clinton moved forward in her own political career—running for the U.S. Senate and then for the U.S. Presidency—her role in her husband's campaigns and presidential terms may have influenced the populace in its opinions of her. Tuman explains, "She [Hillary Clinton] is a brilliant intelligent, politically astute, and observant politician. For whatever reasons, many have known and experienced her primarily through the prism of her husband's political experience, failures, and triumphs."[20] Senator Clinton, who later became Secretary of State for President Obama's administration, used the power of her husband's popularity to her advantage, but Senator Clinton had to overcome many obstacles related to sexism in her own campaign. Senator Clinton's example shows that gender roles are still not defined in politics, but with more women becoming a "supporter" and "partner" in other campaigns and who take on leadership roles can only help expand the opportunities for future female political leadership.

The struggle with women who campaign for their husbands or for other male candidates is that they must ensure that women's roles on the campaign trail leaves room for more than relating to women as mother and wife figures but also as leaders. Carlin and Winfrey explain, "It is possible that a candidate cannot do it [successfully campaign] herself and that at some point a woman with considerable credibility who has been the subject of sexist attacks such as Madeline Albright or Condoleezza Rice needs to take such a speech on the road."[21] Thus, as women are proving invaluable on the campaign trail, they are also proving viable political candidates once their husbands leave office. Additionally, through more modern campaign strategies, the wives of the candidates are lending their names and thus their reputations to help their husbands' political careers. One way they can do that is by communicating on behalf of their candidate-spouses with the electorate, and many are using tools like Twitter, Facebook, and email for that communication. Presidential candidates can be helped by surrogate speakers, whose "primary function is to spread the candidate's messages to audiences that might otherwise not hear them," and these women are effectively communicating and serving as influential supporters for these candidates. [22]

This chapter examines both the issues that the female members of the campaign address and the rhetoric in campaign communication—specifically in emails—that motivates women to advocate for more than generic political support but that ensures that gender does not overshadow their own or other women's political leadership roles and ambitions.

Obama Campaign's Digital Presence

Officially launched on April 4, 2011, the 2012 Obama campaign adopted a similar strategy as the one that his 2008 campaign used, communicating with most of Obama's supporters and constitutes through email, Facebook, Twitter, and text messages. Winograd and Hais assert that the consistency of Obama's message through these channels attracted voters (particularly younger voters) and ultimately stopped the technologically scattered Republican presidential nominee from obtaining the presidency. [23] The 2008 presidential candidates were not the first candidates to use electronic and computer-mediated communication to address and work with supporters. Montgomery argues that 2004 presidential candidates still used traditional piece-mail and telephone calls, but third parties like Moveon.org, Vote or Die Campaign, and The New Voter Project aggressively pursued new online means of accessing various publics. [24] But, for the first time, a candidate's campaign was directly linked to these tools. In the past, such as in the 2004 election, third-party groups campaigning for their candidates were responsible for the politically driven communication that occurred through these mediums. In addition to being novel, the tactics of these organizations were extremely successful at accessing and communicating with (not to) the "Millennials," a group previously deemed politically unenthused and toxic. [25] And the beginning of online communication campaign techniques by these supporting organizations allowed for new campaign methodologies to emerge. Hendricks and Denton say that, in the 2004 campaign, "Social networking software allowed grassroots events to happen where supporters could find events nearest their location. Extensive databases allowed email targeting where a single voter profile could generate a more personalized message." [26]

As a result of the 2004 grassroots communication through electronic media, candidates in the next campaign adopted tools for electronic communication. Obama's campaign in 2008 in particularly adopted these tools and campaign methods that used them. Thus, the success of the 2008 Obama campaign developed a presence on social networking websites such as My Space, Facebook, Twitter, and LinkedIn and also developed an extensive variety of websites and blogs intended to communicate with and inform different demographic and political groups. For example, Obama's campaign created www.my.barackobama.com specifically for younger voters eighteen to twenty-four years old. [27]

However, the presence of Obama's 2008 campaign went beyond websites and approached voters directly and more personally: through emails and text messages. Through these personalized messages, Obama's campaign reached out to subscribers, delivered his messages directly to his supporters, and kept them notified: of new campaign promises (e.g., lowering interest rates on federal student loans), issues (e.g., economic recovery plans), and events (e.g., planned speeches, debates, and rallies). Although the text messages sent by the campaign were shorter than emails—which is appropriate for the messages that each tool is designed to deliver—the two channels always featured similar content. That is, the campaign workers used consistent themes but formatted the messages per the media through which they were delivered. For example, if the campaign was going to send a message to subscribers about universal health care (later termed "Obamacare"), the campaign writers would send a message in email and an abbreviated message in text form. Additionally, the writers might create a Tweet, a status post on the campaign's Facebook page, and a post on the homepage of the Obama campaign website, and the messages would all contain information on that same issue. According to Winograd and Hais, this strategy empowered supporters to access information about Obama and his campaign and to understand his stance on the currently debated issues. [28] Additionally, social media campaigns were useful to Obama's campaign because "Citizens cannot attend every campaign event. Candidates' websites and social media campaigns allow the candidates to publish their stances on the issues as well as to inform readers of the candidates' daily activities." [29] Of course, third-party sites and groups were still active during the 2008 campaign, and many linked to Obama's web presence, which supported the candidate's message. They also forwarded messages from his campaign and thus furthered the influence of his messages.

Considering the widespread success that the mass media and academic researchers have ascribed to these communication campaign techniques, researchers, strategists, and candidates themselves must understand the messages being "consistently" featured. [30] These messages were fully explored in the aftermath of the 2008 campaign, but researchers could feasibly investigate messages of 2011–2012 to gain an understanding of the reelection campaign.

While each email from the Obama campaign was sent to subscribers from the same non-reply webmail address—info@barackobama.com—each message was labeled and signed by different people in the campaign. These authors included President Barack Obama, Vice President Biden, or Campaign Manager Jim Messina but also frequently included women—for example, First Lady Michelle Obama, Caroline Kennedy, and Chief Operating Officer Ann Marie Habershaw—as authors of these emails.

Rhetoric and *Kairos*

Rhetoric, according to Rife, is "the art of persuasion as well as a particular epistemological outlook that emphasizes the ability to generate probable knowledge."[31] In addition, rhetoric's importance (per Asen) rests in its ability to affect public opinion and to influence the creation of public policy, both results that enact a form of leadership.[32] Using historical examples of two separate social security public opinion campaigns—by President Franklin D. Roosevelt and President George W. Bush, Asen argues that those in political power can influence public opinion and channel support for potentially divisive political issues through the use of rhetoric and persuasive appeals.[33] Findings in studies by Simons and Hogan support the strong affects that political rhetoric has on public opinion and emphasize a need to continuously study the rhetoric of politicians to understand the behaviors of the public and the evolution of support of public policy.[34]

In developing a study of rhetoric, scholars must consider the *ethos*, *logos*, and *pathos* as well as the *kairos* of a text. These four concepts were identified and theorized by Aristotle, who considered them as the four intentional strategies or modes of persuasion. *Ethos* (credibility), *logos* (logic), and *pathos* (emotions) are most commonly used to understand political text; however, Rife, Kinneavy and Eskin, and Sullivan have begun to identify *kairos* (timing) as perhaps the most important of the strategies.[35] Longaker and Walker define *kairos* as "both an occasion for discourse and the surrounding conditions that present the rhetor with opportunities and constraints: opportunities or openings to say certain things in certain ways; and constraints that limit what can be said and how."[36] Rife suggests that the study of *kairos* is thus most important in an evaluation of rhetoric and asserts, "*Kairos* trumps the other three rhetorical strategies because no matter how perfect the *ethos*, no matter how strong the *pathos*, and no matter how logical the argument, if the timing is wrong, the audience will not listen."[37] Thus, while *ethos*, *logos*, and *pathos* are important in a rhetorical analysis, scholars should privilege and prioritize the study of *kairos*.

Rhetoric is critical to understand the leadership of women in any given society. Because of this importance, an ongoing debate waged over the cause and effect of women leadership and men's rhetorical dominance is ever-present. Studies by Bashevkin, Campbell, and Hawkesworth suggest rhetoric have made men historically assert dominance over women politically.[38] However, other studies by Sutton and Bourdieu suggest that rhetoric is also how women overcome men's societal dominance and push toward equality.[39] Women's historical push for equality is why examining the contemporary use of rhetoric by women involved in a campaign will help people understand and help influence women's leadership opportunities in campaigns. Paxton and Hughes identified rhetoric as one means of identifying power relationships in campaign representation.[40] These power relations are described through the language and leadership rhetoric used in spoken or written word. While women are often featured in contemporary political campaigns, through rhetoric their power relationships are socially structured. The style and *kairos* of women's rhetoric suggests that specific roles are designated or occupied by women most frequently. These roles include those of "character reference" and emotional support system. While viewed as important, these roles highlight the "support" rather than the "leadership" function that women have completed. Thus, a study of women's political leadership must include an analysis of the content of the text for these implied roles.

METHODS

The Obama campaign sent out 1670 emails since the April 4, 2011 announcement of the President's re-election bid. This study uses both quantitative and qualitative techniques to study the types and rhetoric of emails sent by the women of the Obama campaign.

This study asks the following questions as they related to the two methods used to investigate the sample of emails that made up the data set for this study.

1. What topics do the women of the Obama campaign address more than their male counterparts?
2. What issues are not addressed by women authors?
3. How do the women of the campaign communicate on each topic?
4. What stylistic choices do the writers of each email make?
5. What can the *kairos* or context of these messages tell us about gender in campaigning?

Content Analysis

A quantitative content analysis is a systematic way to look for patterns in text. Defined by Krippendorff, a content analysis is a "research technique for making replicable and valid inferences from text (or other meaningful matter) to the contexts of their use."[41] This form of analysis allows researchers to look at the content, function, form, and structure of a communicated message. White and Marsh identify electronic content, such as webpages and emails, appropriate texts for a content analysis.[42]

In this study, the communicated messages or texts include all emails sent by the Obama Campaign since the April 4, 2011 candidacy announcement. This is the full and complete data set of all emails sent by the campaign. White and Marsh suggest that sampling a large data set correctly is the most important element of a quantitative content analysis.[43] The importance and methods of selecting a random and representative sample is asserted by Standsbury, who suggests a 10 percent sample size is large enough to yield generalizable results without becoming too unmanageable or redundant.[44] This data set includes 1670 emails sent by various authors (all from the same non-reply email address). For this study, we sample 10 percent, or 167 emails. As described by Standsbury, we use a random-number generator to systematically select 167 emails. Then, we code that sample for the quantitative content analysis.

Each email is coded for the author and subject matter. Through an open coding process described by White and Marsh, the authors perform a deep reading of each email, creating a category for each topic addressed.[45] Each email is coded for one subject: When two codes or subjects exist within one email, the primary or dominant subject is coded. The coding process aimed to help discover the frequency of topics addressed by specific email authors. This frequency provides insight into what topics women campaigners took initiative or leadership on. Further, the gender of each email sender is coded in an effort to study the frequency different authors wrote on different subjects (see Table 8.1).

Table 8.1. List of Codes and Descriptions

Code	Description
Gender	1 = women 2= men
Swag	regarding items for purchase or giveaway
Competition-Style Fundraising	asking for a donation for a chance to win a prize
Fundraising	asking for a donation to support the campaign without offer of a prize
Supporting the President	asking to sign an electronic card or using a social media application that signifies support
Supporting Michelle	asking to sign an electronic card or using a social media application that signifies support
Supporting VP	asking to sign an electronic card or using a social media application that signifies support
Recruiting Volunteers	asking for volunteers
Thank You	thanking supporters for emotional or financial contributions

Collapse Support	combination of gender, swag, competition-style fundraising, fundraising, supporting the President, Michelle, VP, volunteer recruits, and thank you
Healthcare	giving information regarding Obamacare or Universal healthcare issues
Immigration	giving information regarding immigration or the Dream Act
Marriage Equality	giving information regarding same-sex marriage or marriage equality
Jobs	giving information regarding jobs
Iraq War	giving information regarding the Iraq War or the end of the Iraq War
Taxes	giving information regarding taxes
Veterans	giving information regarding veterans issues
Collapse Issues	combination of healthcare, immigration, marriage equality, jobs, the Iraq War, taxes, and veterans
Survey	asking the receiver to take survey
Conservative Critique	critiquing the GOP, conservatives, Mitt Romney, Romney's campaign, senate, house, and local GOP campaigns

Material generated by authors

A content analysis yields many benefits in the present study. For example, content analysis is relatively unobtrusive, making it easy to perform a complete analysis without involving the message senders. However, there are problems also associated with a strict content analysis. Anderson illuminates that content analysis simplifies the richness of the text. This is visible in the approach to code every email as having only one topic. This does not take into account the tone, types of examples, use of rhetorical devises, and overall type of email (persuasive, informative, attacking). While it can reveal important statistical measures such as what author is responsible for each issue, it cannot give us information about the language and efforts of the campaign. To delve into the meaning of the messages, the use of rhetorical analysis is needed.

Rhetorical Analysis

Rhetorical analysis allows investigators to examine the quality, intentional strategies, or modes of persuasion used to appeal to certain audiences. Fahnestock explains, ". . . a rhetorical analysis concentrates on a single text or a group of texts related, as the scholar chooses, by author, audience, time, genre, subject, or implication in an intellectual or social movement."[46] One important aspect to a rhetorical analysis is identifying the *kairos* of the set of emails sent by the Obama administration. By studying the *kairos*, we can focus specifically on the context, timing, and surrounding conditions by which text is created and received by an audience. Further, by studying the rhetoric of the emails, we can begin to understand the leadership roles and language used to enact these roles taken on by the women campaigners. Longaker and Walker say such rhetoric can relate to "cultural, political, economic, and technological" conditions by which the reader of a text makes sense of the message.[47]

The results of the content analysis of the emails are examined through a rhetorical lens of *kairos*. As a result, the rhetorical analysis enhances the content analysis because it explores the situation and meaning behind each email message. A complete analysis should look at the relationship of outside events to the rhetoric, but also how different statements relate within the larger data set. Thus, to understand the themes and *kairos* of the text, we should read the emails as a set, which allows us to see the impact that each message plays in the collective whole.

A rhetorical analysis must go beyond looking at the context of the messages and must also consider the linguistic and stylistic choices made in the articulation of each email message. Evaluating the style of these messages rhetorically—a "stylistic analysis"—allows us to evaluate messages for their clarity, correctness, appropriateness, distinction, word choice, tropes, and schemes.[48] We evaluate these various rhetorical considerations when analyzing the set of emails authored by female representatives who were related to the Obama campaign.

For reliability purposes, the findings section includes detailed examples of the rhetoric employed by various emails. This is a method made popular by Polit and Beck's work on qualitative techniques.[49] While not an exhaustive listing of all incidents or appearances of the *kairos* and stylistic choices, these examples do represent an effort to connect the findings to the data set.[50] The later discussion section will draw larger inferences from the findings and relate them to previous and future research.

FINDINGS: CONTENT ANALYSIS

A deep reading is conducted of 165 emails sampled from the 2012 Obama campaign. While a sample of 167 emails is collected, two emails were sent from the author "Obama for America," and thus, because of their genderless authorship are eliminated from the data set. Of the remaining 165 emails, a content analysis where the topics of each email were denoted and a rhetorical analysis of the style and *kairos* is conducted.

Overall, women sent forty-seven of 165 (28.48 percent) emails and men sent 118 of 165 (71.52 percent) emails. A statistical content analysis of the topics of men's and women's emails of the Obama campaign reveals three important and statistically significant findings. First, overall women emailed less frequently than men; second, women emailed more frequently about competition-style fundraising; and third, women emailed less frequently about political issues such as healthcare and taxes.

Frequency

Of the twenty-six authors who sent emails from the Obama campaign, fourteen of the sources were male, and twelve were female. On average, male authors sent eight unique emails, while female authors sent only four. These findings reveal a significant difference in the number of emails sent by each gender. Women were less likely to be a source of an email from the Obama campaign, and when they were a source, they sent fewer emails than their male counterparts. Julianna Smoot, the Deputy Campaign Manager sent the most emails of the female data set, responsible for seventeen of fifty-five emails or 30.9 percent. First Lady Michelle Obama sent fifteen emails of the female data set or 27.2 percent. Five of the female authors sent only one email during the length of the campaign. These findings further reveal that men were significantly more likely to send emails from the Obama campaign due to both the frequency of their emails as well as the number of male authors.

Competition-style fundraising

The first finding is true of almost every topical category except for the category of "competition-style fundraising" in which the authors asked supporters to donate a few dollars to enter a competition to meet or dine with the president and a special guest (Michelle Obama, Beyoncé and Jay-Z, or George Clooney). This campaigning tactic began in early 2012 and accounted for the largest amount of emails sent by women in any category. As detailed in Table 8.2, women sent seventeen emails on the topic of competition-style fundraising accounting for 30.9 percent of their total emails and 54.8 percent of the total emails in that category. Men, however, sent fourteen emails on competition-style fundraising, accounting for 11.8 percent of their total emails and 45.2 percent of emails in that category (see Table 8.3).

Table 8.2. Women and Support Categories

	Swag	Competition-Style Fundraising	Fundraising	Supporting the President	Supporting Michelle	Supporting the VP	Recruiting Volunteers	Thank You
Ann Marie Habershaw, Chief Operating Officer		4	2	1	1			
Caroline Kennedy				2				
Eva Longoria, supporter		1						
Gabrielle Union, supporter							1	
Heather Colburn, National Women's Vote Director							1	
Jill Biden					1	1		
Julianna Smoot, Deputy Campaign Manager	3	5	5	1			1	
Katherine Archuleta,								

National Political Director								
Lilly Ledbetter, supporter					1			
Michelle Obama	1				4	3	7	
Sara El-Amine, National Training Director		1						
Stephanie Cutter, Deputy Campaign Manager		1						
total	1	5	1	2	8	10	17	3

Material generated by authors

Table 8.3. Men and Support Categories

	Swag	Competition-Style Fundraising	Fundraising	Supporting the President	Supporting Michelle	Supporting the VP	Recruiting Volunteers	Thank You
Barack Obama		6	13	4	2			
Bill Clinton		1						
David Axelrod, supporter				1				
Ed Prouty, supporter			1					
James Kvaal, Policy Director		1		2			1	
Jeremy Bird, National Field Director	1	1		1			9	
Jim Messina, Campaign Manager		1	7	4			5	
Joe Biden			1	1			1	
John Kerry, Senator				1				
Marlon Marshall, Deputy National Field Director							4	

Mitch Stewart, Battleground States Director				2		
Reggie Love, body man to President		1				
Robert Diamond, Veterans and Military Families for Obama						
Rufus Gifford, National Finance Director	1	3	8			1
total	2	14	30	16	2	21

Material generated by authors

Importantly, women did send more emails than men in all categories related to fundraising. Men sent thirty emails on regular-form fundraising or 25.4 percent of the total emails for their gender and 75 percent of the total emails in the fundraising category (see Table 8.3). Women sent ten emails or 18.2 percent of their total emails on regular-form fundraising and 25 percent of the emails in that topical category (see Table 8.2).

The distinction between amounts of male and female emails reveals an important gender distinction between emails sent by men and women in regards to fundraising. Women sent significantly more emails in regards to the new, competition-style fundraising, while men sent significantly more emails using traditional fundraising tactics. Thus, a conclusion from the content analysis is that women took on a leadership role when it came to competition-style fundraising.

Further, the majority of emails sent by women were topically included in the overarching category of support, which includes topics such as competition-style fundraising, signing cards for the president or vice-president to show emotional support, and recruiting volunteers. Of the fifty-five emails sent by women, forty-seven or 85.5 percent of them related to the overarching topic of seeking-support (see Table 8.2). Men, however, sent sixty-four or 54.2 percent of their emails on topics of support (see Table 8.3). Again, this reveals emails by women were more likely to include seeking-support messages than emails sent by men.

Political issues

Because women were more likely to send emails with seeking-support messages, they were significantly less likely to send emails regarding campaign issues. Women only sent five of their fifty-five emails or 9 percent on campaign issues (see Table 8.4). The issues they did address were limited to healthcare and immigration. Topics not addressed by women include marriage equality, jobs, the Iraq War, taxes, and veterans issues. Men sent thirty-two emails on campaign issues, accounting for 27.1 percent of their total emails (see Table 8.4). Most emails were sent on the topic of marriage equality, which accounted for eight emails or 6.8 percent of the total emails sent by men.

Table 8.4. Issue Categories

	Healthcare Laws	Immigration	Marriage Equality	Jobs	Iraq War	Taxes	Veterans	Collapse Issues	Survey	Conservative Critique
Ann Marie Habershaw, Chief Operating Officer										
Caroline Kennedy										
Eva Longoria, supporter										
Gabrielle Union, supporter										
Heather Colburn, National Womens Vote Director										
Jill Biden										
Julianna Smoot, Deputy Campaign Manager	1							1		
Katherine Archuleta, National		1						1		

Political Director				1
Lilly Ledbetter, supporter	1			
Michelle Obama				
Sara El-Amine, National Training Director				
Stephanie Cutter, Deputy Campaign Manager	3		3	1
total	4	1	5	2

Material generated by authors

FINDINGS: RHETORICAL ANALYSIS

In conducting a rhetorical analysis on the 165 emails sampled from the Obama campaign, three important findings regarding the *kairos* and stylistic choices of the women's emails are identified. First, emails from women encourage financial contribution for self-esteem and peer recognition reasons. Second, women address the campaign broadly and its ramifications on the present. Third, women personalized messages and addressed readers as singular audience members.

Financial contributions

The most frequent topics of the Obama campaign emails were fundraising in both traditional and competition-style. In addition to differences in the type of fundraising each author requested, the authors displayed a difference in the way they motivated readers to donate to the campaign. Women's emails suggested that donating money increased supporter odds at meeting the president and accompanying celebrities, while men's emails reinforced that donations would help the president achieve reelection. Consider the following quotes from fundraising emails.

Women:

"Pitch in $3 or whatever you can to help build this campaign in these last 82 days—and you'll be automatically entered to be our personal guest in Charlotte. This is a pretty amazing opportunity. The campaign will fly you and a guest to Charlotte and cover your hotel for the three nights you're there. And each night, you'll get some of the best seats in the house to watch the big speeches."
(Michelle Obama, August 16 2012, *Be my guest for the convention*)

"For a chance to hang out with President Obama at George Clooney's house, donate $3 or whatever you can to be automatically entered to win. George Clooney is doing his part to help re-elect the President, but he also knows that it's folks like you who will decide this election. That's why we're reserving a few spots for grassroots supporters. If you donate $3 or whatever you can today, you'll be doing your part to support the campaign, and be automatically entered to join them in Los Angeles."
(Julianna Smoot, August 19, 2012, *Clooney*)

"I have some advice for the two people who will be selected to go to a party for the President at George Clooney's house: Choose your guest wisely. Whoever you pick to join you is going to owe you big time. Think about it— and chip in $3 or whatever you can today to be automatically entered."
(Anne Marie Habershaw, April 23, 2012, *Some advice about Clooney*)

Men:

"And that's OK. But only if we're able to keep the spending gap close enough so that our investments in a truly grassroots campaign pay off. I believe in that model, and I'm betting that you do, too. It's moments like these that I need you to act on that belief. Can you make a donation of $3 or more today?" (Barack Obama, August 9, 2012, *Insurmountable*)

"We knew this moment would come when Romney secured the nomination. What happens next is up to you. Help close the gap right now—make a donation of $3 or more. I want to be clear: We'll always have more people pitching in." (Jim Messina, June 7, 2012, *We got beat*)

These quotes suggest that the female and the male voices of the fundraising messages voice two different motivations to financially contributing to the campaign. Further, men's fundraising emails reflect a sense of urgency due to approaching fundraising deadlines and pressure from Romney's fundraising results. Women's emails often reflect urgency based on the closing deadline of a competition. Through the use of words such as "opportunity" and the positioning of the selected donor as a "winner," women's emails evoke a sense of competition and motivate donors by detailing the victor's spoils. The female authors extend this and describe the social bonus of the donor winning by describing the social and cultural capital that winning invokes.

Breadth of the Campaign

Throughout their emails, women rarely addressed specific issues pertaining to the campaign, but rather discussed the campaign and its current (not future) effects. Women made large over-arching statements about the campaign and its presence in the first-family's life and relationships. For example,

"Every night in the White House, I see Barack up late poring over briefings, reading your letters, and writing notes to people he's met. He's doing that for you—working hard every day to make sure we can finish what we all started together." (Michelle Obama, March 28, 2012, *Up late*)

"I know I don't usually send you emails, but Joe has a birthday coming up this Sunday—and I'm trying something new. The First Family and I are putting together a special card for him—and we'd like as many supporters of this campaign as possible to add their names and messages for Joe." (Jill Biden, November 18, 2011, *Joe's birthday*)

These quotes demonstrate that women's emails often depicted the current status of the campaign through personal reflections of their husband's actions. First Lady Michelle Obama's reflection on her husband's late nights illustrates the character of the President and his efforts to help citizens. Dr. Jill Biden's email asking for supporters to sign her husband's birthday card implies that her husband is need of emotional support now, not just financial contributions for the future. Women in particular provided insight into the current state of the campaign and the political leaders who were running it. Foremost, their emails provided vivid explanations about the burdens of political responsibility through requests for "well wishes" and "support." This language provided a context by which the campaign can ask readers for donations of money and time in other emails.

Personalized Messages

While men often began their emails with "hi" or "hey," women began their emails by addressing the reader as "friend" or by using the first name of the subscriber. This personalization of the email builds the illusion of closeness between the sender and the receiver of the message. Especially when Dr. Jill Biden wrote, "we'd like as many supporters of this campaign as possible to add their names and messages for Joe." In writing this, she helps supporters feel like a part of the family event.

While the use of a receiver's personal name in the body of the email is often created through inserting a computer program into the text, the addition of this personalization in women's emails implies a relationship between the women senders and the audience that is not present in the male emails. This relationship is often reinforced through the use of "you" in the women's emails. Women use this devise much more frequently in the body of their emails, again suggesting that the email is a personal conversation between the sender and the receiver.

> "Campaigns are never easy, and we're lucky to have supporters like you by our side." (Michelle Obama, August 31, 2012, *Deadline:*)

> "Friend—I love seeing 2008 bumper stickers on cars and bicycles when I travel across the country. But as we start to see Republican gear hit the streets, what about making sure people know you're supporting the President in 2012?"
> (Julianna Smoot, September 17, 2011, *Put this on your car*)

Moreover, these emails suggest closeness between the sender and the receiver of the message, but they also place the receiver in a position of action. By making it clear that the message is directed at the reader (because of the personalization), the receiver is left with little option except to act in the manner suggested by the email. It is a direct call to action that specifically suggests what is expected by the campaign.

DISCUSSION

The content and rhetorical analyses reveal the underpinnings of the 2012 Obama campaign strategy in its use of male and female voices in the electronic campaign. Whereas males sent the majority of emails, the presence and stylistic choices in the emails of women showed solid female leadership. Female voices were most evident in emails about fundraising through asking for support and in messages created to build relationships between the candidate and his campaign and the electorate. By presenting women as the voice of competitive fundraising as well as using women to establish closeness and a relationship between supporters and the presidential community, the 2012 Obama campaign developed a set of gendered norms for electronic campaign communication and leadership. Specifically, by using women to evoke a relationship between senders and receivers of the emails, the campaign used familiar women's roles—such as mother, wife, nurturer, and emotional provider—to attract supporters and to help email recipients to have a complete picture of the presidential community.

Interestingly, female authors of emails did not address the same topics as did male authors. The rhetorical analysis suggests the topics that women addressed were specifically designed to give the readers a "big picture" look at the implications for involvement in the Obama campaign and potential victory. The women authors described financial contributions to the Obama campaign as a victory for all, therefore placing responsibility for the success or failure of the campaign into supporters' hands. Emails asking for competition-style fundraising often suggested the elevated social status that a donation could give the donor (especially when the donor won the celebrity inspired prize). These emphases further reinforce the community-building responsibility and leadership that the women's voices took on during the campaign.

Women also took leadership in other areas of seeking support. First Lady Michelle Obama and Dr. Jill Biden both asked supporters to sign electronic cards to their husbands for holidays and birthdays, thus asking supporters to join them in emotionally supporting the candidates. In an effort to develop a powerful image of family-focused men and the candidates' various responsibilities to the country, the candidates' wives also shared personal stories and thus illustrated the character and personal histories of their husbands. They emailed messages that mentioned the candidates doing "late night homework" with their children or the candidates' first dates with their wives. Male email authors rarely shared personal stories about the candidates, even though the candidates could have done so and their supporters and staff members also could have shared stories that reflected Obama's and Biden's characters. Thus, women senders served as the primary character references in these emails to their husbands' lifestyles. These messages gave the campaign the ability to share the important qualities that their spouses had and that would make Obama and Biden good candidates without the candidates seeming too self-centered. This increasingly important role that women took in this presidential campaign is also the reason that the wives of the candidates were given prime-time speaking roles during national conventions and why they often start their own social campaigns during their tenure in the White House.

The campaign emails from women regarding the character of the male leadership came at a cost to other topics. Because women were charged with these big picture roles, they rarely emailed about specific topic-driven issues that often define a campaign. The topics women did and did not address are fully outlined in Table 8.4. Men were more likely to email about specific campaign topics such as immigration, the Iraq War, and veteran's issues. This is ironic because First Lady Michelle Obama and Dr. Jill Biden have taken the lead to help the military members and their families adapt to life during and after deployment. Furthermore, women authors did not address women issues such as the debate over women's reproductive rights. Males— for example, David Axelrod and Robert Diamond—emailed about healthcare and women's reproductive rights (as demonstrated in Tables 8.3 and 8.4; these topics were not addressed in campaign emails by female authors who could have served as leaders to help women supporters understand and personalize the issue for women by women.

As demonstrated by Lazar's work on feminist discourse, power and leadership are closely tied to rhetoric and the language of text.[51] A key aim of the content analysis and Lazar's approach is to show that social practices are not neutral, but rather gendered.[52] The content analysis displays this relationship and the social practices in a fundamentally explicit manner. The 2012 Obama campaign clearly wanted women to take the lead and not to take the lead in certain topics. Thus, the campaign used women's authorship to illustrate and encourage support through fundraising, volunteer recruitment, and emotionally driven e-cards. Because of this focus, however, the women's voices were silent on controversial campaign issues such as immigration, military activity, and jobs. Thus, the women were not positioned as leaders on these specific topics, as Lazar's work suggests, and this is due to the increased attention and knowledge that women require.[53] This is one element of the power relations found in contemporary politics. Women are invited to take on big picture topics, but are discouraged when it comes to smaller issues and policies. Lazar deems this as one of the final remaining areas of the glass-ceiling in politics.[54]

Similar findings by Paxton and Hughes elaborate that these roles are far from accidental, and that women in political support roles is one just one barrier to political equality.[55] While women in the Obama 2012 campaign speak loudly and frequently about fundraising and support, their absence from the tough issues reflects steadfast and stringent gendered norms regarding the leadership and roles political women take on. For example, by the style of women's emails—the use of "you" and "friend" emphasize a close relationship between sender and receiver, meant to reinforce women as the outward voice of the campaign as well as supporters, point of connection to the campaign. The women's emails, such as Dr. Jill Biden's email about the Vice President's birthday, are designed to bridge the amorphous and somewhat abstract campaign and give it a humanitarian and personal touch instead of having the women write about more controversial issues such as women's healthcare rights.

CONCLUSION

Although women appeared frequently in the 1670 emails sent by the 2012 Obama campaign, the women's voice was relegated to only a few categories of topics, specifically those related to the campaign's efforts to seek emotional and financial support for the candidates and Obama's presidential campaign. Through both the frequency and style of emails signed by female supporters, women in Obama's campaign clearly demonstrated leadership on some topics (e.g., financial support, the candidates' characters, relationships with family) but failed to address other topics (e.g., military action, the U.S. economy, jobs, immigration). This pattern represents yet another area of the gendered political divide. Revealed by content and rhetorical analysis, the style of the women's emails suggests an implied relationship between the female senders and the recipients of these emails. This attention to the personal and big-picture topics worked for the Obama 2012 campaign: to help the campaign to develop an image of the candidates for supporters that was both community oriented and based on the contributions of supporters. Although the women's voices functioned in the support-seeking and personal-referencing roles, the lack of women's voices related to specific issues clearly indicated gendered norms. For example, the Obama campaign did not use female leaders to lead on issues pertaining to women's issues. In fact, women authors who sent emails to campaign supporters missed an opportunity to reach an audience on important women issues. The campaign should have used powerful female voices to reach a sector of the audience that could relate rhetorically to the speakers' situation.

Future research in this area should include a detailed narrative analysis of all rhetoric related to the Obama campaign and other campaigns and study of the frequent stories told throughout both male and female emails. Further, a comparison study between this study and the emails from the 2012 campaign of Republican nominee and Governor Mitt Romney would help researchers, strategists, campaign staff, and American citizens to understand the differences and similarities of the roles women took in each campaign and perhaps in each political party. Such a comprehensive study also might reveal possible connections between political orientation and the role of women in these leadership positions.

Supported by previous findings regarding gendered roles in politics, these findings show that the 2012 Obama campaign maintains traditional divides in both the issues women address and the ways that women address those issues. This work contributes to conversations regarding the current state of women leadership in politics while identifying the topics and styles women use while emailing supporters.

NOTES

1. The authors collected emails throughout the campaign, equaling a total of 1670.
2. Morley Winograd and Michael D. Hais, *Millennial omentum: How a New Generation is Remaking America* (New Brunswick: Rutgers University Press, 2011), 90.
3. Jean Edward Smith, *FDR* (New York: Random House Trade Paperbacks, 2007), 183.
4. Ibid.
5. Ibid.
6. Barbara Kellerman, "The Political Functions of the Presidential Family," *Presidential Studies Quarterly* 8, no. 3 (1978): 305.
7. Ibid., 307.
8. Susan A. MacManus and Andrew F. Quecan, "Spouses as Campaign Surrogates: Strategic Appearances by Presidential and Vice Presidential Candidates' Wives in the 2004 Election," *Political Science and Politics* 41, no. 2 (2008): 346.
9. Ibid., 337.
10. Michelle Lazar, ed., *Feminist Critical Discourse Analysis: Gender, Power, and Ideology in Discourse* (New York: Palgrave MacMillan, 2005), 2.
11. Ibid., 4.
12. Norman Fairclough and Ruth Wodak, *Reflections on Gender and Science* (New Haven: Yale University Press, 1997), 6.
13. Ibid.
14. Kathryn A. Remlinger, *Feminist Critical Discourse Analysis: Gender, Power, and Ideology in Discourse*, ed. Michelle Lazar (New York: Palgrave MacMillan, 2005), 10.
15. Ibid., 20.
16. Ibid., 21.
17. Ibid., 6.
18. Ibid., 12.
19. Ibid.
20. Joseph S. Tuman, *Political Communication in American Campaigns* (Los Angeles: Sage Publications, 2008), 118.
21. Diana B. Carlin and Kelly L. Winfrey, "Have you Come a Long Way, Baby? Hillary Clinton, Sarah Palin, and Sexism in 2008 Campaign Coverage, "*Communication Studies* 60, no. 4 (2009): 339.
22. Judith Trent and Robert V. Friedenberg, *Political Campaign Communication: Principles and Practices Fifth Edition* (New York: Rowman and Littlefield Publishers, 2004), 211.
23. Winograd and Hais, *Millennial Momentum: How a New Generation is Remaking America*, 112.
24. Kathryn C. Montgomery, *Generation Digital: Politics, Commerce, and Childhood in the Age of the Internet* (Cambridge: MIT Press, 2009), 90.
25. Ibid., 179.

26. John A. Hendricks and Robert E. Denton, Jr., "Political Campaigns and Communicating with the Electorate in the Twenty-First Century," in *Communicator-In-Chief: How Barack Obama Used New Media Technology to Win the White House,* ed. John Allen Hendricks and Robert E. Denton, Jr. (New York: Lexington Books, 2010), 5.

27. Montgomery, *Generation Digital: Politics, Commerce, and Childhood in the Age of the Internet,* 90.

28. Ibid.

29. Janet Johnson, "Twitter Bites and Romney: Examining the Rhetorical Situation of the 2012 Presidential Election in 140 Characters," *Journal of Contemporary Rhetoric* 2, no. 3–4 (2012): 56.

30. Joshua Green, "The Science Behind Those Obama Campaign E-Mails," *Bloomberg Business Week*, November 29, 2–12, www.businessweek.com/articles/2012-11-20/the-science-behind-those-obama-campaign-e-mails.

31. Martine Courant Rife, "Ethos, Pathos, Logos, Kairos: Using a Rhetorical Heuristic to Mediate Digital-Survey Recruitment Strategies," *Transactions on Professional Communication* 53, no. 9 (2010): 261.

32. Robert Asen, "Reflections on the Role of Rhetoric in Public Policy," *Rhetoric and Public Affairs* 13, no. 1 (2010): 123.

33. Ibid.

34. Herbert W. Simons, "Rhetoric's Role in Context, Beginning with 9/11." *Rhetoric and Public Affairs* 10, no. 2 (2007): 183; Michael J. Hogan, *The Nuclear Freeze Campaign: Rhetoric and Foreign Policy in the Tele-Political Age* (East Lansing: Michigan State University Press, 1994), 11.

35. Rife, "Ethos, Pathos, Logos, Kairos: Using a Rhetorical Heuristic to Mediate Digital-Survey Recruitment Strategies," 261; James L. Kinneavy and Catherine R. Eskin, "Kairos in Aristotle's Rhetoric," *Written Communication* 17, no. 3 (2000): 432; Dale L. Sullivan, "Kairos and the Rhetoric of Belief," *Quarterly Journal of Speech* 78, no. 3 (1992): 317.

36. Mark G. Longaker and Jeffrey Walker, *Rhetorical Analysis: A Brief Guide for Writers* (Boston: Longman, 2011): 10.

37. Rife, "Ethos, Pathos, Logos, Kairos: Using a Rhetorical Heuristic to Mediate Digital-Survey Recruitment Strategies," 262.

38. Sylvia Bashevkin, "Party Talk: Assessing the Feminist Rhetoric of Women Leadership Candidates in Canada," *Canadian Journal of Political Science* 42, no. 2 (2009): 345; Karolyn Kohrs Campbell, "'The Rhetoric of Women's Liberation: An Oxymoron' Revisited," *Communication Studies* 50, no. 2 (1999): 125; Mary E. Hawkesworth, "Feminist Rhetoric: Discourses on the Male Monopoly of Thought," *Political Theory* 16, no. 3 (1988): 444.

39. J. S. Sutton, "Intersections: Women, Rhetoric, and Domination," *American Journal of Semiotics* 22, no. 1 (2006): 136; Pierre Bourdieu, *Outline of a Theory of Practice* (Cambridge: Cambridge University Press, 1977), 20.

40. Pamela Paxton and Melanie M. Hughes. *Women, Politics and Power: A Global Perspective* (Thousand Oaks: Pine Forge Press, 2007), 15.

41. Klaus Krippendorff, *Content Analysis: An Introduction to its Methodology* (Thousand Oaks: Sage, 2004), 18.

42. Marilyn Domas White and Emily E. Marsh, "Content Analysis: A Flexible Methodology," *Library Trends* 55, no. 2 (2006), 28.

43. Ibid., 31.

44. M. C. Standsbury, "Problem Statements in Seven LIS Journals: An Application of the Hernon/Metoyer-Duran Attributes," *Library and Information Science Research* 24, no. 2 (2002), 160.

45. White and Marsh, "Content analysis: A Flexible Methodology," 28.

46. Jeanne Fahnestock, *Rhetorical Figures in Science* (Oxford University Press, 1999), vii.

47. Longaker and Walker, *Rhetorical Analysis: A Brief Guide for Writers,* 12.

48. Ibid., 11.

49. Denise F. Polit and Cheryl T. Beck, *Nursing Research: Principles and Methods* (Philadelphia: Lippincott Williams and Wilkins, 2004), 50.

50. Ibid.

51. Lazar, *Feminist Critical Discourse Analysis: Gender, Power, and Ideology in Discourse*, 20.

52. Ibid.

53. Ibid., 15.

54. Ibid.

55. Paxton and Hughes, *Women, Politics and Power: A Global Perspective*, 159.

Chapter Nine

Western Women's *Ethos* and a Response to Privilege

Advocacy in Hillary Rodham Clinton's "Women's Rights Are Human Rights"

Nancy Myers

Across September 5 and 6, 1995, Hillary Rodham Clinton, then First Lady of the United States, gave four speeches in China during the United Nations Fourth World Conference on Women.[1] Out of those, the speech that was noticed, and continues to be recognized, is the one she addressed to diplomatic delegates from various world countries in the Conference's Plenary Session. Clinton's view is that standing in a country that suppresses women's rights and speaking to an audience representing many more countries that suppress women's rights, she purposefully took a risk on behalf of women worldwide. As she maintains in *Living History*, "I wanted the speech to be simple, accessible and unambiguous in its message that women's rights are not separate from, or a subsidiary of, human rights and to convey how important it is for women to make choices for themselves in their lives."[2] Now known as "Women's Rights Are Human Rights," this speech had impact then and now in both social history and scholarly discussion. The immediate Western response in social history is that the speech offset Clinton's complicated First Lady persona in the United States tied to her political outspokenness related to healthcare and feminism and her personal profile with her ever-changing hairstyles and discourses. The day after this 1995 plenary speech, *The New York Times* had two articles that noted the immediate response to Clinton's words with statements such as: "[M]any delegates applauded, some cheered and others pounded the tables," and "the impact of the speech seemed to reverberate through the hall."[3] Both journalists remarked that Clinton had received this support from world delegates and, more importantly, from the United States delegation to the conference with one stating that the speech "may have been her finest moment in public life."[4] This immediate positive response was at a time in Clinton's role as First Lady, when neither the press nor United States politicians, many of whom did not want her to attend the conference, were particularly friendly to her.[5] In addition, in 2005 the International Women's Health Coalition honored Clinton for her "groundbreaking leadership ten years ago at the United Nations Fourth World Conference on Women, held in Beijing, and for her continuing efforts on behalf of women in the United States and globally."[6] In scholarly discussions, "Women's Rights Are Human Rights" ranks thirty-fifth in the list of top 100 American speeches in the twentieth century by "137 leading scholars of American public address," and, according to Stephen E. Lucas and Martin J. Medhurst, the 100 speeches were chosen "on the basis of social and political impact, and rhetorical artistry."[7] Lucas and Medhurst included Clinton's words in Oxford University Press's 2009 *Words of a Century*, which captures in book form these twentieth-century speeches. Now almost twenty years later as Clinton ends her tenure as United States Secretary of State, outlets as diverse as the esteemed newspaper, the *New York Times*, and the popular woman's fashion magazine *Marie Claire*, draw attention to her long-term commitment as champion of "improving the status of women and children" globally, referring explicitly or implicitly to that speech.[8] Both social history and scholarly discussions in the West continue to analyze her activism and her speech.

This partial rendering of two decades of positive response to "Women's Rights Are Human Rights" is based on United States' sources, and, as such, illustrates a specific Western assessment of a female political leader's representation of other women in speech and writing in global arenas. However, while Clinton's 1995 speech is a historical moment, it also highlights feminist and postcolonial claims that representations of disenfranchised women are unable to, first, speak for others because of the speaker's privileged location, which oppresses and makes invisible the women spoken about, and, second, speak for oneself as representative of a group because of the impossibility of one standing in for all or one standing in at all.[9] No Western female political leader can hope to comprehensively account for women's diverse cultural, linguistic, and geopolitical experiences across worldwide communities, Western nations, or even her own country. Feminist and postcolonial scholars contend that the acclaim resulting from Clinton's speech is nothing more than a reinscription of white Western privilege and status. Thus, these critiques of Clinton and other Western feminist leaders raise the question in what situations a white privileged female political leader's words can speak to or for any other woman's injustice. Can a speech responsibly address women's global political issues to include marginalized and silenced voices?

While not discounting the double bind of Western privilege, I reframe these representational questions for analyzing female political leaders as a rhetorical one, asking *how* does one speak about others in relationship to her *ethos* within the speech? Issues of representation tie to rhetorical *ethos*, as it is a display of character or disposition through language and manner. Status, the speaker's social standing, or what is known about the speaker by the audience also plays a role in this development of *ethos* in a rhetorical situation. In that way, rhetorical *ethos* in a speech operates multiply within three categories: the speaker or rhetor, those spoken on behalf of, and the audience. *Ethos* as the character of the rhetor is distinct from but associated with the *ethos* of those spoken for, about, or on behalf of, and these *ethē*, multiple characters, are distinct from the audiences' constructed *ethē*, or the diversity of characters and attitudes the rhetor believes the audience members have and value.[10] Each and all are discernible rhetorical representations. The rhetor constructs her own, those she speaks on behalf of, and her audience's *ethē*, just as the audience employs the same strategies of construction in listening or reading the discourse. If those spoken for, about, or on behalf of are participants in the hearing or reading of this speech, they too participate in this multiple construction of *ethē*. However, this multiplicity and variety do not exist without the rhetor's initial constructions of her own *ethos* and those she advocates for in recognition of the *ethos* she anticipates in her audience. In global arenas, one must have the authorization to speak for change, to advocate for others, but in order to generate affirmation, cooperation, and persuasion in the audience, one must be heard.

I argue that *ethē* provide one means of re-examining how female political leaders' speeches are rhetorical acts of multiple character constructions distinct from their own, allow for possible accountability on the part of a white privileged Western woman authorized by her status to speak for disenfranchised women, and challenge the limitations of political representation. While Ciceronian legal *ethos* theoretically accounts for this construction of variable *ethē* in forensic speeches, its rhetorical situation correlates issues of the rhetor's location and of audience diversity relevant to white Western women's advocacy in global political arenas. Clinton's Beijing speech serves as an illustration of this argument in its construction of multiple *ethē* to speak for, about, and on behalf of other women as well as to address multiple audiences with differing value systems.[11] Understanding the correlations between Ciceronian legal *ethos* and Western female political leaders' rhetorical situations in global arenas presents a means for a woman of privilege to advocate for women who are marginalized. The following section outlines the problem of political representation and the critique of privileged Western women advocating for others. Next, I address this problem by maintaining that Ciceronian multiple *ethē* in advocacy offers insight into advocacy by the privileged for the voiceless; then I demonstrate the ways Clinton's "Women's Rights Are Human Rights" constructs multiple *ethē* and an engagement with the audience as a means of affirmation, cooperation, and possibly persuasion. I conclude with implications for women political leaders and global leadership.

ADVOCACY AND THE PROBLEM OF POLITICAL REPRESENTATION

Evolving from the Latin *advocāre*, to summon for counsel, advocacy means to speak or argue for a cause or on another's behalf. What was the United Nations Fourth World Conference on Women if it was not to enact in global ways this concept? As both a summoning and speaking for, this rhetorical situation called on delegates as representatives of 189 governments to congregate and address women's issues and concerns globally, to present and represent their nation, to champion women's issues and achievements within these nations as a means to advocate for change. As Nancy J. Adler defines global leadership:

> Global leadership involves the ability to inspire and influence the thinking, attitudes, and behavior of people from around the world. Thus from a process and an outcome perspective, global leadership can be described as "a process by which members of . . . [the world community] are empowered to work together synergistically toward a common vision and common goals . . . [resulting in an] improve[ment in] the quality of life" on and for the planet (based on Astin/Leland 1991, p. 8; Hollander 1985). Global leaders are those people who most strongly influence the process of global leadership. [12]

Clinton's "Women's Rights Are Human Rights" constitutes an instance of global leadership as it attends to both global leadership's claim to inspire others to change and advocacy's agenda to support a cause on behalf of others. The speech is an argument for a global commitment to support and aid women worldwide, including those in China: "Let this Conference be our—and the world's—call to action." [13]

While Clinton received acclaim by many of the United Nations delegates and in the United States for her speech, her argument and call to action were not universally appreciated. The negative responses were twofold: in social history, some of the delegates reacted not only to her status as First Lady but also to her declaration that many countries suppress women; in addition, scholars critique the speech arguing that Clinton conflates America's values with all women's values around the world. At the time of the speech, the United States and Chinese relations were fraught, yet Clinton wanted to attend, if need be "as a private citizen," and to be answerable to women: "I didn't want to squander a rare opportunity to advance the cause of women's rights."[14] The video of her speech shows audience members grimacing and shifting uncomfortably in their seats—not every delegate applauded.[15] The Chinese delegates "sat in rigid silence," and the government blocked her speech from being heard or seen outside the hall.[16] Even though Clinton declared that "it is time to break our silence" about the injustices toward women around the world, her words were silenced by China.[17] In addition, women scholars' assessments claim that Clinton both reinscribes difference and conflates similarity with United States' values and all women's goals and needs worldwide. Zillah Eisenstein declares that "Clinton reinscribes the east/west divide in her depiction of women's lives in south-east Asia."[18] Tani Barlow's assertion is more troubling as in Clinton's speech: "women around the world are seen to heed the U.S. women's achievements even despite their own oppressive states."[19] This double bind of either "one entirely different from me" or "one just as me" is the dilemma of political representation for women political leaders. Their status, their privilege, their Western location suggests that anything they argue on behalf of other women is totally suspect as a statement of building power. As Linda Martín Alcoff concludes, "the practice of speaking for others is often born of a desire for mastery, to privilege oneself as the one who more correctly understands the truth about another's situation or as the one who can champion a just cause and thus achieve glory and praise."[20] The differing responses to Clinton's words both positive and negative show that audience reception is not undivided, nor can one reaction be expected or counted on by the rhetor. In addition, the global arena of the conference highlights the unavoidability of political representation, as one of many means, when trying to enact international change. Because of its historical context, Clinton's speech operates as political representation but also as a rhetorical one that argues for women's rights and possibly inspires and persuades some, but not all, United Nations delegates to affirm her call to action.

As an illustration of political representation—female Western political leaders speaking on behalf of women worldwide—"Women's Rights Are Human Rights" demonstrates the conundrum of promoting a vision and making claims about others, particularly for women from other cultures, languages, and ethnicities. As Inderpal Grewal explains in *Transnational America*, "It is unfortunate but unavoidable that the 'moral superiority' of American geopolitical discourse should have become part of the new global feminism in the United States . . . , constructing 'American' feminists as saviors and rescuers of 'oppressed women' elsewhere within a 'global' economy run by a few powerful states."[21] Clinton's speech includes universalizing lines such as, "Those of us . . . have the responsibility to speak for those who could not," and "I want to speak up for women in my own country."[22]

These types of rhetorical and political claims are ones that Gayatri Chakra-vorty Spivak's 1985 groundbreaking "Can the Subaltern Speak?" brought into stark relief with her question of whether Western thought and activism could speak for nonwestern existence, particularly for women worldwide.[23] She argues that "political representation" of the marginalized—which is what advocacy is as opposed to "literary representation" which she privileges—loses sight of its own construction and contingency, as if language is truth and reality.[24] In moments of advocacy, one can easily recognize the confla-tion of the constructed with the real, the rhetorical with the political, in phrases like "These people need" or "I speak for so-and-so."

Spivak has three concerns about political representation. First, it silences through appropriation of the other's voice, in other words, it speaks "for" rather than "to" the other. Second, it objectifies the marginalized through its construction in the dominant discourse; in other words, it is a re-presentation filtered through the perspective of the rhetor's values. Third, it disregards national practices, meaning the localized and specific class, religious, tribal, and political systems in operation; in other words, it elides the marginalized's multiple value systems. In addressing this issue of reinscription, Alcoff com-plicates the advocacy of speaking "for" or "about" others by showing how both are always working in consort with a woman's words inescapably shap-ing the representation of others: "[T]here is no neutral place to stand free and clear in which my words do not prescriptively affect or mediate the experi-ence of others, nor is there a way to demarcate decisively a boundary be-tween my location and all others."[25] While claiming that most speaking is both self-aggrandizement and political, thus a restatement of the status quo, she argues for self-accountability, as that accountability must be to oneself as well as to the one spoken for and about and must entertain praise and affir-mation as well as criticism and condemnation for the spoken words by asking the question, "Will it [women's words] enable the empowerment of op-pressed peoples?"[26] Female political leaders must speak for other women, but they need to interrogate why they have made that choice, what location they speak from, what responsibility they have to those they speak on behalf of, and what the probable outcomes may be. Thus, advocacy has a twofold purpose to speak for one's own location as well as to support the location of another, meaning that, while global claims are made, local considerations matter and that, while political representation is unavoidable, rhetorical rep-resentation can complicate that construction. Wendy S. Hesford and Wendy Kozol contend that women's human rights require a "transnational and trans-cultural process whereby reading or seeing human rights violations locates the viewer, the reader, and the witness within local and global commu-nities."[27] Given the problem that Grewal identifies with the rhetorical *ethos* of Western feminists, how might the *ethos* of a female political leader's discourse be examined in order to make evident Alcoff's accountability and Hesford and Kozol's locations?

Accountability is also responsibility, so women of privilege have the obligation to use their rhetoric where it may be heard. Rhetorical representation speaks back to the limitations of political representation through an understanding of *ethos* as a constructed location, including those locations of status. The rhetor, those spoken on behalf of, and the audience are distinct constructions but in fragile and ever-altering allegiances with each other. The rhetor's accountability in advocacy, particularly for a woman with status, is in those shifting locations and multiple *ethē* in a speech that enables associations, like-mindedness, and the possibility for making change. Those locations are never neutral nor fixed, but always undulating. The privileged woman rhetor, authorized to speak, employs her status as rhetoric in order to keep these multiple *ethē* in flux with the audience. Advocating through these various associations because it may be heard might result in affirmation, cooperation, and persuasion in the audience on behalf of the disenfranchised. While the *ethē* in the speech cannot speak for the silenced marginalized woman, this multiplicity may at least make her visible to the audience. *Ethos*, as S. Michael Halloran explains, is "[i]n contrast to modern notions of the person or self, *ethos* emphasizes the conventional rather than the idiosyncratic, the public rather than the private."[28] *Ethos* as the rhetorical representation that explains advocacy in global contexts is directly tied to Cicero's legal rhetoric, which accounts for both the dynamic construction of multiple *ethē* and the constraints of those constructions in negotiating relationships between the rhetor and those defended and between the rhetor and the audience who judges that defense.

ADVOCACY AS *ETHOS* AND CICERO'S LEGAL RHETORIC

"Women's Rights Are Human Rights" demonstrates the parallels between white privileged women political leaders' advocacy and rhetorical *ethos* to show how rhetorical representation can complicate political representation. It accounts for both Alcoff's need for accountability of the rhetor and to those women spoken on behalf of and Hesford and Kozol's balancing of local and global views. As a rhetorical strategy, *ethos*, as the construction of the rhetor's and others' credibility and believability across the speech works to create affirmation, cooperation, or persuasion in the audience. This multiple construction of credibility by the rhetor for her audience is a construction of the rhetor's *ethos* as well as a construction of the *ethos* of the women spoken on behalf of and requires a dynamic exchange that keeps both *ethē* in a constant flux so that neither is established in isolation or by conflation but only in relation to the other *ethos*. In this way, the rhetor is addressing the multiplicity of audience *ethē*, what she recognizes as people with diverse views and allegiances. As Susan C. Jarratt argues of rhetorical representation, "differences can be spoken of not in terms of exclusive categories but rather as places, descriptions, or narratives of relation."[29] In addition, the audience with its varied participants dynamically reacts to those *ethē* so that no one reaction can be anticipated and no one response by all participants evolves. This continual exchange and negotiation of rhetorical representation destabilizes a privileged position of rhetor as sole voice and reinforces a dynamic exchange among rhetor, audience, and women spoken on behalf of. Cicero's theory of legal *ethos*, which is a multiply constructed *ethos* of advocate-rhetor—the person speaking—of the client—the person spoken on behalf of—and of the audience offers one understanding of how a woman political leader as rhetor not only locates herself within competing rhetorical, ideological, and political systems but also accounts for her ever-shifting tolerance for and resistance to the agendas and needs of others and the societies she is addressing and speaking about.

Cicero understood political representation as well as rhetorical representation in the dynamic exchange between rhetor and audience when constructing *ethos*. Michael Leff captures this exchange in his discussion of Cicero's rhetorical situation: "Orators [rhetors] work within a bounded but fluid medium, and they must exercise great inventive powers to shift the medium without appearing to subvert it, and this requires a special, delicate, and contextually sensitive relationship between self and community—a relationship that allows individual agents to stand apart as leaders because they stand with and serve the people they lead."[30] As the one authorized to speak by the community, the rhetor must shift but not subvert the situation, so using status to establish and maintain distance from those spoken on behalf of and from the individual audience members is necessary to foster change. Balancing communal constraints and dynamic possibility, Cicero's theory of forensic *ethos* accounts for the advocacy of another as always contingent and the construction of *ethos* as always a negotiation of competing value systems among the rhetor, the one spoken about, and the audience. In Roman trial cases, two *ethē* were being represented—the patron's *ethos* as advocate-rhetor, the one who orally both represents and defends, and the client's *ethos*, the one spoken about. The advocate-rhetors pleaded the case of their clients not to judges but to "fifty to seventy-three" jurors who were upper-class educated male citizens, but each with individualized interests and with individual votes.[31] Cicero's *De Oratore* highlights the advocate-rhetor's need to appeal to various audiences: "For if someone is to decide a case in our favor, it is necessary that he should either lean in our direction because his sympathies are so inclined, or be brought over by our arguments for the defense, or be forced by emotions."[32] This explains that different appeals must be made to different audience members' concerns and ways of thinking about the situation. In addition to the jurors, the advocate-rhetors had another influential group of listeners, the populace. As Richard Leo Enos notes, "By Cicero's time, huge crowds were common at important trials" and yelled "biased praises" for the advocate-rhetors they liked.[33] The larger audience's reactions could influence the result of the trial, so a factor in the case was not only the *ethē* of the principals (plaintiff and defendant) but also the *ethē* of the advocate-rhetors representing them; thus, "a skilled patron like Cicero took advantage of this, often speaking about himself and his opponents as well as about his client and his opponents, and sometimes exploiting differences between himself and his client as a way to strengthen his case."[34] This dynamic of constantly shifting distinctions and associations between advocate-rhetor and client across the speech operates as a distancing from and as an affiliating with but always in partial and contingent ways. Through rhetorical construction of *ethos*, the advocate-rhetor engages with the anticipated *ethē* of the audience members in order to strike up different allegiances with different agendas.

Between the contexts of Cicero's arguing cases in Roman courts and white privileged female political leaders speaking on behalf of women, two correlations arise: the diversity and unreliability of the audience and the locations of the speaker and the one referred to in the speech. Figure 9.1 shows the Roman environment and dynamic of legal representation.

Concerning audience, Cicero practiced law in courts infected with party politics. This meant that Cicero was advocating before unreliable juries comprised of citizens situated within social and political factions vying for power and control of the courts and of Rome. In addition, Cicero was defending clients whom jurors might turn against due to bribery or to fear of repercussions by those more powerful.[35] The individual juror might shift alliances

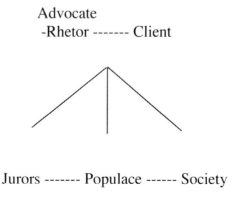

Figure 9.1.

quickly and illogically for both political and physical survival, so the advo-cate-rhetor was speaking to unreliable and unpredictable decision-makers. The jurors' factional diversity and untrustworthiness went directly against Cicero's perceived objective for litigation, which, according to Enos, was "to readjust an imbalance through an interpretation of existing laws on a particu-lar issue."[36] By attaining equity in the courts, this rebalancing of law, the advocate-rhetor demonstrated justice or fair dealing with others, which con-tributed to the balance or re-balancing of the state and the community, not necessarily to maintain the status quo but to shift it even if just slightly. For the advocate-rhetor Cicero, the unstable and competing value systems of the Roman society, which were represented in the shifting political make-up of the juries, made both equity and justice difficult to achieve because the standards were not stable. He must appeal to the audience's diverse interests both through "thoughts drawn from the audience," by understanding the rhetorical situation and the interests involved, and through a speech's organ-ization that must "press" the jurors in order to move them toward affirmation, cooperation, and persuasion.[37] Thus the advocate-rhetor's *ethos* evolved from the ability to appeal to a range of individuals' notions of balanced standards, rather than those of a monolithic community. This evolution was dependent on the rhetor's ability to comprehend the divergent views and agendas of the audience members, their *ethē* as both rhetorically and politi-cally discerned. The result of this instability caused by competing standards is the advocate-rhetor's decision in each situation to turn both away from certain standards and toward others. The awareness of this multidirectional influence could establish distinctions and nuances that commonly held stan-dards might not. Furthermore, the readjustment to societal laws would be a change in the standards, not a reinscription.

The second correlation between Cicero's forensic theories and practices and the privileged Western feminist rhetor is the location of the advocate-rhetor and the woman spoken on behalf of. Unlike the Greek courts where the plaintiff and defendant orally represented themselves, the Roman judicial system with its use of advocate-rhetors complicated this direct physical and auditory presentation of singular *ethos*. Thus the advocate-rhetor had to es-tablish his own *ethos* as well as his client's. George A. Kennedy identifies Cicero's awareness and distinction in developing these multiple *ethē* across his career with examples from his early defense of Sextus Roscius in 80 BCE to his later defense of Cluentuis in 66 BCE.[38] Cicero developed the client's *ethos* as one element of the subject matter in the defense, in other words speaking on behalf of, as the representative for, but not as the client. In *De Oratore*, he acknowledges this value of multiple *ethē* for successful argu-ments: "The character, the customs, the deeds, and the life, both of those who do the pleading and of those on whose behalf they plead, make a very important contribution to winning a case."[39] While the advocate-rhetor rhetorically constructs the client's *ethos* of the past action and/or current situation as a representation, he also must construct his own *ethos* as a second representation by means of his words and the jurors' and populace's *ethē* in anticipation of their interpretations and reactions. This separation of the advocate-rhetor *ethos* from the client *ethos* allows the diverse audience members to individually participate in the construction of both and in doing so become invested in the client's situation.

Similarly, a female political leader as rhetor speaking on behalf of marginalized women is establishing and negotiating her credibility in relationship to the audiences' multiple and possibly antagonistic value systems as well as to the disenfranchised women she is advocating for. The rhetor does this by finding shared interests among all, both those spoken on behalf of and the audience, that convey the need for equity and justice of the represented woman (see Figure 9.2). As Jarratt explains this complicated dynamic, "The aim of this rhetoric is to open the distance between writer and audience rather than close it."[40] It is not only to create a distance but also to establish an allegiance between the rhetor and the voiceless. This distancing is intentional as a pointing at others, both those advocated for and the audience, as well as self. Through this distancing, all of the participants in the rhetorical situation are made visible. No one is hidden, and everyone is accountable. The separation of the *ethos* of the self and of the client in a speech produces *ethē*, a multiplicity of characters. In the rhetor's negotiation of competing value systems, the *ethē* act as a conceptual and linguistic reminder to the rhetor and the audience that both the woman rhetor and the women spoken on behalf of are constructed. These distinct but fluid *ethē* allow for the rhetor to locate herself through witnessing, reasoning, and critique yet offer the space for diverse responses from the audience members. The rhetor approaches this diversity through appealing to affirmation, cooperation, and persuasion. As Cicero explains, "we bring people over to our point of view in three ways, either by instructing them or by winning their goodwill or by stirring their emotions."[41] Jarratt, in "Beside Ourselves: Rhetoric and Representation in Postcolonial Feminist Writing,"

Woman Rhetor ---------- Women

Local Audiences ------ Global Audiences

Figure 9.2.

offers a comparable demonstration of the rhetor's negotiation of authority, when speaking on behalf of others through the work of Spivak, Trinh T. Minh-ha, and Rigoberta Menchú Tum. Playing on the differences in metaphor and metonymy, she maintains that Spivak speaks to the marginalized, Trinh speaks alongside them, and Menchú Tum speaks for them: "For both Spivak and Trinh, the denial of authenticity is a necessary position for the diasporic intellectual, one which forces the first-world academic to notice the difference between another academic and a suppressed history of colonization. For Menchú Tum, the claim to authority—to the truth of her lived experience—is central to her project."[42] In each case, quite different *ethē* rather than one *ethos* are accounted for, yet all are advocating in different ways for marginalized peoples they are more directly in concert with. Their authority as one authorized to speak is tied to the similarities with the marginalized, whether by ethnicity, class, culture, language, or geography, and does not account for the location of the white privileged female political leader, who is mostly removed in all of these ways from the those she advocates for. Jarratt's discussion offers insight for advocacy for the women who have direct political relationships with the disenfranchised. In a parallel way, Cicero's theory of *ethos* provides an avenue of advocacy for the white privileged female political leader.

In its relationship between the rhetor and the audience, its multiple *ethē* of the advocate-rhetor and the client, and its negotiation of competing value systems to create a common interest for communal cooperation and change, Ciceronian legal *ethos*, as rhetorical representation, is one means of addressing Spivak's three concerns of "political representation." First, since the *ethos* of the marginalized woman as spoken for, about, or on behalf of is subject matter and since *ethos* is negotiated between the rhetor and the audience, the rhetor advocates not to elide difference but to find common affiliations or relationships within those differences in order to invoke persuasion and to support change for others. While only a slight shift in perspective, this highlights the social imbalance of the marginalized in the speech and argues either for the need for change or ways to address that imbalance. The second concern of objectifying the marginalized through representation's construction in the dominant discourse ensues, but again with a slight modification. Because of the rhetor's and audience's construction of multiple *ethē* across the speech, these constructions are not unrecognized monolithic objectifications, but constructs that become more visible as such through their multiplicity. The third concern, that "political representation" disregards national practices—meaning the localized and specific class, religious, tribal, and political systems in operation—cannot be fully redressed in one speech, one declaration, one conference, but recognition that those competing value systems are in play can be addressed. The rhetor's values, as Western privilege, are acknowledged as distinct from the audience's and the marginalized's, so they are not argued as universal in the "one answer approach" to the problem, only that the problem is one both rhetor and audience need to address and redress over time with multiple plans of action adapted to local situations and multiple revisiting and revisions of those initial goals. While always partial and contingent, rhetorical representation is one way to move beyond the limitations of political representation. The various *ethē* continually evolving and changing across a speech offer white privileged female political leaders the opportunity to continually acknowledge difference and location and to hold themselves and others accountable for their views and actions.

ETHĒ AS AN ADVOCACY OF ACCOUNTABILITY AND LOCATION

Just as Cicero, Clinton turns away from certain standards to advocate for others to establish a common sense of purpose among the delegates, whether through affirmation, cooperation, or persuasion. As both a positioning of location, or which relationship the speech addresses at a specific moment, and an accountability, as a pointing to difference in the needs, conditions, and issues of the women the speech argues for and in the diverse agendas and dispositions of the audience, "Women's Rights Are Human Rights" demonstrates constantly evolving and changing *ethē*, sometimes the rhetor's, sometimes those advocated for, and sometimes the audience. At each moment an affiliation, alliance, or connection is created. This does not generate universality or uniformity, but multivocal difference, since each is affirming, cooperating, or agreeing in her own interests. Clinton declares, "Speaking to you today, I speak for them, just as each of us speaks for women around the world who are denied the chance to go to school, or see a doctor, or own property, or have a say about the direction of their lives, simply because they are women."[43] She acknowledges that she is speaking for others but reminds her audience that she is not alone in this endeavor as each delegate, with her or his own value system, is also representing others. Clinton positions herself with her audience in terms of their similar purpose at the conference in order to highlight the denied opportunity of most women worldwide to speak and act on behalf of themselves. The local audience at the United Nations Fourth World Conference on Women included delegates from around the world with multiple and competing value systems and, of course, the global audience was even more so. Through its rhetorical representation of *ethē*, "Women's Rights Are Human Rights" addresses the political, social, and economic situations of women both locally and globally. Across the speech *ethē* and the fluctuating allegiances are created through both distancing, as a pointing to, and association, as a being with. Both operate as accountability between those political and rhetorical representations—the ever-shifting locations of privilege in order to be heard. Clinton's speech invokes status in two ways, as difference and as allegiance.

"Women's Rights Are Human Rights" demonstrates this separation of *ethē* as a pointing to difference, the rhetors as distinct from those advocated for, in a listing of six examples of women enacting social change. Each example begins with "I have met" then continues to describe the location of women (Indonesia, Denmark, South Africa, India and Bangladesh, and Belarus and Ukraine), places Clinton has visited but not lived in, and local women's productive work (nutrition, family planning, childcare, political action, literacy development, entrepreneurship, professional medicine), most occupations Clinton has not engaged in.[44] As subject matter Clinton's rhetorical representations provide reverberations of these individual women's voices in dialogue with hers at another place and time, as a witnessing of her experience but not theirs. She employs local examples of her experiences with women working worldwide to change others' lives in order to establish global concerns. With her repetition of "I have met," Clinton underscores that she encountered them publicly, but does not know them privately, thus keeping the audience aware that she is not considering herself one of these women only associated with them through her travels. Through her witnessing, Clinton simultaneously constructs herself and those she speaks on behalf of as *ethē* in an engagement with the audience. She not only is accounting for multiple specific locations, but also doing this in the context that Alcoff suggests, a context of praise and affirmation. In both her positioning with the audience and her positioning with the women she speaks on behalf of, the speech is negotiating the dynamic of rhetorical representation through the construction of *ethē*, thus underscoring the audience's role in generating this dynamic construction of *ethē*.

The speech's second strategy of allegiance is in its use of first-person plural, because it demonstrates these *ethē* through ever-shifting associations with the multiple groupings the speech invokes. In combination with local and specific examples, this fluid use of first person continually reminds the audience members that they too are making differing associations of groups across the speech and in doing so, creating the *ethē* of those in that relationship. The first person is used in five ways: with two uses of "I" narrating what has been witnessed, such as the previous example of "I have met," and claiming what is believed by the rhetor, such as "women's rights are human rights," and with three uses of "we" associating at different moments the rhetor with women worldwide, with the United States as a nation and as women, and with the United Nations conference delegates and by extension all governments.[45] As a rhetorical dynamic, these five uses reflect the fluidity of joining and separating different *ethē*. Each association represents different constructions of *ethos*, such as those who have similar experiences, those who are like-minded, those who hold similar values, those who are female, etc. At two moments, the speech encapsulates this first-person pronoun dynamic, and that is discussed in contrast to the use of "it" to show how the speech's construction of *ethē* operates as a dynamic exchange between rhetor and audience.

The first extended example of first-person plural drawing different alliances is quite early. In paragraphs four and five of the speech, Clinton uses "we" three times to suggest that women globally, including herself, "come together" in their various geographic locations to share "aspirations and concerns."[46] With the third use, she acknowledges differences among these women and herself but suggests that women can find a "common ground."[47] As both an affiliation with and a distancing from those she speaks on behalf of, the speech is creating two *ethē*, the rhetor's and those advocated for. The women may have some common values, goals, and practices, but their lives, languages, and cultures are distinct from the rhetor's. In the next sentence of the same paragraph, the "we," through a slippery shift between the third and fifth use of the pronoun, becomes the delegates, many not women, and the conference's charge is to find those shared and collective interests to enable and empower women now and in the future. This slippery shift is a re-alliance, associating the rhetor's agenda with the goals of the delegates and the conference, creating another *ethos*, that of the audience's character. The final "we" in this sequence, the seventh in three paragraphs, associates this abstract "common ground" to a list of economic, social, and political commonplaces: "access to education, health care, jobs and credit, the chance to enjoy basic legal and human rights and participate fully in the political life of their countries."[48] In less than one minute of the speech, three *ethē* as relationships of different types are established. Clinton's *ethos* is both related to, yet distinct from, the *ethos* of the women she speaks on behalf of and the audience's *ethos* she pleads to. Following this and in contrast to it, the *ethos* of the "I," as reliable witnessing, directs the audience to three other conference assemblies that Clinton attends in Beijing: the Non-Governmental Organization forum at Huairou, China, the World Health Organization forum, and the United Nations Development Fund for Women forum.[49] While all political locations, they are also addressing social and economic issues. These listings of issues and various assemblies work together to keep the audience's attention on the variety and diversity of women's situations and to allow the audience members to make connections between their individual concerns and those being addressed across the entire event.

A second extended first-person example appears at the speech's end after Clinton associates the concept of freedom with allusions to the U.S. Constitution tied to the right of assembly and the right to speak, even if challenging "the views of their governments."[50] "We" is used twice to refer to the United States collectively in her examples of men and women joining together to accomplish women's suffrage and to win World War II.[51] However, both of these "we"s are blurred with the earlier framing statement, "Let us not forget that among those rights are the right to speak freely—and the right to be heard."[52] This is not only what the "we" of the United States know, but what the world delegates should know from U.S. history. The next "we" associates the United States with the United Nations with "We have seen peace prevail in most places for a half century. We have avoided another world war."[53] Whether accurate or not historically and an amazing generalization, it is a rhetorical enthymemic association that establishes relationships among the *ethē* of rhetor, audience, and women worldwide, suggesting that change can happen for men and women in peaceful ways. By contrasting these successes to the "deeply-rooted problems" of women, the next "we" expands this association by adding the delegates "to take bold steps to better the lives of women."[54] The last uses of first-person plural are a direct appeal to the delegates, and by extension the world's governments, to make dramatic change. While one reading of this section might suggest that this is conflating United States' goals with all nations', as rhetorical moves of association and distinction, the pronouns and examples engage the audience by highlighting the struggle and cost of national social and political change on behalf of women and by suggesting the possibility for change in the delegates' countries and communities, but not necessarily the same changes in each location. This association as both local and global among all women's plights, the United States' achievements, and the United Nations delegates operates as a reminder of the delegates' challenge to address the concerns of women in their countries.

In between these two illustrations of shifting *ethē*, through association and difference, across the "we," the speech makes a radical shift in pronoun use with the famous listing of "It is a violation of *human* rights."[55] At this moment the speech points to multiple *ethē* through its shifting associations, the rhetor's *ethos* who focuses on difference and the need for change, the *ethē* of the women spoken on behalf of who are silenced and marginalized in their own environs and at the conference, and the audience's *ethē* who associate the speech's points with local issues and concerns whether positively or negatively. This list details seven violent actions against women: female infanticide, forced prostitution, spousal murder, rape, domestic murder, genital mutilation, and sterilization.[56] The shift from the various groupings of "we" to "it" can be read as universalizing and obfuscating, with the violators no longer local, no longer specific to a person or group, and with women's rights as being subsumed by human rights. In other words, distancing and difference are used to dismiss or hide accountability. However, framed by two multiple and different sets of associations tied to first person as *ethē*, this listing both in its repetition of the initial clause, "It is a violation of *human* rights," and in location within the speech suggests a second understanding. The first-person pronoun use, as both the witnessing of the "I" and the fluid shifting audience associations with "we," point to the "it" as inclusive. All of the various audience members of this speech are now implicated in these violations and through extension all governments, which is made apparent in the second illustration of "we" at the end of the speech. The universalizing is not focused on women worldwide but on the audience's experiencing this speech locally and globally at that moment and later. Each and every country is accountable, just as every human is. Women's positions in society and in the world must be attended to at this United Nations Conference that claims it supports human rights. In addition, while these examples of violence are associated with women's lack of political voice and personal freedoms, the listing focuses on the single social issue of violence toward women, not on their education or economic limitations. In this way, these acts become individualized to a specific woman as victim in each case. This is a local concern that must be dealt with in global forums if change is to occur. Finally, immediately preceding this list, Clinton claims that "the history of women has been a history of silence."[57] Directly following it she appeals to women's right to speak and to be heard.[58] This framing of silence and voicing highlights the difference between Clinton's privileged position as rhetor and other women who are silent and living in the local environs of the United Nations delegates.

Through the speech's multiple and adjusting associations of various groups—women spoken on behalf of, the United States people, and the delegates—in conjunction with the local examples and the abstraction of the "it"—implicating all groups and audiences—"Women's Rights Are Human Rights" keeps those spoken on behalf of visible. Since, as Alcoff claims, no location is neutral, a female political leader, particularly a Western one, can employ accountable rhetorical strategies, maybe not with total efficacy, but still employ them in constructing the *ethē* of their advocacy. Even with the relation of difference, this dynamic and fluid exchange allows participants to affirm the qualities that they understand as worthy and credible in order to generate a tenuous affiliation across disparate value systems of the participants. Through this process recognition, affirmation, cooperation, and persuasion are possible. The words that female political leaders speak become rhetorical representations not only of the women they speak on behalf of but also of themselves. However, these *ethē* are not static and monovocal but fluid and multivocal, continually contingent and negotiated in a dynamic exchange among rhetor, women spoken on behalf of, and audience. These representations are contingent, constructed, and negotiated between the participants in the speech (between the rhetor and the women whose interests are addressed) in the context of the speech (between rhetor and audience), and across time (in the representations through interpretation that critics make of these speeches later). Each representation arises as an *ethos*, the characters of the speaker and the one spoken about. These *ethē* are constructed between rhetor and audience based on qualities that the audience as society deems worthy and credible, suggesting that an affiliation can be crafted between the separate value systems of the rhetor and audience in the hope of productive change.

Clinton as a privileged Western female political leader chose to speak for women worldwide. She was not suggesting that she understood all women in all places, but she advocated for their opportunities to speak, act, and make change in their own regions because the United Nations, at the least, claims that it supports that agenda. The value of considering *ethē* in political representations that advocate on behalf of others is threefold. First, it highlights the construction both of the rhetor and the woman/women represented in the speech. Second, it rhetorically demonstrates the dynamic exchange involved in that multiple construction. Third, it speaks back to the claim that personal motive in a speech is always a "desire for mastery and domination," because the audience's reaction is not universal nor uniform, thus no matter the motive, political representation is contingent.[59] While political representation is in the historical moment, it is only a moment and once over becomes a rhetorical artifact of advocacy whether captured through text, audio, video, or witnessing. If female political leaders, specifically those from Western nations, are to support and champion the cause for all women worldwide, women leaders must acknowledge the major differences as well as the few similarities of women globally. In addition, they must sway their audiences to focus on women's issues in every nation, country, and community. As Adler claims, "Within this emerging cross-culturally interactive context, global leaders must articulate a vision which, in and of itself, is global; that is, global leaders articulate the meaning within which others from around the world work and live."[60] However, this articulation both politically and rhetorically is fraught. Arabella Lyon and Banu Özel maintain that "rhetoric is not limited to the standpoints and traditions within each disparate culture; transnational movements place the activists and industrialists of many nations in struggle and dialogue, creating a polyphony of traditions, rhetorics, and cultures."[61] While this claim is framed within the limitations of Western interpretation, the multiplicity of voices needs to be embraced in every way, always asking how the voices of those authorized to speak because of privilege can be more accountable and how they can support the advocacy of those silenced women. As a historical performance trapped in time and location, a political representation such as Clinton's speech is open to multiple interpretations by the immediate audience and by all who examine it later. It is that opportunity for multiple rhetorical, political, feminist, postcolonial, and transnational interpretations that offers the possibility of responsibility traversing the divide that Spivak acknowledges in "Righting Wrongs": "The difficulty is in the discontinuous divide between those who right wrongs and those who are wronged."[62] *Ethē* as a rhetorical approach to advocacy is one of multiple interpretative frameworks that offer ways to keep this discontinuity visible in an understanding of female global leadership.

NOTES

1. These four speeches are collected in *Remarks by First Lady Hillary Rodham Clinton: United Nations Fourth World Conference on Women, September 5–6, 1995, China*. All quotations and page numbers for "Women's Rights Are Human Rights" are from this government document.

2. Hillary Rodham Clinton, *Living History* (New York: Simon and Schuster, 2003), 304.

3. Patrick E. Tyler, "Hillary Clinton, in China, Details Abuse of Women," *New York Times*, September 6, 1995, A1.

4. "Mrs. Clinton's Unwavering Words," Editorial, *New York Times*, September 6, 1995, A24.

5. Gail Sheehy, *Hillary's Choice* (New York: Random House, 1999), 275–78.

6. International Women's Health Coalition, "January 2005 Gala," www.iwhc.org/index.php?option=com_content&task=view&id=2119&Itemid=603.

7. Stephen E. Lucas and Martin J. Medhurst, "Top 100 Speeches," *American Rhetoric*, www.americanrhetoric.com.

8. " Clinton's Many Choices Hinge on the Biggest One," New York Times Service, *Greensboro News and Record*, December 9, 2012, A10.

9. Feminist and Postcolonial Studies have criticized Clinton's speech for its historical Western elitism (Enlightenment theories of nation and capitalism) and for its ideological stance (often referred to as international United States feminism), both which normalize all women into universal categories and which suggest that Western nations recognize women's concerns while other countries do not.

10. Since I am arguing for Ciceronian legal rhetoric as my basis for analysis, I employ the plural of *ethos*, *ethē*, as it was used during the Greek and Roman Classical periods rather than *ethea*, used in Homer's Greek several centuries earlier.

11. Scholarship on Clinton is impressive and analysis of her rhetoric and rhetorical representations of her is actively being interpreted and explored. Scholars, with the exception of Campbell, are drawing mostly on twentieth-century models and theories of rhetoric for analysis. For instance, Erickson and Thomson analyze Clinton's U.S. Senate run via contemporary seduction theory; Kelley examines First Lady Clinton's rhetorical strategies in moments of crisis. Other scholars, including Anderson and Huglen and Brock, have used Kenneth Burke's theories to explore Clinton's rhetoric. Focusing on two speeches, "Women's Rights Are Human Rights" and Clinton's 2005 speech reaffirming and extending it, Manning uses a 1980s linguistic theory to argue that Clinton is "successfully renegotiating a woman's role in politics" through her adherence to a masculine rhetorical style. Focusing on representations of Clinton's travels while First Lady, Kaplan draws on postcolonial and feminist theories to demonstrate the construction of global feminist subjects. Mandy R. Manning, "The Rhetoric of Equality: Hillary Rodham Clinton's Redefinition of the Female Politician," *Texas Speech Communication Journal* 30.2 (2006): 109.

12. Nancy J. Adler, "Global Leadership: Women Leaders," *MIR: Management International Review* 37 (1997): 174.

13. Hillary Rodham Clinton, *Remarks by First Lady Hillary Rodham Clinton: United Nations Fourth World Conference on Women, September 5–6, 1995, China* (Washington: Government Printing Office, 1995), 7.

14. Clinton, *Living History*, 300, 303.

15. Hillary Rodham Clinton, "Women's Rights Are Human Rights," American Rhetoric video, www.americanrhetoric.com/speeches/hillaryclintonbeijingspeech.htm.

16. Sheehy, *Hillary's Choice*, 277; Clinton, *Living History*, 306.

17. Clinton, *Remarks*, 5.

18. Zillah Eisenstein, "Women's Publics and the Search for New Democracies," *Feminist Review* 57 (1997): 150.

19. Tani Barlow, "International Feminism of the Future," *Signs* 25.4 (2000): 1100.

20. Linda Martín Alcoff, "The Problem of Speaking for Others," in *Who Can Speak? Authority and Critical Identity*, Judith Roof and Robyn Wiegman, ed. (Urbana: University of Illinois Press, 1995), 115–16.

21. Inderpal Grewal, *Transnational America: Feminisms, Diasporas, Neoliberalisms* (Durham: Duke University Press, 2005), 152.

22. Clinton, *Remarks*, 4.

23. Since Spivak's essay, postcolonial theory, feminist theory, and transnational studies worldwide have interrogated that privileged position and explored ethical methods to politically represent the marginalized woman without silencing her. In tandem to and intersecting with that debate has been the discussion of human rights and women's roles and rights within that framework. Across these debates, scholars have worked to support voice for the silenced and marginalized by focusing either on specific and local situations or on incidents of displacement and diaspora with recent work exploring analytical models of networks and circulation. Most importantly, these discussions have highlighted the incongruities between local law and custom and global justice and equity for women.

24. Gayatri Chakravorty Spivak, "Can the Subaltern Speak?," in *Marxism and the Interpretation of Culture*, Cary Nelson and Lawrence Grossberg, ed. (Urbana: University of Illinois Press, 1988), 278–80.

25. Alcoff, "The Problem,"108.

26. Ibid., 116.

27. Wendy S. Hesford and Wendy Kozol, *Just Advocacy? Women's Human Rights, Transnational Feminisms, and the Politics of Representation* (New Brunswick: Rutgers University Press, 2005), 11.

28. S. Michael Halloran, "Aristotle's Concept of *Ethos*, or If Not His Somebody Else's," *Rhetoric Review* 1.1 (1982): 60.

29. Susan C. Jarratt, "Beside Ourselves: Rhetoric and Representation in Postcolonial Feminist Writing," *JAC* 18.1 (1998): 60.

30. Michael Leff, "Tradition and Agency in Humanistic Rhetoric," *Philosophy and Rhetoric* 36.2 (2003): 145.

31. George A. Kennedy, *A New History of Classical Rhetoric* (Princeton: Princeton University Press, 1994), 104.

32. Cicero, *On the Ideal Orator* (*De Oratore*), James M. May and Jakob Wisse, trans. (New York: Oxford University Press, 2001), 157.

33. Richard Leo Enos, *The Literate Mode of Cicero's Legal Rhetoric* (Carbondale: Southern Illinois University Press, 1988), 49.

34. Kennedy, *A New History*, 103–4.

35. Enos, *The Literate Mode*, 1–17.

36. Ibid., 15.

37. Cicero, *On the Ideal Orator*, 211–12.

38. Kennedy, *A New History*, 129–33.

39. Cicero, *On the Ideal Orator*, 171.

40. Jarratt, "Beside Ourselves," 66.

41. Cicero, *On the Ideal Orator*, 208.

42. Jarratt, "Beside Ourselves," 68.

43. Clinton, *Remarks*, 4.

44. Ibid., 3.

45. Ibid., 6.

46. Ibid., 1.

47. Ibid.

48. Ibid.

49. Ibid., 2.

50. Ibid., 6.

51. Ibid., 6–7.

52. Ibid., 6.
53. Ibid., 7.
54. Ibid.
55. Ibid., 5.
56. Ibid., 5–6.
57. Ibid., 5.
58. Ibid., 6.
59. Alcoff, "The Problem," 111.
60. Adler, "Global Leadership," 176.
61. Arabella Lyon and Banu Özel, "On the Politics of Writing Transnational Rhetoric: Possibilities and Pitfalls," in *Feminist Rhetorical Resilience*, Elizabeth A. Flynn, Patricia Sotirin, and Ann Brady, eds. (Logan: Utah State University Press, 2012), 55.
62. Gayatri Chakravorty Spivak, "Righting Wrongs—2002: Accessing Democracy among the Aboriginals," in *Other Asias* (Malden: Blackwell Publishing, 2008), 56.

Chapter Ten

Media and Hillary Clinton's Political Leadership

A Model for Understanding Construction of Collective Memory

Mary Tucker-McLaughlin and Kenneth Campbell

When making significant decisions about whether to trust a political leader with major power, voters are influenced by collective memory that includes perceptions about individual qualities and leadership ability traits.[1] Within that collective memory are conscious and unconscious patterns of thought, such as constraining and demeaning stereotypes that Gordon and Miller recognize as representing "significant obstacles for a woman's candidacy for president."[2] Women, historically, have been absent from collective memory of upper-level U.S. political leadership, whether as governors, U.S. Senators, or Presidents, due to male dominance of those positions. Female presence began to emerge in the 1970s,[3] and Hillary Rodham Clinton almost succeeded in bringing women's leadership to the highest level in her bid for the presidency in 2008, but she fell short of winning the Democratic nomination.[4] However, she still succeeded, we believe, in making a significant change; she altered the basis of collective memory of women as leaders in top-level elective politics. But, the question remains whether she has actually changed the collective memory. Using her campaign, we explore this question and offer a model to illustrate the process of the construction of collective memory. We conclude with implications for women's leadership and political decision-making.

This essay builds upon our grounded theory study of media representations of Hillary Clinton in her quest for what is widely perceived as the ultimate leadership position in the United States—the presidency. In a discussion of "Governance, Leadership, and the Presidency," Gordon and Miller define leadership as "a process that involves influence, occurs in groups, and includes attention to goals." It also includes "individual traits, leader behavior, patterns of interacting, role relationships, relations with followers, and follower perceptions."[5] The concept of leadership provides context for interpreting Clinton and her presidential race, a context that is created, in part, by collective memory. Journalists, for their part, routinely incorporate collective memory into their reporting,[6] which means voters are ultimately influenced by it. Thus, the collective memory of women in political leadership, or a specific female politician such as Clinton, can be significant in voters' decision-making. This contention is consistent with literature which shows that journalists turn to stereotypes and familiar themes for stories about women in politics[7] (and voters turn to stereotypes to help them process political decision-making).[8]

We also explore the basis of future collective memory of Clinton and female political leaders seeking high office; that is, coverage of Clinton's 2008 presidential campaign will contribute to collective memory that will be used by voters in the future to support, or not support, her political leadership or that of other women.

THEORETICAL FRAMEWORK

Conceptually, collective memory studies are split into two realms: the study of memory from the perspective of the individual, and the study of memory from the perspective of society. The split reflects the intellectual influences on French sociologist Maurice Halbwachs, the originator of collective memory, who defines it as a group's shaping of the past to give meaning to the present.[9] His conception of the theory embodies influences of his mentors, French philosopher Henri Bergson and sociologist Emile Durkheim. Bergson saw reality as a combination of representations as individuals experience or perceive them. Durkheim saw memory as a construction, which is influenced by an individual's social context. In this view, leadership as a concept is constructed from what is represented as leadership, whether it is success in attaining high-level political office or the ability to overcome barriers. That representation may be based in collective memory and may become a new version of it since collective memory is "the ongoing collaborative recasting of 'the past'—of a particular group, event or experience—in the present."[10] For example, leadership can be constructed and remembered as masculine or feminine, decisive or collaborative, and successful or failed.[11] The social context in which the remembering takes place determines the meaning in the collective memory.[12] The concept that memory is constructed, and not retrieved from the past, is crucial to understanding collective memory. Essentially, collective memory is how the past is remembered or constructed, or the meaning given to the remembered or constructed past.[13] Even though collective memory is about the past, the memory and meaning are in the present. Therefore, whatever triggers the construction of memories contributes to the reconstructed memories.[14] A collective memory of leadership, then, begins with what initiated the construction of the memory and ends with the meaning assigned to it. We will discuss this more in relation to Clinton and leadership in the conclusion.

Since the late 1980s, the body of literature on the theory of collective memory has flourished, especially as societies and groups within societies seek to remember their past and create identity,[15] including how significant individuals contribute to memory and culture.[16] However, collective memory has it critics, who argue that there is fuzziness and overlap in the theory. Kammen goes so far as to suggest that "collective memory is now regarded by many with a certain mistrust," in part because of underlying assumptions that go unexamined such as a "misleading notion of consensus" conveyed by the term.[17] We acknowledge the criticisms but disagree with them. Collective memory does not rule out the possibility of a variety of memories being held by individuals and groups coexisting with a broadly held collective memory. Some historians express dissatisfaction with the distinction between history and collective memory.[18] As we see it, both are social constructions, but history documents and interprets the past while collective memory is concerned with how the past is remembered.[19] Thus, history identifies women leaders, their positions, and their leadership style, explaining what they were and meant at the time they occurred while collective memory addresses how their leadership is constructed, which can be disconnected from the documented history, and connects its relevance to the present. History is the past; collective memory is the present.[20]

Collective memory and journalism are inextricably linked. Information in journalists' stories often becomes facts of history and stories are used for ideas or as sources and background in subsequent stories.[21] According to a 2010 study by the Pew Center for Research, traditional news outlets—television, print, and radio—continue to provide the largest percentage of Americans with news, as large as 75 percent combined on a given day compared to 44 percent who use online, mobile, and social media.[22] Many people use traditional and new sources of information, but TV news still has the largest share. Our study seeks to illuminate the implications of television news representations on the individual and society's collective memory, using Hillary Clinton as a focus. According to a 2009 comprehensive study on women and leadership, "Women leaders in politics are the most visible manifestation of women's leadership in our culture. Because they operate in the public eye, they have the potential to transform the perception of women in a far greater sphere than in any other sector."[23] Clinton is the epitome of that leadership.

GROUNDED THEORY METHODOLOGY FOR ORIGINAL STUDY

We use grounded theory methodology to explore the use and development of collective memory of Clinton's leadership because it requires close familiarity with the data. Glaser and Strauss[24] developed the methodology during the late 1960s as a response to a call by some scholars to move away from quantitative methods, which they claimed required preconceived notions because the data collection is based on guidance from previous literature. Grounded theory methodology is appropriate when there is reason to believe qualitative research data may reveal patterns for the development of new theory. Essentially, when using the grounded theory method, researchers examine the data multiple times to put themselves in the place of the individual viewer of a news story. Notes of remarkable statements and images are recorded in an attempt to go beyond the surface story and determine what the news story is trying to tell the viewers. The ability to derive meaning in terms of societal and sociological implications exists in the researcher's ability to unearth themes in the data that have implications for the individuals' and society's memory. This process frees the research from being locked into concepts produced by previous literature, a freedom which increases the possibility of new theory being developed. Our research goal was to explain news media representation of Clinton's leadership in ways other than the typical discussion of stereotypical portrayals. We believe grounded theory methodology allows the results of our study to reflect the uniqueness of Hillary Clinton's role and leadership in public and political life in the study of collective memory.

We selected thirty news stories about Hillary Clinton, nearly three hours total, from among 3,000 shown on the three major news networks—the American Broadcasting Company (ABC), the National Broadcasting Company (NBC), and the Columbia Broadcasting System (CBS)—during the period 1993 through 2008. We chose stories that clustered around significant events in Clinton's public life, such as her tenure as First Lady, her entrance into the U.S. Senate race, her entrance into the 2008 presidential campaign, the New Hampshire town hall meeting where she was said to have cried, and her exit from the 2008 presidential campaign. Representations to determine the collective memory were identified in stories.

COLLECTIVE MEMORY AND MEDIA RELATIONSHIP MODEL

Our original grounded theory analysis of the network news stories about Clinton found two representations, or conceptual themes, not present in the scholarly literature: Innovator and Voiceless. Previous research found that Clinton was presented as nontraditional as a First Lady and as a political leader,[25] but we found dimensions that expanded the representation of Clinton beyond nontraditional. She was an innovator as the only former First Lady to run for political office in her U. S. Senate contest, and a pioneer in one of the most highly financed presidential campaigns in history.[26] But, as Clinton made strides as a powerful political leader, her efforts were at times mitigated by media representations that presented her as voiceless, which is the opposite of what might be expected of someone who is an innovator.[27] Both themes address aspects of the development of collective memory of women's leadership in top-level elective politics. We discuss them in relation to our Collective Memory and Media Relationship Model (see Figure 10.1).

The model is a graphic illustration of how personal, historical, and mass media memory contribute to the development of collective memory. This three-fold approach is consistent with Schudson's contention that ". . . memory is a process of encoding information, storing information, and strategically retrieving information, and there are social, psychological, and historical influences at each point."[28] It is also consistent with studies that separately address contributions of personal, historical, and mass media memory. The model depicts how each of the three types of memory is influenced by the other and how the ultimate product—collective memory—is a social construction. The model is circular because it is impossible to determine a beginning and an end in the development of collective memory. For purposes of discussion, we begin with personal memory, and then we discuss historical memory and mass media memory, respectively, acknowledging that personal memory is undoubtedly influenced by historical and mass media memory. The intersection of the three types of memory is discussed throughout.

PERSONAL MEMORY

The illustration shows that the components of personal memory (the bubble at the bottom of the model) are myths, oral history, and personal experience. Myths are signs that often take on the wider ideological role of a value in society until they feel natural,[29] while oral history refers to stories and ways of thinking handed down informally from the past to the present, or from generation to generation. These myths and stories are not necessarily truths or factual but they are the constructed memory that people believe.

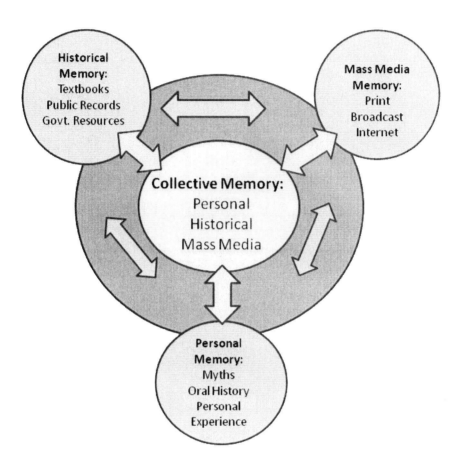

Figure 10.1.

Personal memory, we believe, is an appropriate starting point for our discussion because collective memory theory maintains that personal memory is created in a group, or collective, context. Thus, while personal memory is generally based on individual experience, it can also be memory beyond physical experience, such as that which comes through oral stories and experiences handed down, history and myths an individual closely identifies with, as well as virtual personal experience created by mass media. Because memory is social, it allows individuals to personally experience something that happened long before they were born or in a place far removed. They share experiences as members of a group with which they identify.[30] "Individual memory, in this sense, refers to what, why, and how individuals remember in relation to past experience."[31] What an individual remembers should also be attributed to a "meaning" shared by the collective in question. "It should, for example, evoke similar thoughts or emotions in group members."[32]

In a national election campaign like Clinton's, only a few people get to have a personal experience with a candidate such as a handshake or attendance at a live speech or campaign rally. But media expand our personal experience by bringing experiences to us, such as bringing persons of national stature, like Clinton, into our living rooms. In our increasingly media-afflicted world,[33] media can tell us what is important and what is not important in the experience. In fact, media can transform or redefine personal experience so that what people remember is not their actual experience but the experience as mediated or reconstructed by the media.[34]

Often, what we remember has to do with that which is emotional or causes an emotional reaction.[35] That is the basis for what has become known as flashbulb memories,[36] described by Brown and Kulik as "distinctly vivid, precise, concrete, long-standing memories of the personal circumstances surrounding people's discovery of shocking events, such as assassinations of public figures."[37] Clinton's so-called emotional moment is an example of the role of emotion. Although the moment does not rise to the level of a flashbulb memory, it has some of the qualities, which suggests it would be a more lasting memory than a typical memory. One of the clusters of stories we analyzed reported on Clinton crying—according to reporters—and showed her supposedly wiping away a tear at a New Hampshire speech during the presidential primary campaign. This type of story can create a personal experience for viewers, as if they witnessed the emotion and tears in person. It is a legitimate news story, but how it is handled makes all of the difference. It is not at all clear whether she, in fact, cried. Nonetheless, the memory, even by those who were there, is that she cried. The considerable coverage of the New Hampshire emotional moment emphasized sound bites like the one from primary opponent John Edwards who questioned Clinton's strength as a leader when he said, ". . . I think what we need in a Commander in Chief is strength and resolve and . . . Presidential campaigning is a tough business . . . but being President of the United States is also a very tough business."[38] The implications are echoed by female politicians everywhere who have experienced what political communications scholar Kathleen Hall Jamieson calls women's "double-bind" of balancing what is perceived to be feminine with what is perceived to be masculine traits.[39] "Clinton became a national test case, subjected in fact to *all* the binds traditionally deployed against women," according to Jamieson, who also posited that the press perpetuates the binds.[40] Clinton was portrayed in the press for being too tough, like a man, but when a situation arose where it was appropriate to become misty eyed, she was criticized as being too soft, like a woman.[41] Some incidents of male politicians crying, like that of Senator Edmund Muskie during his 1972 presidential campaign when he responded to questions about his wife's alcoholism, also have been damaging; he pulled out of the race for the Democratic nomination.[42] Yet, it has become acceptable for male politicians, like House Speaker John Boehner, to shed a tear and show a softer side[43] because it does not perpetuate a negative collective memory. Conversely, the ramifications of a female politician caught-on-tape in an emotional moment can be devastating because it feeds into a collective memory of women as emotional and weak rather than affirming her passion for her candidacy and desire to serve. Former Colorado Congresswoman Pat Schroeder still hears from voters about a moment in 1987 when she withdrew from the presidential race, and could be seen holding back the tears in a three-second pause as she caught her breath. "Guys have been tearing up all along and people think it's marvelous," Schroeder said in an interview several years later.[44] Those guys have included Presidents Ronald Reagan, George W. Bush, and Bill Clinton, whose political careers were not hurt by showing emotion.

The powerful role of mass media in constructing personal memory was also shown in how Hillary Clinton is represented in the stories about the Whitewater and Monica Lewinsky affairs. Because this was such an emotional issue, it is like a personal experience, and it was brought to the public by mass media. As Clinton negotiated the negative implications of her husband's affair with Lewinsky, the media represented First Lady Clinton as an innovator but also as voiceless: at times, she was visible through file footage or still photos, but was not interviewed. We contend that she was an innovator because she took a public stand and defended her husband in a controversial personal matter, unlike more traditional First Ladies, such as Jacqueline Kennedy who reserved comment in the midst of many allegations that her husband, John F. Kennedy, had relationships outside of their marriage. During the Lewinsky affair, all three networks positioned Clinton as a silent but strong supporter of her husband. NBC represented her as protecting him stating, "Hillary Clinton has taken a lead role in a damage control effort."[45] ABC quoted a Clinton friend describing her "steely resolve and full battle regalia,"[46] and CBS stated that Clinton had told friends that "she considered the whole thing a schemer campaign."[47] Although Hillary Clinton was represented in a fairly positive light during the Lewinsky affair, in the stories we examined she was simultaneously silenced, either by choice or by the networks, and was not shown speaking for herself. Additionally, the very nature of this story is a derogatory female stereotype—the wife defending her husband's sexual indiscretion. Why was this public issue for the wife, rather than a private marital issue? Why was someone of Clinton's stature relegated to such gossipy "news"? Collective memory promoting old gendered notions about marriage was perpetuated at a time when Clinton's leadership in a controversial personal situation could have been given more of a focus. As a personal memory for viewers, both those who sympathized with Clinton and those who did not, this representation of her in the situation pointed to gender and traditional notions rather than leadership.

HISTORICAL MEMORY

Historical memory, which is positioned in the top left bubble of the model, is what is considered to be the official version of history; its components are textbooks, public records, and other government resources.[48] It also includes "public memory," which is official memory contained in landmarks, museums, images, and architecture of buildings, among other government sources. Historical memory can be influenced by mass media while at the same time it can be an influence on mass media. Journalists are television viewers long before they become journalists and so they absorb information uncritically at that time. They continue to view and absorb even more through media as they enter the world of journalism. Thus, their collective memory is affected by it. Journalists' historical memory becomes part of the media texts they produce. The reliance on government sources for information and historical perspective is also a fundamental part of journalistic routines. The media also convey historical memory when they use historical documents as resources, and when, for example, they use government buildings or landmarks as background for a news story. Additionally, history itself is influenced by mass media as journalists tell and re-tell historical events, selecting facts and perspective to fit their story. These revisions can become the basis for retelling the story, the history, in the future. Historical memory can lead journalists to practice what Carolyn Kitch calls "anniversary journalism," or the reporting of stories only because it is the anniversary of a previous newsworthy event.[49] Such stories are the epitome of collective memory, as they continue to tell a tale of the past, oftentimes trying to present the past in a way to make sense of and to the present.

As an innovator, Clinton provided a new chapter in the historical record of women's political leadership. She was not the first woman to be an innovator in national politics, but she was the first to be so successful at the top level. Although, at times, Clinton was presented as voiceless as a First Lady and adviser on national healthcare reform, speaking on camera less and less frequently, she garnered more attention than any other female politician in the history of American politics. This media attention adds to a historical awareness of women in political leadership, which had previously been sparse and, at times, absent. The experience of previous women running for president, including Victoria Woodhull (1872), Margaret Chase Smith (1964), Shirley Chisholm (1972), and Elizabeth Dole (2000), suggested women's lack of success in high-level politics; Clinton was sometimes presented through that same collective memory rather than as the innovative leader who led the vote count during much of the 2008 presidential primary season. Journalists who prepare stories about female political leaders seeking top-level positions need to recognize they now have different context for future stories because of Clinton's performance in the campaign as well as her political leadership as First Lady and a U.S. Senator. In her role as an innovator, Clinton has now become a part of historical memory that is a component of collective memory.

MASS MEDIA MEMORY

Mass media memory, positioned in the top right bubble of the model, is created by representations in broadcast, print, and Internet content. Relying on Halbwachs, media scholar Jill Edy observes that "mass communication is a critical element of collective memory."[50] She continues, the media are "evermore responsible for our memory of events, including those that oc-curred in the years since we left school."[51] Television is both a sustainer and disturber of reality; it presents and negates perceptions and assists in the creation of memories of both people and events. "For most of us, the way in which we 'know' Hillary Rodham Clinton is through mediated discourse," says Shawn Parry-Giles, and the discourse was generally stereotypical.[52] As viewers are repeatedly exposed to coverage of an event or a person, the viewers incorporate those images and texts into their memories, and their perceptions of that event or individual are augmented.

Although mass media memory can be created by the way historical mem-ory is used in the media, it is different than historical memory. For example, a broadcast journalist may start with a historical memory but the story may debunk that memory or alter it so that it becomes the basis of a new memory. Because of the treatment received in the story, viewers may "remember" a historical event very differently than they had previously remembered it, just as viewers may "remember" a personal experience very differently than it occurred after seeing a media account of it. Television news representations have helped shape the collective memory of important movements in U.S. history, including the Civil Rights Movement and the Women's Movement. News representations of both movements implanted images and perceptions in the memories of those who saw them. During her public life, Clinton's image in the media changed a number of times, but the dominant image she projected, based on the stories we analyzed, was innovator. Clinton's prac-tice at image-making contributed to her positioning as an innovator and paid off during the most difficult times.

In a study of Clinton's favorability ratings while she was First Lady, there are highs and lows. Her first year as First Lady was a "honeymoon" period in which she garnered favorability ratings in the high 1960s and low 1970s among the American public. She experienced a substantial drop in favorability ratings during her second year when Whitewater—an investigation suggesting improper financial deals involving Clinton—emerged as a controversial issue, and healthcare as an unpopular political issue. At this point in office, Clinton's ratings were around 50 percent. As Clinton withdrew from the public eye, her favorability ratings rose, breaking 60 percent by the end of 2000.[53] The opinion polls suggest the public negotiated Clinton's role as innovator with roles of more traditional past First Ladies and at times rejected her leadership. Thus, innovative representations of Clinton as a First Lady were both positive and negative. But it helped set the stage for her acceptance as a presidential primary candidate, where Clinton was an all-out innovator. Clinton's representations as a soon-to-be and then newly elected U.S. Senator were positive and included photo-ops that were strategically managed by the campaign. Some stories we examined show a happy smiling Clinton headed to the polls to vote for herself at the school in their suburban New York neighborhood, and later a smiling Clinton under a shower of confetti celebrating her victory. Clinton's career in the Senate helped to launch her campaign as a presidential primary candidate in 2007. Image-making in politics is a large part of campaigning. As politicians attempt to construct their images with campaign slogans and carefully crafted speeches, they often tap into historical memory of viewers. Clinton tapped into feminists' collective memory of leaders such as Woodhull, Smith, and Chisholm as path-breakers and used it to define herself. Whether through campaign speeches, photo-ops with voters, appearances on shows like *The Daily Show* with Jon Stewart or *Late Night* with David Letterman, Clinton refined her image to reflect the desires of the voters for masculine traits in leadership.

Sound bites in the stories analyzed often pointed to Clinton's gender. In an interview, ABC's Diane Sawyer asked Clinton in reference to the so-called emotional moment in New Hampshire, "Do different standards apply to women?"[54] Former President Bill Clinton, her husband, in an interview with NBC's Andrea Mitchell declared: "I can't make her younger, taller . . . or a man."[55] In these instances, the media were treating her in the gendered collective memory of a country that has never had a female president rather than acknowledging her innovativeness and leadership. Another example of journalists not being able to see her leadership was evidenced in stories when Senator Obama won the nomination as Democratic presidential nominee in August 2008. Stories in our analysis criticized Clinton, who was runner-up to Obama, for not conceding the nomination quickly. However, none of the stories mentioned that although Clinton did not win the nomination, she was the first woman in history to garner so many votes and in early June in Puerto Rico before Obama's nomination, she was leading by over 100,000 votes in the primary contests.

CONCLUSION

We sought to explain how collective memory develops and relate it to how women's leadership may be perceived as a result. We used television news representations of First Lady and presidential candidate Hillary Rodham Clinton because of her political prominence and people's continued reliance on TV for political news. The Collective Memory and Media Relationship Model we introduce shows that collective memory is comprised of three sets of memories, which can be categorized as personal, historical, and mass media memories. The model clearly shows an inter-relatedness, or connections, among the types of memory before they combine into collective memory. This intersection of memories supports Halbwachs' original explanation that memory, or remembering, is social; it is not an individual activity. In the model, even personal memory, which is the most isolated of the three, is connected to a social context. It is the context that triggers memory in the first place and gives it meaning. In this analysis where the context is high-level politics, despite Clinton's aggressive imaging-making of herself as an innovative candidate breaking barriers by skillfully using her leadership abilities, media at times tapped into collective memory that prompted gender stereotypes of leadership which Watson and Gordon said create expectations based on "personal characteristics" and "presumed competence in dealing with particular issues."[56] As explained by Ford, author of *Women and Politics: The Pursuit of Equality*, "Women candidates need to *earn* the voters' judgment of competence, whereas for males a certain threshold of competence is implied by their very presence in the race."[57] This suggests collective memory of Clinton that was relied on was constructed in a context that devalues the participation and leadership of women in high-level politics. Collective memory is fluid and changes to fit the needs of the times, but rather than creating the basis for new collective memory of women's leadership in high-level politics, the media stories analyzed in our research largely perpetuated traditional negative thinking about women in leadership.

The model suggests a more powerful role played by mass media in the construction of collective memory than we expected. We acknowledge that this role may appear to be so powerful because we examined mass media content. Had we chosen to use a different kind of content to illustrate the model, our results might have been different as to the role of mass media in the construction of collective memory. But, we doubt it. Further study is needed to address the role of mass media in the construction of mass media.

We conceptualized our study to examine how collective memory about Hillary Clinton as First Lady and a presidential candidate may be constructed. In doing so, we addressed collective memory of women's leadership at the highest level of politics and its implications for the future. To the degree that Clinton was presented as an innovator as both a First Lady and a female political leader, she may have contributed to a new collective memory of women in high-level political leadership. The visibility of Clinton, although at times diminished, was far more prominent than that of other First Ladies or other female presidential candidates. Yet, rather than focusing on her innovativeness, journalists focused on her uniqueness as a non-traditional First Lady and as a "woman for President," which genderized her campaign and political leadership. While her gender was obviously a part of the ongoing story, journalists may have unnecessarily allowed gender stereotypes embedded in collective memory of high-level political leadership to overshadow her innovativeness. Journalists asked questions and wrote stories about gender rather than leadership. Representing Clinton's gender as a focus of the news has significant implications for voter decision-making and shaping collective memory of Clinton and female political leadership. It suggests the collective memory of her puts gender first, rather than innovativeness or positive leadership. The media's use of collective memory filled with gender notions fraught with limitations for women in high-level political leadership may have reaffirmed and perpetuated those stereotypes.

Judith Butler, Kathleen Hall Jamieson, and Gaye Tuchman, among other feminist scholars, argue that genderization—the focus on gender—can detract from an individual's ability to present herself or himself as a human being versus a female or a male.[58] Butler describes it as a cultural function of performing gender, stating, "Performing one's gender wrong initiates a set of punishments both obvious and indirect, and performing it well provides the reassurance that there is an essentialism of gender identity after all."[59] This presents what Jamieson calls a "double bind"[60] for female political leaders, essentially trying to be feminine enough and masculine enough at the same time. In the realm of politics, all that is, is constructed in the masculine: to be feminine is negative and to be masculine is positive.[61] As Clinton shaped and re-shaped her image as a political leader, she was in a constant battle between being dubbed an innovator because of her gender and presenting herself as having sufficient masculine leadership abilities and skills to be accepted by voters in high-level politics. News practices, at times, by relying on traditional collective memory of female leadership and their own journalistic routines, mitigated Clinton's ability to present a focused image of herself as a political leader, leaving her voiceless or representing her negatively at times.

Television news representations are an omnipresent part of the daily life of most individuals. According to communications scholar James Carey, journalists should report on individuals and events with the knowledge that they are contributing to a body of history, to be reviewed and acknowledged by present and future generations. Journalists have a duty, Carey said, to contribute to journalism history by making sense of the stories they cover as cultural history, which is concerned with the thoughts within the events, the consciousness contained in them, not simply the events themselves.[62] In this way of thinking, journalists should always be mindful that they are tapping into collective memory and at the same time are possibly creating the basis for future collective memory. Reporting isn't just for the moment, particularly when they are dealing with cultural stereotypes as a basis for their stories. As journalists report the stories of the day, it is essential that they reflect upon the purpose of journalism as a non-negotiable part of history. They must begin to understand that collective memories of female politicians contribute to the stories that they produce and add to a historical record that becomes a part of collective memory of, in this case, Hillary Clinton and women's leadership.

NOTES

1. Regina Lawrence and Melody Rose, *Hillary Clinton's Race for the White House* (Boulder: Lynne Rienner, 2010), 47–48.

2. Ann Gordon and Jerry Miller, "Gender, Race and the Oval Office," in Robert P. Watson and Ann Gordon, eds., *Anticipating Madam President* (Boulder: Lynne Rienner, 2003), 146.

3. Judith Nies, "Ms. President," *Women's Review of Books* 21, no. 2 (Nov. 2003): 13.

4. Nichola Gutgold, "Girls Need to See Women Rise to Political Power," *Women's Media Center*, www.womensmediacenter.com/blog/entry/girls-need-to-see-women-rise-to-political-power; Anne E. Kornblut, *Notes from the Cracked Ceiling* (New York: Crown Publishers, 2009), 2; Lawrence and Rose, *Hillary Clinton's Race for the White House*; Theodora F. Sheckels, *Cracked but Not Shattered: Hillary Rodham Clinton's Unsuccessful Campaign for the Presidency* (Plymouth, UK: Lexington Books, 2009), 30.

5. Gordon and Miller, "Gender, Race, and the Oval Office," 164.

6. Jill Edy, "Journalistic Uses of Collective Memory," *Journal of Communication* 49, no. 2 (1999): 73; Michael Schudson, *The Power of News*, vol. 4 (Cambridge, MA: Harvard University Press, 1995) 347–348; Barbie Zelizer, *Covering the Body: the Kennedy Assassination, the Media and the Shaping of Collective Memory* (Chicago: University of Chicago Press, 1992), 3.

7. Erica Scharrer and Kim Bissell, "Overcoming Traditional Boundaries: The Role of Political Activity in Media Coverage of First Ladies," *Women and Politics*, 21, no. 1 (2000): 56.

8. Kim Fridkin, Patrick J. Kenney, and Gina Serignese Woodall, "Bad for Men, Better for Women: The Impact of Stereotypes during Negative Campaigns," *Political Behavior*, 31, no. 1 (2009): 53–77. Shanto Iyengar and Donald R. Kinder, *News That Matters: Television and American Opinion* (Chicago: Chicago University Press, 1987), 90–98; Lynne E. Ford, *Women and Politics: The Pursuit of Equality* (Boston: Wadsworth, 2011), 131.

9. Maurice Halbwachs, *Les Cadres Sociaux Des Memoires* [On Collective Memory], trans. Lewis Coser (1952; repr., 1992); Maurice Halbwachs, *On Collective Memory*, trans. Lewis Coser (Chicago: University of Chicago, 1992; repr., 1992), 72; Schudson, *The Power of News*.

10. Andrew Hoskins, "An Introduction to Media and Collective Memory," *Department of Media and Communication Studies* (Swansea, Wales: Center for Media History, 2001), 1.

11. Ford, *Women and Politics: The Pursuit of Equality*.

12. Schudson, *The Power of News*; Halbwachs, *On Collective Memory*.

13. Esref Aksu, "Global Collective Memory: Conceptual Difficulties of an Appealing Idea," *Global Society* 23, no. 3 (2009): 15; Paul Connerton, *How Societies Remember*, (Cambridge, MA: Cambridge University Press, 1989), 2; Michael Kammen, "Frames Of Remembrance: The Dynamics of Collective Memory by Iwona Irwin-Zarecka," *History and Theory* 34, no. 3 (1995) 245–61; Wulf Kansteiner, "Finding Meaning in Memory: A Methodological Critique of Collective Memory Studies," *History and Theory* 41, no. 2 (2002): 181; James W. Pennebaker and Becky L. Banasik, "On the Creation and Maintenance of Collective Memories: History as Social Psychology" in *Collective Memory of Political Events: Social Psychological Perspec-

tives, ed. James W. Pennebaker, Dario Paez, and Bernard Rime (Mahwah, NJ: Lawrence Erlbaum, 1997), 3–21; Barry Schwartz, "Collective Memory and History: How Abraham Lincoln Became a Symbol of Racial Equality," *The Sociological Quarterly*, 38, no. 3 (1997): 470–71; James Schwoch, "Television Today and Tomorrow: It Won't Be What You Think," *Historical Journal of Film, Radio and Television* 16, no. 2 (1996): 109–21.

14. F. C. Bartlett, *Remembering* (Cambridge, MA: Cambridge University Press, 1932), 197–214; Donald P. Spence, *Narrative truth and historical truth* (New York: Norton, 1984), 279–99.

15. Esref Aksu, "Global Collective Memory: Conceptual Difficulties of an Appealing Idea,"; Paul Connerton, *How Societies Remember*, 6–40; E. Zerubavel, *Time Maps: Collective Memory and the Social Shape of the Past* (Chicago: University of Chicago Press, 2003), 11–14.

16. Barry Schwartz, "Iconography and Collective Memory: Lincoln's Image in the American Mind," *The Sociological Quarterly* 32, no. 3 (1991): 302–303; Barry Schwartz, "Collective Memory and History: How Abraham Lincoln Became a Symbol of Racial Equality," *The Sociological Quarterly* 38, no. 3 (1997): 471; Mitch Kachun, "Cities of the Dead: Contesting the memory of the Civil War in the South 1865–1914," *Alabama Review* 58, no. 3 (2005): 211; Jeff Larson and Omar Lizardo, "Generations, Identities and the Collective Memory of Che Guevara," *Sociological Forum* 22, no. 4 (2007): 431–33; Amber Roessner, 'Remembering "The Georgia Peach': Popular Press, Public Memory, and the Shifting Legacy of an (Anti) Hero," *Journalism History* 36, no. 2 (2010): 84; Howard Shuman, Barry Schwartz, and Hannah D'Arcy, "Elite Revisionist and Popular Beliefs: Christopher Columbus, Hero or Villain?" *Public Opinion Quarterly* 69, no. 1 (2005): 6–10.

17. Kammen, "Frames of Remembrance: The Dynamics of Collective Memory by Iwona Irwin-Zarecka," 258.

18. Judith Butler, "Performative Acts and Gender Constitution: An Essay in Phenomenology and Feminist Theory," *Theatre Journal* 40, no. 4 (1988): 528.

19. Kansteiner, "Finding Meaning in Memory: A Methodological Critique of Collective Memory Studies"; Connerton, *How Societies Remember*, 14.

20. Aksu, "Global Collective Memory: Conceptual Difficulties of an Appealing Idea."; Denise Bostdorff and Steven Goldzwig, "History, Collective Memory, and the Appropriation of Martin Luther King Jr.: Reagan's Rhetorical Legacy," *Presidential Studies Quarterly* 35, no. 4 (2005): 661; James Fentriss and Chris Wickham, *Social Memory* (Oxford: Blackwell 1992), 60–63.

21. Edy, "Journalistic Uses of Collective Memory"; Schudson, *The Power of News*; Zelizer, *Covering the Body: the Kennedy Assassination, the Media and the Shaping of Collective Memory*.

22. *Americans Spending More Time Following the News* (Washington DC: Pew Research Center for the People and the Press, 2010). www.people-press.org/2010/09/12/americans-spending-more-time-following-the-news/; "The State of the News Media," Project for Excellence in Journalism; *News Interest Index* (Washington DC: Pew Research Center, 2007).

23. The White House Project Report: Benchmarking Women's Leadership. 2009. thewhitehouseproject.org/.

24. Barney Glaser and Anselm Strauss, *Awareness of Dying* (Chicago: Aldine Publishing Co., 1967), 292.

25. Lisa M. Burns, *First Ladies and the Fourth Estate* (Dekalb, IL: Northern Illinois University Press, 2008), 42–77; Betty Houchin Winfield, "The Making of an Image: Hillary Rodham Clinton and American Journalists," *Political Communication* 14, no.2 (1997): 242.

26. Karlyn Kohrs Campbell, "Hillary Clinton's 2008 Presidential Bid: The View from Academia," *Presidential Studies Quarterly* 41, no. 1 (2011): 192–95.

27. Mary Tucker-McLaughlin and Kenneth Campbell, "A Grounded Theory Analysis: Hillary Clinton Represented as Innovator and Voiceless in TV news," *Electronic News* 6, no. 1 (2012): 7.

28. Schudson, *The Power of News*, 347–48.

29. Roland Barthes, 1957. *Mythologies* (2000 ed. London: Vintage), 26–29.

30. Connerton, *How Societies Remember*; Zerubavel, *Time Maps: Collective Memory and the Social Shape of the Past*.

31. Aksu, "Global Collective Memory: Conceptual Difficulties of an Appealing Idea," 319.

32. Ibid., 321; Kansteiner, "Finding Meaning in Memory: A Methodological Critique of Collective Memory Studies."

33. Hoskins, "An Introduction to Media and Collective Memory."

34. Zelizer, *Covering the Body: the Kennedy Assassination, the Media and the Shaping of Collective Memory*.

35. Pennebaker and Banasik, "On the Creation and Maintenance of Collective Memories: History as Social Psychology."

36. Roger Brown and James Kulik, "Flashbulb Memories," *Cognition* 5, no. 1 (1977): 191; Catrin Finkenauer et al., "Flashbulb memories and the underlying mechanisms of their formation: toward an emotional-Integrative model," *Memory and Cognition* 26, no. 3 (1998): 516.

37. Roger Brown and James Kulik (1977), "Flashbulb memories," *Cognition* 5 (1): 73–99, 91. Accessed September, 10, 2012.

38. Kate Snow, *Hillary Clinton's Emotional Meeting in New Hampshire*, Story, Reported by Kate Snow, (2008; Manchester, New Hampshire). Television News.

39. Kathleen Hall Jamieson, *Beyond the Double Bind: Women and Leadership* (New York: Oxford, 1995), 17.

40. Ibid., 165.

41. Jim Axelrod, *Hillary Clinton's Emotional Moment,* Story, Reported by Jim Axelrod (2008; Manchester, New Hampshire: CBS), Television News.

42. Harry Rosenthal, "Muskie's Intellect, Honesty Recalled," *Telegram and Gazette*, Mar 27, 1996, 2.

43. Mary Kate Cary, "John Boehner, Sarah Palin, and When Crying is OK in Politics," *U.S. News and World Report,* Dec 2010, 1. www.usnews.com/articles/opinion/2010/12/22/john-boehner-sarah-palin-and-when-crying-is-ok-in-politics.html; www.usnews.com/articles/opinion/2010/12/22/john-boehner-sarah-palin-and-when-crying-is-ok-in-politics.html.

44. Nancy Benac, "Has the Political Risk of Emotion, Tears, Faded?" *USA Today*, December 19 2007, 1. Accessed January 2, 2009. usatoday30.usatoday.com/news/politics/election2008/2007-12-19-emotion-politics_N.htm.

45. David Bloom, *Lewinsky Investigation*. Story, produced by David Bloom (1998, Washington, DC, NBC), television news.

46. Linda Douglas, *Lewinsky Investigation*. Story, produced by Linda Douglas (1998,Washington, DC, ABC).

47. Dan Rather, *Lewinsky Investigation*. Story, produced by Dan Rather (1998, Washington, DC. CBS).

48. Schudson, *The Power of News*.

49. Carolyn Kitch, "Anniversary Journalism, Collective Memory, and the Cultural Authority to Tell the Story of the American Past," *Journal of Popular Culture* 36, no. 1 (2002): 44–47.

50. Edy, "Journalistic Uses of Collective Memory," 72

51. Edy, "Journalistic Uses of Collective Memory, 14.

52. Shawn J. Parry-Giles, "Mediating Hillary Rodham Clinton: Television News Practices and Image Making in the Post Modern Age," *Critical Studies in Mass Communication* 17, no. 2 (2000): 206.

53. Pew Research Center for the People and the Press, *Hillary Clinton's Career of Comebacks* (Washington DC: Pew Research Center, [2012]).

54. Diane Sawyer, *Interviews Hillary Clinton,* Interview, Performed by Diane Sawyer (2008, New York, ABC), television news.

55. Andrea Mitchell, *Hillary Clinton's Emotional Meeting in New Hampshire*, Interview, performed by Andrea Mitchell (2008, Manchester, New Hampshire, NBC) television news.

56. Gordon and Miller, "Gender, Race, and the Oval Office," 147.

57. Ford, *Women and Politics: the Pursuit of Equality*.

58. Judith Butler, "Performative Acts and Gender Constitution: An Essay in Phenomenology and Feminist Theory," *Theatre Journal* 40, no. 4 (1988), 519–31; Kathleen Hall Jamieson, *Beyond the Double Bind: Women and Leadership* (New York: Oxford, 1995); Gaye Tuchman, "Women's Depiction by the Mass Media," *Signs* 4, no. 3 (1979), 528–42.

59. Judith Butler, *Performative Acts and Gender Constitution: An Essay in Phenomenology and Feminist Theory*, 519–31.

60. Jamieson, *Beyond the Double Bind: Women and Leadership*.

61. Ford, *Women and Politics: the pursuit of equality*.

62. James Carey, *The Struggle Against Forgetting* (Remarks at graduation, Columbia University School of Journalism, New York, NY, January 17, 2007), 1.

Chapter Eleven

Electing the Commander in Chief

*The Gender Regime and Hillary Clinton's 2008
Campaign Rhetoric*

Maria Daxenbichler and Rochelle Gregory

Since Victoria Woodhull's nomination by the Equal Rights Party in 1872, more than thirty women have sought the Presidency, yet no one has come as close to securing the nomination as Hillary Clinton did on the Democratic ticket in 2008. Clinton was the most "well-funded, well-connected, and famous female candidate"[1] who consistently polled higher than other candidates throughout 2007, leading Senator Obama by more than fifteen points in June and by twenty in September 2007.[2] As author and political strategist Leslie Sanchez describes it, "Senator Hillary Rodham Clinton came into the 2008 presidential campaign as the presumptive Democratic nominee. Indeed, the word most often used to describe her candidacy was 'inevitable.'"[3]

However, Clinton did eventually lose the nomination to Senator Barack Obama, whose campaign and eventual win marked an historic moment for racial equality. Still, considering her political clout, name recognition, and financial resources, how did Clinton lose a nomination that was considered all but hers? As Sanchez reiterates: "When you consider all of the factors aligning in Clinton's favor—the path breaking nature of her campaign to become the first women president, her strong early lead, the data attributing this lead in large measure of support from women voters, and the fact that women make up a majority of Democratic primary voters—her failure to capture the nomination is that much more stunning."[4]

While many factors contributed to the failure of the Clinton campaign and to the success of Obama's, one contributing factor to Clinton's loss is an American political and social system based on what R. W. Connell calls the "gender regime" of the state. Gender, in this context, refers to what Joan Scott describes as "a socially agreed upon system of distinction rather than an objective description of inherent traits."[5] This system is "a social product, an institution of power relations learned through and perpetuated by culture."[6] It relies on repeated public performance of gender roles through gender specific rhetoric and behavior.[7] Qualities that are connected to political leadership such as toughness, dominance, and assertiveness are coded as masculine;[8] feminine qualities are connected to traditional women's roles as mothers and caregivers.[9] Men and women who assume gendered qualities that contradict traditional gender roles challenge the social gender system and potentially encounter criticism for acting outside their gender roles.

Connell argues that this system also manifests itself in government structures. The state is "an active player in gender politics" because it is "a significant vehicle of sexual and gender oppression and regulation"[10] that institutionalizes social gender roles and patriarchy. The gender regime is visible insofar as "women and men tend to occupy particular positions within the state, and work in ways structured by gender relations."[11] Men, for example, disproportionately hold positions of political power, because the system of political representation "has also been socially organized on gender lines."[12] Gendered division of labor, gendered power structures, and gendered political representation reinforce each other and result in a gendered electoral process. Clinton's unsuccessful responses and eventual loss to Obama exemplifies the gender regime because "it appears consistent with many Americans' perception of a competitive electoral environment that is biased against women, but also because it likely reinforces these perceptions."[13]

This gender regime heavily influenced and limited Clinton's campaign strategies. Some observers of the presidential primaries expected that in the case of a well-known politician such as Clinton, "her individual persona would trump general gender stereotypes and that she would be judged more as an individual and less as a typical woman."[14] Yet, even with a high-profile candidate, gender dominated the public discussion around Clinton's candidacy. Much like in any campaign, Clinton faced challenges to her aptitude and capacity for leadership; however, as a woman, Clinton was repeatedly condemned as being shrewd, harpy, unlikable, emasculating, and disingenuous. Critics described Clinton as a nag and "stereotypical bitch" whose voice reminded men of "nails on the blackboard"[15] and a Nurse Ratched figure that kept men's testicles stowed away in "lockboxes."[16] Clinton, like other female political candidates, could not circumvent the interconnectedness of gender, patriarchy, and the institutions of the state and she was "forced to navigate a sexist environment and craft a strategic response."[17]

One of the tools Clinton used to try to overcome the limits of the gender regime was a masculine campaign rhetoric that fit the gendered expectations of the electorate. Rhetoric was a powerful tool for her because all discourses, including presidential campaign rhetoric, occur in relation to "history and context;"[18] therefore, effective campaign rhetoric situates the rhetor by drawing upon the experiences of past presidents and connects to ongoing events. Previous presidents have increasingly masculinized and militarized the Office of the President through rhetoric mobilizing the nation for war; therefore, Clinton used masculine and militaristic rhetoric to fit into the presidential tradition. In other words, Clinton tried to overcome the restrictions of the gender regime through rhetoric. The gender regime is flexible enough to allow some women into political offices,[19] but they have to use masculine rhetoric to avoid being perceived as too feminine,[20] which would hurt their chances at a masculinized political office. This chapter will first explore the militarized gender regime and then discuss how, in an effort to overcome the conventional gender regimes for the President, Clinton framed herself in masculine terms by drawing attention to her expertise and leadership qualities. Clinton's failure to secure the nomination as a presidential candidate indicates that while masculine campaign rhetoric is unavoidable for candidates, the gender regime's exclusion of women from political power was persistent enough to withstand Clinton's strategy.

RHETORIC OF THE MILITARIZED GENDER REGIME

Women as speakers and reformers have historically endured censure and public ridicule since "rhetorical action of any sort was, as defined by gender roles, a masculine activity."[21] In *Man Cannot Speak For Her*, Karlyn Kohrs Campbell analyses nineteenth-century women's political rhetoric and discusses how, ideally, effective public speakers were the authoritative experts who "called attention to themselves, took stands aggressively, initiated action, and affirmed their expertise."[22] They were competitive and ambitious but prone to "lustful, ruthless, competitive, amoral" behaviors.[23]

This ideal speaker, however, hardly fit the model for appropriate feminine behavior. "Traditional concepts of womanhood" emphasized "passivity, submissiveness, and patience,"[24] and women's natures were to be "pure, pious, domestic, and submissive."[25] Likewise, because women were considered intellectually inferior, they were also inherently unsuited for public speaking and deliberation. After all, a woman's place was the home, "a haven from amoral capitalism and dirty politics, where 'the heart was,' where the spiritual and emotional needs of husband and children were met by a 'ministering angel.'"[26] Women were to occupy entirely the "private sphere of the home, eschewing any appearance of individuality, leadership, or aggressiveness."[27]

Presently, this rhetorical style, as Campbell argues, continues to conflate femininity with traditional gender roles. She writes that for female rhetors, "performing or enacting femininity has meant adopting a personal or self-

disclosing tone (signifying nurturance, intimacy, and domesticity) and assuming a feminine persona, for example, mother, or an ungendered persona,
for example, mediator or prophet, while speaking."[28] Based on women's
social role, which made it almost impossible for them to speak publicly,
female activists developed a style of rhetoric that tries to combine appropriate feminine behavior with public speaking. Also, if women want to be
perceived as feminine and gender appropriate they are expected to use "strategies associated with women—such as domestic metaphors, emotional appeals to motherhood."[29] Consequently, while female public speakers today
do not face the same obstacles as their predecessors, the conflict between
traditional women's roles and their presence as public speakers "persists."[30]

Women's social and political power is often deemed as emasculating and
threatening, and their familial obligations keep women from following political careers and render them reproducers of the nation.[31] Jacqueline Stevens
argues that "*political societies* constitute the intergenerational *family* form
that provides the pre-political seeming semantics of *nation*."[32] In other
words, the political society of the state has a vested interest in the family as a
place of cultural and physical reproduction of the nation. Because women
have been seen as the reproducers for the nation, their bodies have been and
still are regulated for this reason. After all, women are supposed to produce
new citizens, and through traditional family structures, new citizens learn and
reproduce the gendered power dynamics of the state. To keep this system of
ideological and physical reproduction in place, the state regulates families
and social gender dynamics. Women are encouraged by the state to embrace
traditional gender roles as mothers and caregivers in traditional, heterosexual
families.

While women who pursue political offices are not censured and ridiculed
as overtly anymore, society and the state still hold on to established social
conditions that deter women from seeking political power. These conditions
reinforce themselves: women do not run for office because they are responsible for their families; therefore, women cannot change the state's expectation toward and definition of the family and their roles within it (even though
not all women are interested in changing this dynamic). Consequently, the
state apparatus institutionalizes "men's domination" and helps reinforce patriarchal social structures.[33] Connell calls this system that keeps women out
of elected offices an "electoral patriarchy."[34] The term implies that the state
is not by definition or institution patriarchal but that the patriarchal structures
prevalent in society show themselves at the voting booth.[35] Connell locates
the source of gender inequality in representative offices in the structures of
society that reinscribe the state as a male-led, patriarchal institution. This
structure is the "gender regime" of the state. While this gender regime can
change because it "is linked to . . . the wider gender order of society," social
gender relations have to change before women are going to occupy more

traditionally masculine "positions within the state,"[36] and thus, positions of power such as that of a Senator, Representative, or even the President.

Consequently, while women have been the targets of state policy, they have not been the authors of these policies because they are vastly underrepresented in governments. In the United States in 2013, for example, only 18.1 percent of the Congress are women.[37] According to political scientist Jennifer Lawless, a small number of women occupy political offices because too few of them run in elections. She points out that 51 percent of respondents to two different surveys "believe that Americans are not 'ready to elect a woman to high office'" such as the presidency, and 40 percent of those surveyed "conceded that women are discriminated against in all realms of society."[38] As a result, women who are in positions that would make them possible candidates for political offices are more pessimistic about their chances to get elected and are less likely to run than men. Lawless and Fox find:

> [Women] are less likely than men to be willing to endure the rigors of political campaign. They are less likely than men to be recruited to run for office. They are less likely than men to have the freedom to reconcile work and family obligations with a political career. They are less likely than men to think they are "qualified" to run for office. And they are less likely than men to perceive a fair political environment.[39]

The gendered structures of the state thus repeat and reinforce themselves through the electorate's expectations toward politicians and the social constraints women face.

The gendered division of labor within the state further intensifies in times of war. Women's service for the nation at war used to be celebrated as "republican motherhood"—women give birth to and raise sons who can fight for the country.[40] Still today, women are expected to be mothers and caregivers when the state is at war but not act as its defenders.[41] Likewise, women are seemingly the subjects of male violence who need to be protected. For example, in the past decade, President George W. Bush's administration used the idea of the defenseless Afghan woman to justify its war on terror. In speeches that were supposed to gather support for the invasion of Afghanistan, members of the administration presented Afghan women as deprived of human rights and dependent on American protection. This rhetoric appealed to the idea of feminine vulnerability in general, and the protection of Afghan women was an extension of the need to protect American women. Michaele Ferguson argues that this "feminized security rhetoric"[42] suggests that women are "victims, vulnerable, in need of masculinist protection, here embodied in the figure of the United States."[43] Using the image of women in need of protection from their own barbaric countrymen, this rhetoric "reinscribes traditional gender roles of chivalrous male protectors rescuing female damsels-in-distress."[44] As Iris Marion Young points out, these chivalrous forms of masculinist protection "express and enact concern for the wellbeing of women, but they do so within a structure of superiority and subordination."[45]

The idea of the chivalrous protector does not only work for a pro-war rhetoric, but Young argues that it also works within American society. In a paternalistic family structure, the "good" American man shields his family from outside "aggressors"; those in "protected positions," like women, concede "critical distance and decision making autonomy."[46] Young translates this structure of chivalrous protection to the American state that after 9/11 established a "security regime": "the state and its officials assume the role of protector towards its citizens, and the citizens become positioned as subordinates, grateful for the protection afforded them."[47] A nation's citizens therefore take on a feminine role, whereas the leaders of the state embody a masculine role. American men still act as the protector of their families, but concede the protection of the nation to the state. This "security regime" consequently is a "gender regime" in which the state is masculinized and the citizens feminized; the Bush administration's security rhetoric reinforced this system.

The figure who most prominently represents this masculine character of the state is the President, and one of the most important duties of the president that has steadily gained importance in the course of the twentieth century is that of Commander in Chief.[48] Although Article 2, Section 2 of the Constitution designates the president as the "Commander in Chief of the Army and Navy of the United States and of the Militia of the several States, when called into the actual Service the United States," Commanders in Chief both declare war and establish the "series of rhetorical acts that lay the foundation for it."[49] As Commander in Chief, the president offers the "commencement address that defends preemptive military action" and presents "vivid, dramatic narratives that arouse us to an anger that justifies putting our sons and daughters in harm's way" before national audiences and in speeches to the United Nations General Assembly.[50]

Since Ronald Reagan's invasion of Grenada in 1983, presidents have enlarged the "role of commander in chief [. . .] significantly through executive assertion of that role."[51] Both Reagan and his successor George H. W. Bush justified invasions of countries "by the threat posed to U.S. nationals"[52] in speeches they gave, and the term "Commander in Chief" has become equivalent to "president." After 9/11 and with the start of the "war on terror," George W. Bush picked up on this trend and, in addition, infused "his presidential authority with [a] militarized masculinity"[53] and thus deepened "even further the masculinized militarization of a legally gender-neutral, civilian institution, the American presidency."[54] Georgia Duerst-Lahti points out how the "2004 [presidential] election dripped with projections of masculinity": "George W. Bush flew a fighter jet, drove a racing boat, cleared brush, and continually talked tough about killing terrorists."[55] Enloe calls this "a profoundly gendered distortion"[56] of the Office of the Presidency because it "legitimizes masculinized men as protectors, as actors, [and] as rational strategists" and renders feminized persons as passive and in need of protection.[57]

Considering the masculinized gender regime, the role that the American president plays as commander in chief might be the single most important reason why it is so hard for women to win the Presidency, because the president's gender reflects the gendered character of a nation. Todd Reeser writes:

> Leaders of nations have more frequently been male than female, and since the image of the nation is closely connected to the gender of its leader or leaders, the masculinity of a president [. . .] influences how the nation is perceived and how it perceives itself.[58]

A male president, consequently, recreates the image of a masculine nation. The United States as a nation presents itself, in Ferguson's terms, as masculinist protectors, with the president as Commander in Chief and main representative of this masculinist protection. Women could step into this role and perform the gender of the nation and the role of the Commander in Chief as masculine, yet their gender performance would have to be masculine.

For example, this image was crucial throughout George W. Bush's administration since the invasion of Afghanistan started partially on the pretext of protecting Afghan women from the Taliban. Since the invasion in Afghanistan was justified by presenting Afghan women as in need of protection, the reason to go to war was justified, in part, with gendered arguments. Americans were reminded that women are victims, not aggressors, in a war. While it was specifically Afghan women who were portrayed in this way, the argument also affected how Americans thought about gender and war in general. This idea was reinforced through the military's continuing exclusion of female soldiers from combat. Moreover, George W. Bush promoted a "masculinized militarization"[59] and reinforced the masculine gender regime of the presidency, thus making it more difficult for women to present themselves as masculine enough to fill the role. Combined with the gender regime within American society that prevents women from being elected to "high office,"[60] this masculinized gender regime of the presidency suggests the difficulty that women face when running for president because voters do not expect women to present the nation as masculine enough to justify the United States' role as "protector" of women's rights worldwide.

Yet, Reeser argues, the perceived gender of a nation is performative. Only through "repetition of that national-gendered style" does it come to "be seen over time as stable, as natural-like, or as inextricably characteristic of that culture."[61] Consequently, the nation's gender is fluid, especially when it is connected to the leader's gender, and can be influenced, among other things, by rhetorical acts. Since the gender performances of nations' leaders vary, many "national-gendered style[s]" are possible, or "a leader may act in a certain gendered manner in order to gender the nation by analogy."[62] For example, Campbell points out that Ronald Reagan used "elements of feminine [rhetorical] style" which earned him a "positive response" from the public.[63] Yet female leaders of states cannot use feminine rhetorical styles, but have to act in masculine ways to gain their positions. Only through masculine rhetoric as part of a masculine gender performance "female masculinity can come to signify the nation."[64] Margaret Thatcher's nickname "Iron Lady," for example, shows that she managed to be perceived in masculine terms and to "maintain a perception of a kind of national masculinity."[65] The gendered character of a nation thus can change with the election of a new president. More difficult to change is the gender regime of the state, because, as Connell points out, "the wider gender order of society" has to change to dismantle it.[66] A president who changes the gender character of the nation by embodying a less militaristic masculinity might influence voters' ideas about gender, but that in itself is not enough to change the gender regime of the state.

HILLARY CLINTON: COMMANDER IN CHIEF

When women challenge the gender regime of the state, especially when they want to enter traditionally masculine arenas such as political offices, they have to negotiate paradoxical consequences of the gender regime. On the one hand, as Carroll points out, the "very role of presidential candidate demands that a woman demonstrate her ability to be dominant, and campaigning certainly requires self-promotion and disagreement with one's opponent,"[67] which means that women have to embrace traits that are associated with masculinity. On the other hand, "in proving that they are qualified to be leaders, women can easily cross the line and appear to be insufficiently feminine—that is, not 'nice' enough."[68] In her 2008 presidential election campaign, Clinton was faced with this paradox as she struggled to overcome the gender regime and present herself as Commander in Chief.

Before she announced her candidacy, Clinton's status in the realm of American politics was that of an established Washington politician. Her supporters admired her for her intelligence and her forthright, outspoken, and direct character.[69] Also, Clinton had made a name for herself as champion for women's rights, thus fitting into a feminine gender role because the political cause she was most prominently working for was "women's issues." But the ways in which she promoted her ideas were perceived as "masculine."[70] Writing about Clinton's political work in the 1990s, Campbell argues, "Hillary Rodham Clinton's style of public advocacy typically omits virtually all of the discursive markers by which women publicly enact their femininity," because "she speaks forcefully and effectively, manifesting her competency in meeting rhetorical norms" and omitting personal anecdotes and personal appeals.[71]

While many voters responded favorably to this masculine rhetorical style, some voters perceived Clinton as "[o]verly aggressive" or "overbearing."[72] The discomfort Clinton's leadership style evoked suggests that she had been pushing the limits of the gender regime throughout her political career. As long as she was known as a champion for women's issues, Clinton's rhetorical style did not disturb voter's expectations too much.[73] Yet when she entered the primary race, Clinton entered a highly masculine realm of American politics. One might suggest that this shift of focus—from women's issues to the highest executive office, including that of Commander in Chief—threw off the balance between the masculine and feminine appeals Clinton balanced more effectively before.

Her campaign, as Carroll points out, tried to negotiate this gender dilemma but failed.[74] For example, Regina Lawrence and Melody Rose argue that Clinton tried to approach this paradox with a campaign that had a "putatively gender-neutral appeal," but that also included "coded appeals to female solidarity" in her initial campaigning to mobilize female voters.[75] In this early period of her campaign she focused on women's issues such as health care. She sometimes even used feminine rhetorical styles, such as personal anecdotes and "a rare story about Chelsea as a baby"[76] to show a feminine side. Later in the campaign, when Obama gained popularity and she started losing her frontrunner position, she switched to a "heavily masculinized message strategy."[77] For example, she "refused to apologized for her vote" authorizing the Iraq war and "telling the ABC News program *Good Morning America* that under her presidency the United States would 'totally obliterate' Iran if it launched nuclear weapons at Israel."[78]

Despite Clinton's attempts to appear as the toughest, most experienced candidate, many responses during her campaign focused on her gender. For example, after Clinton had lost the primary in Iowa in early January 2008, she campaigned in New Hampshire, where a campaign stop at a café turned, in the media's view, into the "key moment" of her campaign.[79] Answering a supporter's question as to how she was handling all the campaigning and keeping "upbeat and so wonderful," Clinton choked up and spoke with a slightly broken voice: "It's not easy. And I couldn't do it if I just didn't, you know, passionately believe it was the right thing to do."[80] This brief dialogue was read as heavily feminine by the media because it was one of the rare moments Clinton spontaneously used feminine gender performance. The question evoked feminine rhetoric because it had a personal tone, encouraged self-disclosure, was not confrontational, and did not mention Clinton's opponents.[81] Clinton's response was not specifically feminine in its rhetoric—it did not differ substantially from any of the other statements she gave throughout the campaign, saying that the future of the country was important to her and that she thought some other candidates were not ready to take on the job of president—but in its emotionality. The combination of a rhetorically feminine question with an emotionally feminine response was enough for the media to label it as a feminine campaign moment.

As Lawrence and Rose point out, "Hillary Clinton's near-tears in Portsmouth illustrate the highly gendered aspects of some defining campaign moments,"[82] and this incident likely made the news because it fit the "stereotype of feminine emotionality (and manipulativeness)."[83] Moreover, Clinton was caught by the media in a lose-lose situation: When she demonstrated a reluctance to show emotion throughout the campaign, it was perceived in the media "as an inherent character flaw"; yet when Clinton showed emotion in the New Hampshire café, she was charged with being manipulative and calculating.[84] As Carroll points out, "Reporters and commentators rarely recognized or analyzed Clinton's tactical decisions as in a way gender related."[85] In this way, the media's analyses of the campaign repeated the gender stereotype that links women to emotionality and "manipulativeness," not to strategic thinking. The media, as Connell argues, is an agent in the gender regime;[86] it perpetuates patriarchal social structures and reinforces gender stereotypes such as masculine aggression.[87] Since it is part of the gender regime, the media was unable to reflect critically on its own complicity in the system. It focused heavily on gender issues but reported only in perfect conformity with the gender regime.

While Clinton's emotional responses did not seem to hurt her credibility as a presidential candidate initially when she won the New Hampshire primary, this key moment from Clinton's campaign illustrates the tensions that women face as they present themselves as commanding while compassionate. On the one hand, Clinton's emotional reactions in the roundtable discussion on the day before the election illustrated her wit and compassion that appealed to New Hampshire voters and catapulted her to success in the polls. After all, while Clinton was initially the frontrunner at the beginning of the primaries, her victory had not been anticipated by polls conducted the weekend before the primary held on Tuesday, and polls "showed Obama with a double-digit lead."[88] Also, the voter turnout was much higher than expected. For example, on the Monday between the polls and the election, the day Clinton had this "key moment," many Democratic voters seem to have changed their minds about their choice of candidate. Although it is difficult to find the ultimate reasons for this sudden change, polls suggest that especially female voters decided to vote for Clinton in the primaries. Whereas 34 percent of women said they planned to vote for Clinton in polls conducted on the weekend,[89] it was 46 percent who voted for her the day after the incident.[90] Clinton also gained among male voters, increasing her share of votes from twenty[91] to 29 percent[92] between weekend polls and Election Day. Social researcher Frank Newport suggests that "voters may have been closely attuned to election events in the final days before the election, which, in turn, may have had a greater influence on their behavior in the ballot booth."[93]

An analysis of Clinton's rhetorical choices illustrates how she asserted a masculine approach and left out personal appeals from her campaign rhetoric, as Carroll argues, in order to manipulate the reactions of the media, and in turn, the workings of the gender regime. Even after her early win in New Hampshire, in which she seemed to have succeeded through personal appeal, Clinton and her campaign chose to keep the focus on her experience and toughness. While Clinton spoke on numerous occasions throughout the campaign about the war in Iraq, military intervention in Afghanistan, and American foreign relations, two significant moments from her campaign demonstrated Clinton's deliberate attempt to frame herself as commander in chief. Specifically, in February 2008, Clinton's political TV advertisement "Three a.m." began with images of children sleeping in their beds when a phone began to ring in the background, and a speaker announces: "It's three a.m. and your children are safe and asleep. But there's a phone in the White House and it's ringing."[94] The advertisement continued:

> Something is happening in the world. Your vote will decide who answers that call. Whether it's someone who already knows the world's leaders, knows the military, someone tested and ready to lead in a dangerous world. It's 3 a.m. and your children are safe and asleep. Who do you want answering the phone?[95]

The ad evoked associations between a military crisis and the legendary "red phone" that connected the White House with the Kremlin during the Cold War.[96] In the advertisement, Clinton attempted to convey the message that she was the most experienced candidate in military and foreign policy questions.

While ultimately the advertisement helped Clinton gain momentum as she moved into the Ohio primaries, the ad seemed reminiscent of previously controversial campaign advertisements, including Lyndon B. Johnson's "Daisy Girl" ad in 1964 and Walter Mondale's "Teach the Parents" advertisement in 1984. For audiences, fear appeals provoke "unpleasant emotional" reactions that work by "presenting a threat to which the recipient is susceptible and which is severe" and by "recommending protective action" to neutralize the threat.[97] Like the other two advertisements, Clinton's advertisement appealed to audiences' fear of terrorism, violence, and war. It used the image of a young, vulnerable, sleeping child to motivate audiences to vote for the experienced Clinton. In the wake of the George W. Bush presidency, in which the masculine gender regime of the presidency was reinforced by Bush's focus on the militaristic component of the Office of the Presidency, it is understandable that Clinton presented a more masculinized image in order cast doubts regarding Obama's preparedness to become Commander in Chief. As Carroll puts it, "because of the negative gender stereotype of women as too weak and too emotional, Clinton had no choice but to portray herself as tough and strong."[98]

While Clinton had never held an office that would have brought her close to having experiences in any of these fields, she claimed that she had gained experience with war, the military, and foreign policy when she was first lady. On several occasions, Clinton tried to prove her claims by talking about her trips to "more than eighty countries," about being "on the front lines as the United States made peace in Bosnia and Northern Ireland and [about helping] save refugees from ethnic cleansing in Kosovo."[99] She described her role as First Lady in dramatic terms by stating, "There was a saying around the White House that if a place was too small, too poor, or too dangerous, the president couldn't go, so send the First Lady."[100] She even asserted to have been under attack from "sniper fire" in Bosnia, evoking the idea that she had been in a quasi-combat situation.[101] Later, Clinton admitted that she "misspoke" on her claims to have been under sniper fire.[102] These incidents show that Clinton was trying to prove that she was not only experienced in foreign policy but that she also was acquainted with the militaristic aspects of the presidential office. Just as the Commander in Chief's first acts are always rhetorical, not militaristic,[103] Clinton attempted to present herself as the Commander in Chief and represent the United States as a masculine, militaristic nation. Still, it seems that voters might not have been comfortable with the narrative of fear, especially when projected by a woman.

While "political language is political reality"[104] and Clinton was constructing a narrative in which voters identified her as Commander in Chief, this strategy ultimately proved unsuccessful. Clinton's campaign illustrates the "fine line" that female candidates must walk between being appealing, sensitive, and "likeable enough" while also projecting a commanding, calculating, and assertive authority as the military leader who is responsible for sending young men and women into combat. After all, the Commander in Chief engages in the rhetoric of "investiture": "In identifying a threat to the community and to its fundamental values, presidents implicitly argue that now is the appropriate time for them to assume the office of the commander in chief. Presidential war rhetoric legitimizes that role in the face of the identified threat and seeks support for its assumption from Congress and the public."[105] Yet especially when it comes to issues of war and the military, the gender regime draws distinct lines between the roles men and women are supposed to play: men act as protectors of women. After all, while more American women served in Afghanistan and Iraq than in any other military engagement, it was not until 2013 that American women were officially allowed to serve in combat roles, a decision that suggests just how pervasive the gender regime is.

CONCLUSION

It is difficult for women to break the gender regime of social and institutional barriers that keep them from assuming high political offices. As Clinton's unsuccessful campaign shows, it was impossible for her to convincingly argue that she was the right person to assume the role of the Commander in Chief in the face of threat to the country. Since Clinton did not win the Democratic primary, we still cannot tell how much femininity American voters might tolerate when it comes to the presidency. Clinton and her campaign staff thought they could win by participating in the gender regime and portraying Clinton as tough and experienced. While there certainly were many reasons for this tactic, it implies that they speculated that the American nation is not ready to elect a woman who shows feminine characteristics as president. As Lawrence and Rose point out, Clinton's strategy "seems to have backfired to some extent because pre-existing narratives about Clinton already framed her as overly ambitious [. . .] leaving us to wonder whether a campaign more grounded in a distinctly feminine voice might have actually succeeded."[106] Also Carroll concedes, "Clinton was so successful in demonstrating toughness that many observers thought she did not show enough emotion."[107] Yet the media's readiness to overemphasize Clinton's "feminine" moments show how readily they framed her as a sensitive woman, or as a woman still occupied with fighting blatant sexism. Still, a campaign strategy that focused on women's interests or underlined Clinton's femininity might have ended up similarly.

There were certainly many reasons for Clinton's loss, but one of them might be that America's electorate actually was ready to elect a feminine woman as president. As Carroll points out, a majority of voters wanted to have a change in office because they were "dissatisfied and looking to throw the rascals out."[108] By focusing solely on experience, Clinton "ceded the issue of change to Obama, who made that the centerpiece of his campaign."[109] In other words, the desire to change the country's political leadership was so strong that voters were ready to give up the traditional identity regime of the presidency. Clinton's partial success in the primaries (after all, she won "1,640 pledged delegates compared, [*sic*] to 1,763 for Obama")[110] shows that a substantial amount of voters were willing to vote for a woman as presidential candidate.

The election of the first female president of the United States would change the gender regime of the state more than the election of a woman into any other office. Women running for presidency are an important way to change the gender regime of the state. As Georgia Duerst-Lahti points out,

> [W]omen's presence in top posts that have never been held by a woman and in agencies consistent with masculine expectations count as the most important gains. Because practices themselves are gendered, the possibility of achieving transgendered understandings is greatest with the first female appointment to a highly masculinized policy area.[111]

So, while Clinton did not win the Democratic primary in 2008, her experiences continued to mark the trail for other women to follow, including Sarah Palin's run for Vice-President on the McCain ticket in 2008 and the record number of women elected to the House and Senate in 2012. Many voters were ready to counteract the gender regime of the state, which implies that "the wider gender order of society,"[112] and the basis for the gender regime of the state may be slowly changing.

NOTES

1. Anne E. Kornblut, *Notes from the Cracked Ceiling: Hillary Clinton, Sarah Palin, and What It Will Take For a Woman to Win* (New York: Crown Publishers, 2009), 8.

2. Leslie Sanchez, *You've Come a Long Way, Maybe: Sarah, Michelle, Hillary, and the Shaping of the New American Woman* (New York: Palgrave Macmillan, 2009), 20.

3. Ibid., 19.

4. Ibid., 21.

5. Joan W. Scott, *Gender and the Politics of History* (New York: Columbia UP, 1999), 29.

6. Evelyn Nakano Glenn, *Unequal Freedom* (Cambridge: Harvard UP, 2002), 12.

7. Karlyn Kohrs Campbell, "The Discursive Performance of Femininity: Hating Hillary," *Rhetoric and Public Affairs* 1, no. 1 (Spring 1998): 4, accessed January 7, 2013, Project Muse.

8. Susan Carroll and Richard Fox, *Gender and Elections: Shaping the Future of American Politics* (Cambridge: Cambridge University Press, 2006), 2.

9. Karlyn Kohrs Campbell, "The Discursive Performance of Femininity: Hating Hillary," 5.

10. R. W. Connell, "The State, Gender, and Sexual Politics: Theory and Appraisal," *Theory and Society* 19, no. 5 (October 1990): 519, accessed January 13, 2008, JSTOR, 519.

11. Ibid., 523.

12. Ibid., 526.

13. Jennifer Lawless, "Sexism and Gender Bias in Election 2008. A More Complex Path for Women in Politics," *Politics and Gender* 5, no. 1 (March 2009): 74, accessed May 1, 2012, doi: dx.doi.org/10.1017/S1743923X09000051.

14. Susan Carroll, "Reflections on Gender and Hillary Clinton's Presidential Campaign. The Good, the Bad, and the Misogynic," *Politics and Gender* 5, no. 1 (March 2009): 2, accessed May 1, 2012, ProQuest, 2.

15. "CNN's, ABC's Beck on Clinton: '[S]he's the Stereotypical Bitch,'" *Media Matters*, March 15, 2007, accessed February 17, 2013.

16. "Limbaugh: 'We Created This Whole Concept of a Testicle Lockbox in Connection with Mrs. Clinton,'" *Media Matters*, August 26, 2005, accessed February 17, 2013.

17. Jennifer Lawless, "Sexism and Gender Bias in Election 2008. A More Complex Path for Women in Politics," 73.

18. Karlyn Kohrs Campbell and Kathleen Hall Jamieson, *Presidents Creating the Presidency: Deeds Done in Words* (Chicago: University of Chicago Press, 2008), 22.

19. Todd W. Reeser, *Masculinities in Theory. An Introduction* (Hoboken: John Wiley and Sons, 2011), 173.

20. Karlyn Kohrs Campbell, "The Discursive Performance of Femininity: Hating Hillary," 5.

21. Karlyn Kohrs Campbell, *Man Cannot Speak for Her* (New York: Greenwood Press, 1989), 10.

22. Ibid.

23. Ibid., 11.

24. Ibid., 13.

25. Ibid., 10.

26. Ibid.

27. Ibid.

28. Karlyn Kohrs Campbell, "The Discursive Performance of Femininity: Hating Hillary," 5.

29. Ibid.

30. Ibid.

31. Nira Yuval-Davis, *Gender and Nation* (London: Sage Publications, 1997), 22.

32. Jacqueline Stevens, *Reproducing the State* (Princeton: Princeton University Press, 1999), 9.

33. R. W. Connell, "The State, Gender, and Sexual Politics: Theory and Appraisal," 514.

34. Ibid., 526.

35. Ibid., 524.

36. Ibid., 523.

37. "Facts on Women in Congress 2011," *Center for American Women and Politics. Rutgers.* 2013. Accessed January 31, 2013, www.cawp.rutgers.edu/fast_facts/levels_of_office/Congress-CurrentFacts.php.

38. Jennifer Lawless, "Sexism and Gender Bias in Election 2008. A More Complex Path for Women in Politics," 74.

39. Jennifer Lawless and Richard Fox, "Why Are Women Still Not Running for Public Office?," *Governance Studies. Brookings Institute.* 2008. 1–20. Accessed May 12, 2012, 2, www.brookings.edu/~/media/research/files/papers/2008/5/women%20lawless%20fox/05_women_lawless_fox.pdf.

40. Evelyn Nakano Glenn, *Unequal Freedom*, 41.

41. Nira Yuval-Davis, *Gender and Nation*, 22.

42. Michaele Ferguson, "'W' Stands for Women: Feminism and Security Rhetoric in the Post-9/11 Bush Administration," *Politics and Gender* 1, no. 1 (March 2005): 9–38. Accessed May 1, 2012, 11.

43. Ibid., 3.

44. Ibid., 5f.

45. Iris Marion Young, "Feminist Reactions to the Contemporary Security Regime," *Hypatia* 18, no. 1 (Winter 2003): 223–31. Accessed May 1, 2012. Project Muse, 230.

46. Ibid., 224.

47. Ibid., 225.

48. Cynthia Enloe, *The Curious Feminist: Searching for Women in a New Age of Empire* (Berkeley: University of California Press, 2004), 153.

49. Karlyn Kohrs Campbell and Kathleen Hall Jamieson, *Presidents Creating the Presidency: Deeds Done in Words*, 23.

50. Ibid.

51. Ibid., 12.

52. Ibid.

53. Cynthia Enloe, *The Curious Feminist: Searching for Women in a New Age of Empire*, 152.

54. Ibid., 153.

55. Georgia Duerst-Lahti, "Masculinity on the Campaign Trail," *Rethinking Madame President*, in *Are We Ready for a Woman in the White House?*, edited by Lori Cox Han and Caroline Heldman, 87–112 (Boulder: Lynne Rienner Publications, 2007), 87f.

56. Cynthia Enloe, *The Curious Feminist: Searching for Women in a New Age of Empire*, 154.

57. Ibid.

58. Todd W. Reeser, *Masculinities in Theory. An Introduction*, 272f.

59. Cynthia Enloe, *The Curious Feminist: Searching for Women in a New Age of Empire*, 152.

60. Jennifer Lawless, "Sexism and Gender Bias in Election 2008. A More Complex Path for Women in Politics," 2.

61. Todd W. Reeser, *Masculinities in Theory. An Introduction*, 282.

62. Ibid., 173.

63. Karlyn Kohrs Campbell, "The Discursive Performance of Femininity: Hating Hillary," 5.

64. Todd W. Reeser, *Masculinities in Theory. An Introduction*, 173.

65. Ibid.

66. R. W. Connell, "The State, Gender, and Sexual Politics: Theory and Appraisal," 523.

67. Susan Carroll, "Reflections on Gender and Hillary Clinton's Presidential Campaign. The Good, the Bad, and the Misogynic," 3.

68. Ibid.

69. Frank Newport and Joseph Carroll, "Personal Characteristics Loom Large in Americans' Views of Hillary Clinton," *Gallup*. July 6, 2006. Accessed April 20, 2012. www.gallup.com/poll/23578/Personal-Characteristics-Loom-Large-Americans-Views-Hillary-Clinton.aspx.

70. Shanto Iyengar et al, "Running as a Woman: Gender Stereotyping in Political Campaigns," In *Women, Media, and Politics*, edited by Pippa Norris, 77–98. (New York: Oxford University Press, 1997), 80.

71. Karlyn Kohrs Campbell, "The Discursive Performance of Femininity: Hating Hillary," 6.

72. Shanto Iyengar et al., "Running as a Woman: Gender Stereotyping in Political Campaigns," 80.

73. Ibid., 78.

74. Susan Carroll, "Reflections on Gender and Hillary Clinton's Presidential Campaign. The Good, the Bad, and the Misogynic," 6.

75. Regina Lawrence and Melody Rose, *Hillary Clinton's Run for the White House. Gender Politics and the Media on the Campaign Trail* (Boulder: Lynne Rienner Publications, 2009), 9.

76. Ibid., 121.

77. Ibid., 109.

78. Ibid., 116.

79. Ibid., 65.

80. "Clinton Wells Up: 'This Is Very Personal.'" *YouTube*. January 07, 2008. Accessed February 13, 2013. www.youtube.com/watch?v=pl-W3IXRTHU.

81. Karlyn Kohrs Campbell, "The Discursive Performance of Femininity: Hating Hillary," 5.

82. Regina Lawrence and Melody Rose, *Hillary Clinton's Run for the White House. Gender Politics and the Media on the Campaign Trail*, 65.

83. Ibid., 67.

84. Susan Carroll, "Reflections on Gender and Hillary Clinton's Presidential Campaign. The Good, the Bad, and the Misogynic," 4.

85. Ibid.

86. R. W. Connell, "The State, Gender, and Sexual Politics: Theory and Appraisal," 532.

87. Ibid., 535.

88. Frank Newport, "Post-N.H.: Explaining the Unexpected," *Gallup*. July 6, 2006, accessed April 20, 2012. www.gallup.com/poll/103663/PostNH-Explaining-Unexpected.aspx.

89. Joseph Carroll, "Dissecting the New Hampshire Primary Vote." *Gallup*, January 7, 2008, accessed April 20, 2012, www.gallup.com/poll/103621/Dissecting-New-Hampshire-Primary-Vote.aspx.

90. "NYT Election Guide 2008 New Hampshire: Profile of the New Hampshire Primary Voters," *New York Times*, January 8, 2008, accessed January 31, 2013, politics.nytimes.com/election-guide/2008/results/states/NH.html.

91. Joseph Carroll, "Dissecting the New Hampshire Primary Vote."

92. "NYT Election Guide 2008 New Hampshire: Profile of the New Hampshire Primary Voters."

93. Frank Newport, "Post-N.H.: Explaining the Unexpected."

94. "Hillary Clinton 3 AM Ad." *YouTube*. May 15, 2008. Accessed February 13, 2013. www.youtube.com/watch?v=7yr7odFUARg.

95. Ibid.

96. Katharine Seelye and Jeff Zeleny, "Clinton Questions Role of Obama in a Crisis." *New York Times*. March 1, 2008. Accessed April 20, 2012. www.nytimes.com/2008/03/01/us/politics/01campaign.html?_r=1.

97. Robert A. C. Ruiter, Charles Abraham, and Gerjo Kok, "Scary Warnings and Rational Precautions: A Review of the Psychology of Fear Appeals," *Psychology and Health* 16 (2001): 613–30. Accessed February 13, 2013, 614.

98. Susan Carroll, "Reflections on Gender and Hillary Clinton's Presidential Campaign. The Good, the Bad, and the Misogynic," 4.

99. Katharine Seelye and Jeff Zeleny, "Clinton Questions Role of Obama in a Crisis."

100. Katharine Seelye, "Clinton 'Misspoke' About Bosnia Trip, Campaign Says," *New York Times*, March 24, 2008, 1, accessed April 20, 2012, thecaucus.blogs.nytimes.com/2008/03/24/clinton-misspoke-about-bosnia-trip-campaign-says/.

101. Ibid.

102. Ibid.

103. Stephen E. Lucas, "George Washington and the Rhetoric of Presidential Leadership," in *The Presidency and Rhetorical Leadership* edited by Leroy G. Dorsey (College Station: Texas A and M University Press, 2002), 45.

104. Murray J. Edelman, *Constructing the Political Spectacle* (Chicago: University of Chicago Press, 1988), 104.

105. Karlyn Kohrs Campbell and Kathleen Hall Jamieson, *Presidents Creating the Presidency: Deeds Done in Words*, 234.

106. Regina Lawrence and Melody Rose, *Hillary Clinton's Run for the White House. Gender Politics and the Media on the Campaign Trail*, 137.

107. Susan Carroll, "Reflections on Gender and Hillary Clinton's Presidential Campaign. The Good, the Bad, and the Misogynic," 4.

108. Ibid., 3.

109. Ibid.

110. Ibid., 2.

111. Georgia Duerst-Lahti, "Reconceiving Theories of Power: Consequences of Masculinism in the Executive Branch," in *Gendering American Politics. Perspectives from the Literature* (New York: Pearson, 2006), 312.

112. R. W. Connell, "The State, Gender, and Sexual Politics: Theory and Appraisal," 523.

Bibliography

Adler, Nancy J. "Global Leadership: Women Leaders." *MIR: Management International Review* 37 (1997): 171–96.

Aksu, Esref. "Global Collective Memory: Conceptual Difficulties of an Appealing Idea." *Global Society* 23, no. 3 (2009): 15.

Alcoff, Linda Martín. "The Problem of Speaking for Others." In *Who Can Speak? Authority and Critical Identity*, edited by Judith Roof and Robyn Wiegman, 97–119. Urbana: University of Illinois Press, 1995.

Althusser, Louis. "Ideology and Ideological State Apparatuses." In *Lenin and Philosophy: and Other Essays* (New York: Monthly Review Press, 2001), 85–126.

Alvarez, Walter C. "Shirley Black Lauded." *The Evening Independent*, March 5, 1973, 15–A.

Anderson, Benedict. *Imagined Communities: Reflections on the Origin and Spread of Nationalism*. London: Verso, 2006.

Anderson, Karrin Vasby. "Hillary Rodham Clinton as 'Madonna': The Role of Metaphor and Oxymoron in Image Restoration." *Women's Studies in Communication* 25, no. 1 (2002): 1–24.

Appadurai, Arjun. *Modernity at Large: Cultural Dimensions of Globalization.* Minneapolis: University of Minnesota Press, 1993.

Aristotle. *On Rhetoric: A Theory of Civic Discourse*. Translated by George A. Kennedy. New York: Oxford UP, 1991.

Arthur, Anthony. *Radical Innocent: Upton Sinclair*. New York: Random House, 2006.

Axelrod, Jim. *Hillary Clinton's Emotional Meeting in New Hampshire.* News Package. Performed by Jim Axelrod. Manchester, New Hampshire: CBS, 2008, television.

Bacon, Perry. "Ferraro Leaves Clinton Camp Over Remarks About Obama." *Washington Post*, March 13 2008. Accessed www.washingtonpost.com

Balibar, Etienne. "The Nation Form: History and Ideology." In *Race Critical Theories*, edited by Philomena Essed et al., 220–230. Malden, MA: Blackwell Publishing, 2002.

Banwart, Christine. "Constructing Images in Presidential Primaries: An Analysis of Discourse Strategies in the Dole and Bush Iowa Straw Poll Speeches." *Argumentation and Advocacy* 43, no. 2 (Fall 2006): 65–78.

Barlow, Tani. "International Feminism of the Future." *Signs* 25, no. 4 (2000): 1099–1105.

Barnhurst, Kevin G., and Ellen Wartella. "Young Citizens, Americans TV Newscasts and the Collective Memory." *Critical Studies in Mass Communication* 15, no. 3 (Sept. 1995): 26.

Barthes, Roland. *Mythologies*. 2000 ed. London: Vintage, 1957.

Bartow, Charles L. "Just Now: Aimee Semple McPherson's Performance and Preaching of Jesus." *Journal of Communication and Religion* 20, no. 1 (1997): 71–79.

Baumgartner, Jody C. "The Veepstakes: Forecasting Vice Presidential Selection in 2008." *PS: Political Science and Politics* 41, no. 1 (October 2008): 765–72. Accessed March 31, 2012. doi: 10.1017/S1049096508081043.

Bee, Samantha. "Ready for a Woman President?"; 5 min., 5 sec.; TV show; from *The Daily Show* 9/17/2007. Accessed February 5, 2013. www.thedailyshow.com/watch/tue-september-18-2007/ready-for-a-woman-president.

Benac, Nancy. "Has the Political Risk of Emotion, Tears, Faded?" *USA Today*, Dec.19, 2007.

Bennett-Smith, Meredith. "Republican Women: Female GOP Politicians Look More Feminine Congressional Physiognomy Study Suggests." *Huffington Post*. Accessed September 29, 2012. www.huffingtonpost.com.

Bennhold, Katrin. "In Sweden, Men Can Have It All," *The New York Times*, June 9, 2010, Accessed February 8, 2013. www.nytimes.com/2010/06/10/world/europe/10iht-sweden.html?pagewanted=all&_r=0.

Bergson, Henri. *Matter and Memory* [*Matiere et memoire*]. Translated by Nancy Margaret Paul and W. Scott Palmer. Fifth ed. New York: Zone Books, 1988. 1908.

Bhutto, Benazir. *Daughter of Destiny: An Autobiography*. New York: HarperPerennial, 2007.

Bindel, Julie. "Iceland: The World's Most Feminist Country," *The Guardian*, March 25, 2010. Accessed February 8, 2013. www.guardian.co.uk/lifeandstyle/2010/mar/25/iceland-most-feminist-country.

Black, Shirley Temple. Commentary on "AGENDA ITEM 49: Report of the United Nations High Commissioner for Refugees." United Nations General Assembly. Twenty-Fourth Session. Official Records. Third Committee, 1729th Meeting. December 8, 1969. New York. 465–67.

———. Commentary on "AGENDA ITEM 12: Reports of the Economic and Social Council (UNICEF)." United Nations General Assembly. Twenty-Fourth Session. Official Records. Third Committee. 1721st Meeting. December 2, 1969. New York. 409–13.

———. Commentary on "AGENDA ITEM 48: Draft Declaration on Social Progress and Development." United Nations General Assembly. Twenty-Fourth Session. Official Records. Third Committee. 1664th Meeting. October 10, 1969. New York. 93–95.

———. Commentary on "AGENDA ITEM 47: General Review of the Programmes and Activities in the Economic, Social, Technical Cooperation and Related Fields of the United Nations . . ." United Nations General Assembly. Twenty-Fourth Session. Official Records. Third Committee. 1834th Meeting. December 15, 1969. New York. 6–7.

———. Commentary on "AGENDA ITEM 21: Problems of the Human Environment." United Nations General Assembly. Twenty-Fourth Session. Official Records. Third Committee. 1278th Meeting. November 12, 1969. New York. 219–23.

———. "Don't Sit Home and Be Afraid." *McCall's* 100 (February 1973): 82, 114–16.

———. "Chief of Protocol Inauguration Speech." July 20, 1976. Accessed October 12, 2012. www.youtube.com/watch?v=x4Yfm0pdtDk.

———. "Prague Diary." *McCall's Magazine* (January 1969): 75–76, 91, 93–94.

———. "Sex at the Box Office." *McCall's Magazine* (January 1967): 45, 110.

Black, Susan. "Shirley Temple Black in Africa." *Ladies Home Journal* 92 (October 1975): 72+.

Bloom, David. *Lewinsky Investigation*. Interview. Performed by David Bloom.1998, Washington, DC: NBC, 1998, Television news.

Bordin, Ruth. *Frances Willard: A Biography*. Chapel Hill, NC: University of North Carolina Press, 1986.

Bourdieu, Pierre. "Conclusion: Classes and Classifications," in *Distinction: A Social Critique of the Judgment of Taste*, trans. Richard Nice. (Cambridge, MA: Harvard University Press, 1984), 466–84.

———. *Outline of a Theory of Practice*, trans. Richard Nice. Cambridge, UK: Cambridge University Press, 1977.

———. *Practical Reason*. Stanford: Stanford University Press, 1998.

Bourdon, Jerome. "Some Sense of Time." *History and Memory* 15, no. 2 (2003): 31.

Boyle, Margery O'Rourke. "A Likely Story: The Autobiographical as Epideictic." *Journal of the American Academy of Religion* 57 (1898): 23–51. JSTOR.

Braidoitti, Rosi. *Transpositions: On Nomadic Ethics*. Cambridge, U.K.: Polity Press, 2006.

Brown, Mary Aline. "Organized Mother Love." *Arthur's Home Magazine*, April 1897. Pro-Quest. American Periodicals.

Brown, Mary Ellen. "Feminism and Cultural Politics: Television Audiences and Hillary Rodham Clinton." *Political Communication* 14, (1997): 15.

Brown, Roger, and James Kulik. "Flashbulb Memories." *Cognition* 5, no. 1 (1977): 13.

Brox, Brian, and Madison Cassels. "The Contemporary Effects of Vice Presidential Nominees: Sarah Palin and the 2008 Presidential Campaign." *Journal of Political Marketing*. 8 (2009): 349–63. Accessed March 30, 2012. doi: 1080/1537785090326870.

Brummer, Alex. "Ferraro Struggles with the 'Etiquette Gap,' Advisors." *The Guardian* (London). July 26, 1984. 1. Accessed March 31, 2012. www.lexisnexis.com.zeus.tarleton.edu:81/hottopics/lnacademic/.

Bumiller, Elisabeth. "The Rise of Geraldine Ferraro, Mastering the Process of Politics With a Careful Eye Ahead." *Washington Post*. April 29, 1984: K2. Accessed March 31 2012. www.lexisnexis.com.zeus.tarleton.edu:81/hottopics/lnacademic/.

Burns, Lisa M. *First Ladies and the Fourth Estate*. Dekalb, IL: Northern Illinois University Press, 2008.

Burrell, Barbara. *Public Opinion, the First Ladyship, and Hillary Rodham Clinton*. New York: Garland, 1997.

Butler, Judith. "Performative Acts and Gender Constitution: An Essay in Phenomenology and Feminist Theory." *Theatre Journal* 40, no. 4 (1988): 519–31.Accessed January 13,2013. links.jstor.org/sici?sici=0192-2882%28198812%2940%3A4%3C519%3APAAGCA%3E2.0.CO%3B2-C.

Campbell, Karlyn Kohrs. *Man Cannot Speak for Her: A Critical Study of Early Feminist Rhetoric, Vol. 1*. New York: Praeger, 1989.

———. "The Discursive Performance of Femininity: Hating Hillary." *Rhetoric and Public Affairs* 1.1 (1998): 1–19.

Campbell, Karlyn Kohrs, and Jamieson, Kathleen Hall. *Presidents Creating the Presidency: Deeds Done in Words*. Chicago: University of Chicago Press, 2008.

Carey, James. "The Problem of Journalism History." *Journalism History* 1, no. 1 (Spring 1974): 3–5.

———. "The Struggle against Forgetting." Edited by Columbia University Graduate School of Journalism. New York, 1995.

Carroll, Joseph. "Dissecting the New Hampshire Primary Vote." *Gallup*, January 7, 2008. Accessed April 20, 2012. www.gallup.com/poll/103621/Dissecting-New-Hampshire-Primary-Vote.aspx.

Carroll, Susan. "Reflections on Gender and Hillary Clinton's Presidential Campaign: The Good, the Bad, and the Misogynic." *Politics and Gender* 5 (2009): 1–20.

Carroll, Susan J. and Richard L. Fox. *Gender and Elections: Shaping the Future of American Politics*. Cambridge: Cambridge University Press, 2006.

Carter, Michael F. "The Ritual Functions of Epideictic Rhetoric: The Case of Socrates' Funeral Oration." *Rhetorica* 9 (1991): 209–32. JSTOR.

Cary, Mary Kate. "John Boehner, Sarah Palin, and When Crying is OK in Politics." *U.S. News and World Report* (Dec 22, 2010): 1. Accessed November 9, 2010. search.proquest.com.jproxy.lib.ecu.edu/docview/845041126?accountid=10639.

Chung, Connie. *State of the First Lady/Health Care*. Interview. Performed by Connie Chung. 1995, New York: CBS, television.

Cicero. *On the Ideal Orator* (*De Oratore*). Translated by James M. May and Jakob Wisse. New York: Oxford University Press, 2001.

Clark, Dean. "Getting Paid for Parenting," *U.S. News and World Report*, March 18, 2007. Accessed February 8, 2013. www.usnews.com/usnews/news/articles/070318/26childcare.htm.

Cleveland, Grover. "Woman's Mission and Woman's Clubs." *Ladies Home Journal*, May 1905. ProQuest. American Periodicals.

Clinton, Hillary Rodham. *Living History*. New York: Simon and Schuster, 2003.

———. *Remarks by First Lady Hillary Rodham Clinton: United Nations Fourth World Conference on Women, September 5–6, 1995, China.* Washington: Government Printing Office, 1995.

———. "Women's Rights Are Human Rights." *American Rhetoric* video. www.americanrhetoric.com/speeches/hillaryclintonbeijingspeech.htm.

"Clinton's Many Choices Hinge on the Biggest One." New York Times Service. *Greensboro News and Record*, December 9, 2012, A10.

Coates, Ta-Nehisi. "Is Obama Black Enough?" *Time*, February 1, 2007, Accessed February 8, 2013. www.time.com/time/nation/article/0,8599,1584736,00.html.

Cohen, Jeffrey E. "The Polls: Public Favorability toward the First Lady, 1993–1999." *Presidential Studies Quarterly* 30, no. 3 (2000): 575–85.

Connell, R. W. "The State, Gender, and Sexual Politics: Theory and Appraisal." *Theory and Society* 19 (October 1990): 519. Accessed January 13, 2008. www.jstor.org/stable/657562.

Council of Women World Leaders. Accessed October 22, 2012, www.cwwl.org.

Corley, Matt. "Laura Ingraham Mocks Meghan McCain As Being 'Plus-Sized.'" *Think Progress*. March 12, 2009. Accessed June 30, 2012. thinkprogress.org.

Couric, Katie. *Interview with Hillary Clinton.*Interview. Performed by Katie Couric. 2008,Columbus, OH: CBS, television.

Culbert, David. "Television's Visual Impact on Decision-Making in the USA, 1968: The Tet Offensive and Chicago's Democratic National Convention." *Journal of Contemporary History* 33 (1998): 419–49.

Curtis, Heather D. "'God is Not Affected by the Depression:' Pentecostal Missions During the 1930s." *Church History* 80, no. 3 (2011): 579–89.

Delahunty, Andrew. *Goldenballs and the Iron Lady: A Little Book of Nicknames*. New York: Oxford University Press, 2004.

De Landtsheer, Christ'l. "Introduction to the Study of Political Discourse." Edited by Ofer Feldman and Christ'l De Landtsheer. In *Politically Speaking: A Worldwide Examination of Language Used in the Public Sphere*. Westport, CT: Praeger, 1998.

Duerst-Lahti, Georgia. "Reconceiving Theories of Power: Consequences of Masculinism in the Executive Branch." In *Gendering American Politics. Perspectives from the Literature*, edited by Karen O'Connor, Sarah Brewer, and Michael Fisher, 307–14. New York: Pearson, 2006.

———. "Masculinity on the Campaign Trail." *Rethinking Madame President. In Are We Ready for a Woman in the White House?*, edited by Lori Cox Han and Caroline Heldman, 87–112. Boulder: Lynne Rienner Publications, 2007.

Dochuk, Darren. *From Bible Belt to Sunbelt: Plain Folk Religion, Grassroots Politics, and the Rise of Evangelical Conservatism*. New York: Norton, 2010.

Douglas, Linda. *Lewinsky Investigation.* News Package. Performed by Linda Douglas. 1998, Washington, DC: ABC, television news.

Dow, Bonnie. "Feminism, Miss America, and Media Mythology." *Rhetoric and Public Affairs* 6, no. 1 (2003): 127–49.

duCille, Anne. "The Shirley Temple of My Familiar." *Transition* 73 (1997): 10–32.

Durkheim, Emile. *Elementary Forms of the Religious Life*. Translated by J.W. Swain. New York: Free Press, 1971. 1912.

Edelman, Murray J. *Constructing the Political Spectacle*. Chicago: University of Chicago Press, 1988.

Edgerton, Gary R., and Peter C. Rollins. *Television Histories: Shaping Collective Memory in the Media Age.* Lexington: University of Kentucky Press, 2001.

Edy, Jill. "Journalistic Uses of Collective Memory." *Journal of Communication* 49, no. 2 (1999): 14.

Eidenmuller, Michael E. "Geraldine Ferraro." *American Rhetoric*. Accessed October 28, 2008. www.americanrhetoric.com.

———. "Sarah Palin." *American Rhetoric.* Accessed December 2, 2008. www.americanrhetoric.com.

Eisenstein, Zillah. "Women's Publics and the Search for New Democracies." *Feminist Review* 57 (1997): 140–67.

Enloe, Cynthia. *The Curious Feminist: Searching for Women in a New Age of Empire*. Berkeley: University of California Press, 2004.

Enos, Richard Leo. *The Literate Mode of Cicero's Legal Rhetoric*. Carbondale: Southern Illinois University Press, 1988.

Epstein, Daniel M. *Sister Aimee: The Life of Aimee Semple McPherson*. Orlando: Harcourt Brace and Company, 1993.

Erickson, Keith V., and Stephanie Thomson. "Seduction Theory and the Recovery of Feminine Aesthetics: Implications for Rhetorical Criticism." *Communication Quarterly* 52.3 (2004): 300–19.

"Facts on Women in Congress 2011." *Center for American Women and Politics*. 2013. Accessed January 31, 2013. www.cawp.rutgers.edu/fast_facts/levels_of_office/Congress-CurrentFacts.php.

Fahnestock, Jeanne. *Rhetorical Figures in Science*. New York: Oxford University Press, 1999.

Falk, Erica. *Women for President*. Champaign, IL: University of Illinois Press, 2008.

"Fashion, Fact, and Fancy." *Godey's Magazine*, April 1896. ProQuest. American Periodicals.

Fentriss, James, and Chris Wickham. *Social Memory*.Oxford: Blackwell 1992.

Ferguson, Michaele. "'W' Stands for Women: Feminism and Security Rhetoric in the Post-9/11 Bush Administration." *Politics and Gender* 1 (March 2005): 9–38. Accessed May 1, 2012. dx.doi.org/10.1017/S1743923X0505014.

Ferraro, Geraldine. *Changing History: Women, Power, and Politics*. 2nd ed. Kingston, Moyer Bell Ltd., 1998.

———. *Concession Speech Following the 1984 Presidential Election*. Michigan State University: Vincent Voice Library. CNN TV broadcast recording, 1984. Wav Open-Reel. CD.

———. *Ferraro: My Story*. Evanston: Northwestern University Press, 2004.

"Fine Figures." *The McCook Tribune*, September 12, 1898. Library of Congress. Chronicling America.

Finkenauer, Catrin, Olivier Luminet, Lydia Gisle, Abdessadek El-Ahmadi, Martial Van der Linden, and Pierre Philpott. "Flashbulb Memories and the Underlying Mechanisms of Their Formation: Toward an Emotional-Integrative Model." *Memory and Cognition* 26, no. 3 (1998): 15.

Foss, Sonja K. and Karen A. Foss. "Constricted and Constructed Potentiality: An Inquiry into Paradigms of Change." *Western Journal of Communication* 75.2 (2011): 205–38.

———. "Our Journey to Repowered Feminism: Expanding the Feminist Toolbox." *Women's Studies in Communication* 32.1 (Spring 2009): 36–62.

Foust, Christina. "A Return to Feminine Public Virtue: Judge Judy and the Myth of the Tough Mother." *Women's Studies in Communication*. September 2004. Accessed February 10. 2004. www.questia.com.

"Frances E. Willard and Her Work: The Outlook." *Current Literature*, April 1898. ProQuest. American Periodicals. Chronicling America.

Frankovic, Kathleen A. "The 1984 Election: The Irrelevance of the Campaign." *American Political Science Association* 18.1 (1985): 39–47. Accessed February 6, 2010. www.apsanet.org/search.

Fridkin, Kim, Patrick J. Kenney, and Gina Serignese Woodall. "Bad for Men, Better for Women: The Impact of Stereotypes During Negative Campaigns." *Political Behavior* 31 (2009): 53–77.

Gifford, Carolyn De Swarte, and Amy R. Slagell, eds. *Let Something Good Be Said: Speeches and Writings of Frances E. Willard*. Urbana, IL: University of Illinois Press, 2007.

Gitlin, Todd. "Spotlights and Shadows: Television and the Culture of Politics." *College English* 38, no. 8 (April 1977): 789–801.

Glaser, B. *Emergence vs. Forcing: Basics of Grounded Theory Analysis*. Mill Valley, CA: Sociology Press, 1992.

Glenn, Cheryl. *Rhetoric Retold: Regendering the Tradition from Antiquity Through the Renaissance*. Carbondale: Southern Illinois University Press, 1997.

Glenn, Evelyn Nakano. *Unequal Freedom*. Cambridge: Harvard University Press, 2002.

Goleman, Daniel. *Emotional Intelligence*. New York: Bantam Books, 1995.

Goodman, Ellen. "Ferraro's First." *Washington Post*. July 19, 1984: A21. Accessed April 1, 2012. www.lexisnexis.com.zeus.tarleton.edu:81/hottopics/lnacademic/.

Greenstein, Fred I. "Re: Interview." *Message to the author*. February 17, 2010. E-mail.

———. *The Presidential Difference: Leadership Style from FDR to George W. Bush.* New Jersey: Princeton University Press, 2004.

Grewal, Inderpal. *Transnational America: Feminisms, Diasporas, Neoliberalisms.* Durham, NC: Duke University Press, 2005.

Grewal, Inderpal and Caren Kaplan, eds., *Scattered Hegemonies: Postmodernity and Transnational Feminist Practices*. Minneapolis: University of Minnesota Press, 1994.

Griffin, Cindy L. and Sonja K. Foss. "Beyond Persuasion: A Proposal for an Invitational Rhetoric." *Communication Monographs* 62 (March 1995): 2–18.

Gutgold, Nichola. "Girls Need to See Women Rise to Political Power." *Women's Media Center*, Accessed December 12, 2010. www.womensmediacenter.com/blog/entry/girls-need-to-see-women-rise-to-political-power.

Halbwachs, Maurice. *Les Cadres Sociaux Des Memoires [On Collective Memory]*. Translated by Lewis Coser. 1952. 1992.

Halloran, S. Michael. "Aristotle's Concept of *Ethos*, or If Not His Somebody Else's." *Rhetoric Review* 1, no. 1 (1982): 58–63.

Haskins, Ekaterina. "Endoxa, Epistemological Optimism, and Aristotle's Rhetorical Project." *Philosophy and Rhetoric* 37, no. 1 (2004): 1–20.

Heflick, Nathan and Jamie L. Goldenberg. "Sarah Palin, a Nation Object(ifie)s: The Role of Appearance Focus in the 2008 U. S. Presidential Election." *Sex Roles*. 65 (2011): 149– 55. Accessed March 15, 2012. doi: 10.1007/s11199-010-9901-4.

Herndl, Carl G. and Adela C. Licona. "Shifting Agency: Agency, *Kairos*, and the Possibilities of Social Action." *The Cultural Turn: Perspectives on Communicative Practices in Workplaces and Professions*, ed. Mark Zachery and Charlotte Thralls. New York: Baywood Publishing, 2007. 133–54.

Hesford, Wendy S., and Wendy Kozol. *Just Advocacy? Women's Human Rights, Transnational Feminisms, and the Politics of Representation.* New Brunswick: Rutgers University Press, 2005.

Hollinger, David. "Obama, the Instability of Color Lines, and the Promise of a Postethnic Future," *Callaloo,* 31 (2008): 1033–37.

Hollitz, John. *Contending Voices, Volume II: Since 1865.* 3rd ed. New York: Cengage, 2010.

Hoskins, Andrew. "An Introduction to Media and Collective Memory." Swansea, Wales: *Center for Media History*, 2001.

Huglen, Mark E., and Bernard L. Brock. "Burke, Clinton, and the Global/Local Community." *North Dakota Journal of Speech and Theatre* 16 (2003): 19–29.

Hulu.com. "Bait and Tackle," Accessed on January 2012, www.hulu.com.

———. "McCain QVC Cold Open." Accessed Feb. 9, 2012, www.hulu.com.

———. "Palin/Hillary Cold Open." Accessed Feb.11, 2012. www.hulu.com/#!watch/34465#i0,p0.

Hume, Janice. "Press, Published History and Regional Lore: Shaping the Public Memory of a Revolutionary War Heroine." *Journalism History* 30, no. 4 (2005): 9.

"In Memory of Miss Willard." *Kansas City Journal*, February 25, 1898. Library of Congress. Chronicling America.

International Women's Health Coalition. "January 2005 Gala." Accessed February 19, 2013. www.iwhc.org/index.php?option=com_content&task=view&id=2119&Itemid=603.

Iyengar, Shanto, and Donald R. Kinder. *News That Matters: Television and American Opinion.* Chicago: Chicago University Press, 1987.

Iyengar, Shanto, Nicholas A. Valenino, Stephen Ansolabehere, and Adam F. Simon. "Running as a Woman: Gender Stereotyping in Political Campaigns." In *Women, Media, and Politics*, edited by Pippa Norris, 77–98. New York: Oxford University Press, 1997.

Jagan-Brancier, Nadira. *Cheddi Jagan Research Centre*. www.jagan.org. Accessed February 8, 2013.

Jamieson, Kathleen. *Beyond the Double Bind: Women and Leadership*. Oxford Press, 1995.

Jarratt, Susan C. "Beside Ourselves: Rhetoric and Representation in Postcolonial Feminist Writing." *JAC* 18.1 (1998): 57–75.

Jarvis, Jeff. "Picks and Pans Review: Saturday Night Live." *People*. 22 no.17 (Oct. 22, 1984): 1. Accessed March 31, 2012. www.people.com/people/archive/article/02008891900.html.

Jennings, C. Robert. "Her Eyes are Still Dancing." *Saturday Evening Post* 238, no.11 (June 5, 1965): 93–97.

Jensen, Jane S. *Women Political Leaders: Breaking the Highest Glass Ceiling*. New York: Palgrave Macmillan, 2008.

Joseph, Suad. "Women Between Nation and State in Lebanon," in *Between Woman and Nation: Nationalisms, Transnational Feminisms, and the State*. Ed. Caren Kaplan et al.,162–81. Durham, NC: Duke University Press, 1999.

Kachun, Mitch. "Cities of the Dead: Contesting the Memory of the Civil War in the South 1865–1914." *Alabama Review* 58, no. 3 (2005): 1.

Kammen, Michael. "Frames of Remembrance: The Dynamics of Collective Memory by Iwona Irwin-Zarecka." *History and Theory* 34, no. 3 (1995): 16.

Kansteiner, Wulf. "Finding Meaning in Memory: A Methodological Critique of Collective Memory Studies." *History and Theory* 41, no. 2 (2002): 18.

Kaplan, Caren. "Hillary Rodham Clinton's Orient: Cosmopolitan Travel and Global Feminist Subjects." *Meridians* 2.1 (2001): 219–40.

Kaplan, Caren, Norma Alarcon, and Minoo Moallem, eds. *Between Woman and Nation: Nationalisms, Transnational Feminisms, and the State*. Durham, NC: Duke University Press, 1999.

Kasson, John F. "Shirley Temple's Paradoxical Smile." *American Art* 25, no.3 (2011): 16–19.

Kelley, Colleen Elizabeth. *The Rhetoric of First Lady Hillary Rodham Clinton: Crisis Management Discourse*. Westport: Praeger, 2001.

Kennedy, George A. *A New History of Classical Rhetoric*. Princeton: Princeton University Press, 1994.

Kennedy-Minott, Rodney. *The Sinking of the Lollipop: Shirley Temple Vs. Pete McCloskey*. Diablo Press, 1968.

Kitch, Carolyn. "Anniversary Journalism, Collective Memory, and the Cultural Authority to Tell the Story of the American Past." *Journal of Popular Culture* 36, no. 1 (2002): 23.

Kornblut, Anne E. *Notes from the Cracked Ceiling*. New York: Crown Publishers, 2009.

Lanham, Richard A. *A Handlist of Rhetorical Terms*. Los Angeles: University of California Press, 1991.

Larson, Jeff, and Omar Lizardo. "Generations, Identities and the Collective Memory of Che Guevara." *Sociological Forum* 22, no. 4 (2007): 26.

Lawless, Jennifer. "Sexism and Gender Bias in Election 2008: A More Complex Path for Women in Politics." *Politics and Gender* 5, no. 1 (2009): 70–81.

Lawless, Jennifer and Richard Fox. "Why Are Women Still Not Running for Public Office?" *Governance Studies. Brookings Institute*. 2008. 1–20. Accessed May 12, 2012. www.brookings.edu/~/media/research/files/papers/2008/5/women%20lawless%20fox/05_women_lawless_fox.pdf.

Lawrence, Regina, and Melody Rose. *Hillary Clinton's Race for the White House*. Boulder: Lynne Reiner, 2010.

Leff, Michael. "Tradition and Agency in Humanistic Rhetoric." *Philosophy and Rhetoric* 36.2 (2003): 135–47.

Leonard, Mary. "Saturday Diary: Storming the Barricades with Gerry Ferraro." *Pittsburgh Post-Gazette.com*. April 2, 2011. Accessed on April 8, 2012. www.post-gazette.com.

Libit, Daniel. "Crashing the Republican Party." *Politico*. April 11, 2009. www.politico.com.

Lopez, Juan Carlos, Willie Lora, Bill Schneider, Xuan Thai, and Jessica Yellin. "Clinton Claims Victory in Puerto Rico." *CNN Politics.Com* (2008). Accessed November 17, 2009, www.cnn.com/2008/POLITICS/06/01/puerto.rico/.

Lucas, Stephen E., and Martin J. Medhurst. "Top 100 Speeches." *American Rhetoric*. www.americanrhetoric.com.

Lucas, Stephen E. "George Washington and the Rhetoric of Presidential Leadership." In *The Presidency and Rhetorical Leadership*, edited by Leroy G. Dorsey, 44–72. College Station: Texas A and M University Press, 2002.

———. *Words of a Century: The Top 100 American Speeches, 1900–1999*. New York: Oxford University Press, 2009.

Lyon, Arabella, and Banu Özel. "On the Politics of Writing Transnational Rhetoric: Possibilities and Pitfalls." In *Feminist Rhetorical Resilience*, edited by Elizabeth A. Flynn, Patricia Sotirin, and Ann Brady, 54–56. Logan: Utah State University Press, 2012.

Maddow, Rachel. "The Rachel Maddow Show, Transcript." *Lexis-Nexis*. March 11, 2009. Accessed July 2, 2012. www.lexisnexis.com.

Maddux, Kristy. "The Feminized Gospel: Aimee Semple McPherson and the Gendered Performance of Christianity." *Women's Studies in Communication* 35, no. 1 (2012): 42–67.

———. "The Foursquare Gospel of Aimee Semple McPherson." *Rhetoric and Public Affairs* 14, no. 2 (2011): 291–326.

Manning, Mandy R. "The Rhetoric of Equality: Hillary Rodham Clinton's Redefinition of the Female Politician." *Texas Speech Communication Journal* 30, no.2 (2006): 109–20.

Marilley, Suzanne M. "Frances Willard and the Feminism of Fear." *Feminist Studies* 19 (Spring 1993): 123–46. JSTOR.

Massaquoi, Hans J. "Ghana's Love Affair with Shirley Temple Black." *Ebony* 31 (March 1976): 114–116, 123.

Matviko, John. "Television Satire and the Presidency: The Case of *Saturday Night Live*," In *Hollywood's White House: The American Presidency in Film and History*, edited by Peter C. Rollins and John E. O'Connor. Lexington, KY: University Press of Kentucky, 2003: 333–348.

McCain, Meghan. "What I Learned From the Democrats: The Mistakes Liberals like Harry Reid and Nancy Pelosi are Making Can Teach Republicans How to Regain Power—and How to Hold Onto It." *The Daily Beast*. April 7, 2009. Accessed June 30, 2012. www.thedailybeast.com.

———. "Republican in Name Only? Try the Future of the GOP. The Following is Meghan McCain's Address to the Log Cabin Republicans Convention—A Group that Promotes Gay Issues within the GOP." *The Daily Beast*. April 18, 2009. Accessed June 30, 2012. www.thedailybeast.com.

———. "My Beef with Ann Coulter: As the Pundit Begins a Series of National Debates this Week—Including an Event with Bill Maher Last Night—Meghan McCain Says that Having Her as the Face of the Republican Party is a Recipe for Disaster." *The Daily Beast*. March 9, 2009. Accessed June 30, 2012. www.thedailybeast.com.

———. "Quit Talking About My Weight, Laura Ingraham." *The Daily Beast*. March 14, 2009. Accessed June 30, 2012. www.thedailybeast.com.

———. "Hillary and Sarah's Common Theme." *The Daily Beast*. November 8, 2009. Accessed June 30, 2012. www.thedailybeast.com.

———. "Stop the Fat Jokes." *The Daily Beast*. October 14, 2009. Accessed June 30, 2012. www.thedailybeast.com.

———. "Meghan McCain's 7 Tips for Republican Hopefuls: 2012 Election." *The Daily Beast*. June 20, 2011. Accessed June 30, 2012. www.thedailybeast.com.

———. "Shut Up About My Body Glenn Beck." *The Daily Beast*. May 12, 2011. Accessed June 30, 2012. www.thedailybeast.com.

———. "Rick Perry Is George W. Bush 2.0." *The Daily Beast*. September 16, 2011. Accessed June 30, 2012. www.thedailybeast.com.

———. "My Day at Occupy Wall Street." *The Daily Beast*. October 24, 2011. www.thedailybeast.com.

———. "Meghan McCain: Is It Too Late for Mitt Romney and Republicans?" *The Daily Beast*. April 6, 2012. Accessed June 30, 2012. www.thedailybeast.com.

———. "Meghan McCain on Why Newt Gingrich Should Quit After Florida Primary." *The Daily Beast*. January 31, 2012. Accessed June 30, 2012. www.thedailybeast.com.

McGerr, Michael. *A Fierce Discontent: The Rise and Fall of the Progressive Movement in America, 1870–1920*. Bloomington: Indiana University Press, 2003.

McPherson, Aimee Semple. *This Is That: Personal Experiences, Sermons and Writings of Aimee Semple McPherson.* Los Angeles: Bridal Call, 1936.

McTavish, James. "The *Ethos* of the Practice of Rhetoric." *Philippiniana Sacra* XLV, no.133 (January–April 2010): 66–78.

Media Matters. "CNN's, ABC's Beck on Clinton: '[S]he's the Stereotypical Bitch.'" Last modified March 15, 2007. Accessed February 17, 2013. mediamatters.org/research/2007/03/15/cnns-abcs-beck-on-clinton-shes-the-stereotypica/138303.

———. "Limbaugh: 'We Created This Whole Concept of a Testicle Lockbox in Connection with Mrs. Clinton.'" Last modified August 26, 2005. Accessed February 17, 2013. mediamatters.org/video/2005/08/26/limbaugh-we-created-this-whole-concept-of-a-tes/133728.

Meir, Golda. *My Life.* New York: G.P. Putnam's Sons, 1975.

Merton, Robert. "The Self-Fulfilling Prophecy." *Antioch Review*, 1948. www.jstor.org.

Metacafe.com. "Saturday Night Live-Gerry Ferraro Season: 10." Accessed on Jan. 4, 2012. http:www.metacafe.com/watch/hl40034368/saturday_night_live_gerry_ferraro_season_10/.

Michael Parkinson Show. Interview with Shirley Temple. BBC One, June 1972. Accessed October 12, 2012. www.youtube.com/watch?v=M02C-aubxLY.

"Miss Willard." *The Times*, February 19, 1898. Library of Congress. Chronicling America.

Mitchell, Andrea. *Hillary Clinton's Emotional Meeting in New Hampshire.* News Package. Performed by Andrea Mitchell. 2008, Manchester, New Hampshire: NBC, television news.

———. *Ohio and Texas Primaries* (2008, Columbus, OH: NBC), television news.

———. *Super Tuesday* (2008, New York: NBC), television news.

Mitchell, Greg. "Upton Sinclair's EPIC Campaign." *The Nation*, November 1, 2010.

———. *Campaign of the Century: Upton Sinclair's Race for Governor of California and the Birth of Media Politics.* New York: Random House, 1992.

Mohanty, Chandra Talpade. *Feminism Without Borders: Decolonizing Theory, Practicing Solidarity.* Durham, NC: Duke University Press, 2003.

"Mrs. Clinton's Unwavering Words." Editorial. *New York Times,* September 6, 1995, A24.

"The National Vehicle." *The Courier*, July 20, 1895. Library of Congress. Chronicling America.

"Nation's Uncrowned Queen. Eloquent Tribute to Memory of Frances E. Willard." *Kansas City Journal*, March 21, 1898. Library of Congress. Chronicling America.

Nelson, Dana D. *National Manhood: Capitalistic Citizenship and the Imagined Fraternity of White Men.* Durham: Duke University Press, 1998.

Newport, Frank. "Post-N.H.: Explaining the Unexpected." *Gallup*, July 6, 2006. Accessed April 20, 2012. www.gallup.com/poll/103663/PostNH-Explaining-Unexpected.aspx.

Newport, Frank and Joseph Carroll. "Personal Characteristics Loom Large in Americans' Views of Hillary Clinton." *Gallup*, July 6, 2006. Accessed April 20, 2012. www.gallup.com/poll/23578/Personal-Characteristics-Loom-Large-Americans-Views-Hillary-Clinton.aspx.

Nolen, William. "What Men Don't Understand About Premenstrual Tension." *McCall's* 100 (February 1973): 12.

Norris, Michelle. "Are U.S. Voters Ready to Elect a Woman President?" 12 min., 21 sec.; audio file; from *National Public Radio*, www.npr.org/templates/story/story.php?storyId=6648890 (accessed February 8, 2013).

Nussbaum, Martha C. "Objectification." *Philosophy and Public Affairs* 24, no. 4 (1995): 249–91.

"NYT Election Guide 2008 New Hampshire: Profile of the New Hampshire Primary Voters." *New York Times*, January 8, 2008. Accessed January 31, 2013. politics.nytimes.com/election-guide/2008/results/states/NH.html.

Olick, Jeffrey. "Collective Memory: The Two Cultures." In *Sociological Theory* 17, no. 3 (1999): 15.

O'Reilly, Bill. "Beck Responds to Meghan McCain's Criticism." *The O'Reilly Show Transcript, Lexis-Nexis.* May 13, 2011. Accessed June 30, 2012. www.lexisnexis.com.

Osterweil, Ara. "Reconstructing Shirley: Pedophilia and Interracial Romance in Hollywood's Age of Innocence." *Camera Obscura* 24, no.3 (2009): 1–29.

Palin, Sarah. *Going Rogue: An American Life.* New York: HarperCollins, 2009.

———. "Michele Bachmann Rally in Minneapolis: Part 2;" 5 min., 1 sec.; video; from You-tube.com Accessed February 7, 2013. www.youtube.com/watch?v=O0YeydDCWIQ.

———. "Sarah Palin Michele Bachmann in Minneapolis;" 4 min., 47 sec.; video; from You-tube.com. Accessed February 7, 2013. www.youtube.com/watch?v=oMnaRFZNn7I.

Parker, Kathleen. "Another McCain Throws Down a Challenge." *The Washington Post*, March 25, 2009. www.washingtonpost.com.

Parry-Giles, Shawn J. "Mediating Hillary Rodham Clinton: Television News Practices and Image Making in the Post-Modern Age." *Critical Studies in Mass Communication* 17, no. 2 (2000): 21.

Pateman, Carole. *The Sexual Contract*. Cambridge, U.K: Polity Press, 1988.

Pennebaker, James W., and Becky L. Banasik. "On the Creation and Maintenance of Collective Memories: History as Social Psychology." In *Collective Memory of Political Events: Social Psychology*. Mahwah, N.J. : Lawrence Erlbaum Associates, 1997.

Perlez, Jane. "Mrs. Ferraro for Vice President." *New York Times.* 23 Dec. 1983: A14. *Lexis-Nexis*. Accessed March 31, 2012. www.lexisnexis.com.zeus.tarleton.edu:81/hottopics/lnaca-demic/.

Pew Research Center for the People and the Press. Hillary Clinton's Career of Comebacks. Washington DC: Pew Research Center, 2012, Accessed February 23, 2013, www.people-press.org/2012/12/21/hillary-clintons-career-of-comebacks/.

Phillips, Peter. "The 1934-35 Red Threat and the Passage of the 1934 National Labor Relations Act." *Critical Sociology* 20, no.2 (1994): 27–50.

Poulakos, Takis. "Isocrates' Use of Doxa," *Philosophy and Rhetoric* 34, no. 1 (2001): 61–78.

Probyn, Elspeth. "Bloody Metaphors and Other Allegories of the Ordinary," In *Between Wom-an and Nation: Nationalisms, Transnational Feminisms, and the State*, Caren Kaplan et al., eds., 47–62. Durham, N.C.: Duke University Press, 1999.

Radcliffe, Donnie. "Fashioning a 'Ferraro Look;' The New Conventions, Credibility, and the Candidate's Clothes." *Washington Post.* (July 23, 1984): C1. Accessed April 1, 2012. www.lexisnexis.com.zeus.tarleton.edu:81/hottopics/lnacademic/.

Ramirez, Francisco O., Yasemin Soysal, and Suzanne Shanahan. "The Changing Logic of Political Citizenship: Cross-National Acquisition of Women's Suffrage Rights, 1890 to 1990." *American Sociological Review* 62, no. 5 (1997): 735–45.

Rather, Dan. *Lewinsky Investigation.*Interview. Performed by Dan Rather. Washington DC:CBS, 1998.Television News.

Ray, Donna E. "Aimee Semple McPherson and her Seriously Exciting Gospel." *Journal of Pentecostal Theology* 19, no. 1 (2010): 155–69.

"Real Story Behind the Iron Lady," *The Daily Telegraph*, February 26, 2006, 26.

Reeser, Todd W. *Masculinities in Theory. An Introduction*. Hoboken: John Wiley and Sons, 2011.

Rhode, Deborah L. "Media Images, Feminist Issues." *Signs* 20, no. 3 (Spring 1995): 685–710.

Richards, Rebecca S. "Cyborgs on the World Stage: Hillary Clinton and the Rhetorical Perfor-mances of Iron Ladies." *Feminist Formations.* 23, no. 1 (2011): 1–24.

———. "From Daughters of Destiny to Iron Ladies: Transnational Feminist Rhetorics and Gendered Leadership in Global Politics" (book manuscript, forthcoming).

Riedner, Rachel and Kevin Mahoney. *Democracies to Come: Rhetorical Action, Neoliberal-ism, and Communities of Resistance*. Lanham, MD: Lexington Books, 2008.

Roessner, Amber. "Remembering 'The Georgia Peach': Popular Press, Public Memory, and the Shifting Legacy of an (Anti) Hero." *Journalism History* 36, no. 2 (2010): 12.

Rosenblatt. Roger. "Mondale: This is an Exciting Choice." *Time.* 124 no. 4 (July 23, 1984): 1. *Academic Search Complete.* (57880387). Accessed 7 March 2012. ehis.ebscohost.com.zeus.tarleton.edu:81/ehost/search/advanced?sid=ae7acf92 c5ea-48dd-9896-59a57057ef5c%40sessionmgr110&vid=1&hid=116.

Rowe, Amy Carrillo. "Subject to Power—Feminism without Victims." *Women's Studies in Communication* 32, no. 1 (Spring 2009): 12–35.

Rubeck, Tracie. "Racial Harmony through Clenched Teeth: Remembering the Civil Rights Movement in Newsweek and the CBS Evening News 1990–1999." Dissertation, University of Michigan, 2006.

Ruiter, Robert A. C., Charles Abraham, and Gerjo Kok. "Scary Warnings and Rational Precautions: A Review of the Psychology of Fear Appeals." *Psychology and Health* 16 (2001): 613–30. Accessed February 13, 2013. www.tandfonline.com/doi/abs/10.1080/08870440108405863#.UZKTUis6Vk0.

Ryan, Michael. "As Ambassador to Prague, Shirley Temple Black Watches a Rebirth of Freedom." *People* 33, no.1 (January 8, 1990). Accessed September 26, 2012. www.people.com/people/archive/article/0,,20116493,00.html

Safire, William. "On Language: Goodbye Sex, Hello, Gender." *New York Times*. (Aug. 5, 1984): 8. Accessed 31 Mar. 2012. www.lexisnexis.com.zeus.tarleton.edu:81/hottopics/lnacademic/.

Sandoval, Chela. *Methodology of the Oppressed*. Minneapolis: University of Minnesota Press, 2000.

Sanchez, Leslie. *You've Come a Long Way, Maybe: Sarah, Michelle, Hillary, and the Shaping of the New American Woman*. New York: Palgrave Macmillan, 2009.

Sawyer, Diane. *Diane Sawyer Interviews Hillary Clinton*. Interview. Performed by Diane Sawyer. (New York: ABC, 2008), television news.

Sawyer, Diane, and Roberts, Robin. "Does Size Really Matter? The Great Weight Debate. Good Morning America." *ABC News Transcript, Lexis-Nexis*. March 17, 2009. www.lexisnexis.com.

Schillinger, Liesl. "Daughter of John McCain Is a Rebel." *New York Times*, September 10, 2010. www.nytimes.com.

Schudson, Michael. *The Power of News. Vol. 4*, Cambridge, MA: Harvard University Press, 1995.

Schwartz, Barry. "Collective Memory and History: How Abraham Lincoln Became a Symbol ofRacial Equality." *The Sociological Quarterly* 38, no. 3 (1997): 27.

———. "Iconography and Collective Memory: Lincoln's Image in the American Mind." *The Sociological Quarterly* 32, no. 3 (1991): 18.

———. "Social Change and Collective Memory." *American Sociological Review* 56 (1991).

Schwoch, James. "Television Today and Tomorrow: It Won't Be What You Think." *Historical Journal of Film, Radio and Television* 16, no. 2 (June 6, 1996): 301–02. *Social Perspectives*, edited by James W. Pennebaker, Dario Paez and Bernard Rime. Mahwah, New Jersey: Lawrence Erlbaum, 1997.

Scott, Joan W. *Gender and the Politics of History*. New York: Columbia University Press, 1999.

Seelye, Katharine. "Clinton 'Misspoke' About Bosnia Trip, Campaign Says," *New York Times*, March 24, 2008. Accessed April 20, 2012. thecaucus.blogs.nytimes.com/2008/03/24/clinton-misspoke-about-bosnia-trip-campaign-says/.

Seelye, Katharine and Jeff Zeleny. "Clinton Questions Role of Obama in a Crisis." *New York Times*, March 1, 2008. Accessed April 20, 2012. www.nytimes.com/2008/03/01/us/politics/01campaign.html?_r=1.

Shales, Tom and James Andrew Miller. *Live from New York: An Uncensored History of Saturday Night Live*. Boston: Little, Brown and Co., 2002.

Sheard, Cynthia Miecznikowski. "The Public Value of Epideictic Rhetoric." *College English* 58 (1996): 765–94. JSTOR.

Sheckels, Theodora F. *Cracked but Not Shattered: Hillary Rodham Clinton's Unsuccessful Campaign for the Presidency*. Plymouth, England: Lexington Books, 2009.

Sheehy, Gail. *Hillary's Choice*. New York: Random House, 1999.

"Shirley Black Discusses Issues." *St. Petersburg Times*, March 11, 1968.

"Shirley Black Offered Job as Protocol Chief." *The Miami News*, May 31, 1976.

"Shirley Black in Line for Post." *The Miami News*, June 9, 1976.

Shoemaker, Pamela, and Steven Reese. *Mediating the Message: Theories of Influences on Mass Media Content*. 2nd ed. Longman: Longman, 1996.

Shuman, Howard, Barry Schwartz, and Hannah D'Arcy. "Elite Revisionist and Popular Beliefs: Christopher Columbus, Hero or Villain?." *Public Opinion Quarterly* 69, no. 1 (2005): 27.

Sinclair, Upton. "Letter to Norman Thomas." *Spartacus Educational*. Accessed December 27, 2012. www.spartacus.schoolnet.co.uk.

———. *End Poverty in California: The EPIC Movement. Virtual Museum of the City of San Francisco*. Accessed January 31, 2012. www.sfmuseum.org/hist/sinclair.html.

———. "An Evangelist Drowns." Accessed February 1, 2013. xroads.virginia.edu/~ug00/robertson/asm/sinclair.html.

Smith, Robert A. *A Social History of the Bicycle: Its Early Life and Times in America*. New York: American Heritage Press, 1972.

SNL Archives. "Geraldine Ferraro." Accessed April 4 2012, snl.jt.org/imp.php?i=457.

———. "Sarah Palin." *SNL Archives*. "Sarah Palin." Accessed April 4, 2012, snl.jt.org/imp.php?i=2673.

Snow, Kate. *Hillary Clinton's Emotional Meeting in New Hampshire.* News Package. Performed by Kate Snow. Manchester, New Hampshire: ABC, 2008.Television News.

Spivak, Gayatri Chakravorty. "Can the Subaltern Speak?" In *Marxism and the Interpretation of Culture*, edited by Cary Nelson and Lawrence Grossberg, 271–313. Urbana: University of Illinois Press, 1988.

———. *Outside in the Teaching Machine*. New York: Routledge, 1993.

———. "Righting Wrongs—2002: Accessing Democracy among the Aboriginals." In *Other Asias*, 14–57. Malden: Blackwell Publishing, 2008.

Starr, Kevin. *Endangered Dreams: The Great Depression in California*. New York: Oxford University Press, 1996.

Stein, Judith. *Pivotal Decade: How the United States Traded Factories for Finance in the Seventies*. New Haven: Yale University Press, 2010.

Stein, Karen F. "The Cleavage Commotion: How the Press Covered Senator Clinton's Campaign," In *Cracked but Not Shattered: Hillary Rodham Clinton's Unsuccessful Campaign for the Presidency*, edited by Theodore F. Heckles. Lanaham, MD: Lexington Books, 2009: 125–47.

Steinem, Gloria. "Women Are Never Front-Runners." *New York Times*, January 8, 2008. Accessed June 30, 2012. www.nytimes.com.

Stevens, Jacqueline. *Reproducing the State*. Princeton: Princeton University Press, 1999.

Stolberg, Sheryl Gay. "In Defining Obama, Misperceptions Stick," *The New York Times*, August 18, 2010. Accessed February 8, 2013. www.nytimes.com/2010/08/19/us/politics/19memo.html.

Sullivan, Dale L. "The Ethos of Epideictic Encounter." *Philosophy and Rhetoric* 26 (1993): 113–33. JSTOR.

Sullivan, Meg. "The GOP has a Feminine Face, UCLA Study Finds." *UCLA Newsroom*. Accessed September 27, 2012. newsroom.ucla.edu.

Sutton, Matthew Avery. *Aimee Semple McPherson and the Resurrection of Christian America*. Cambridge: Harvard University Press, 2007.

———. "Clutching to 'Christian' America: Aimee Semple McPherson, the Great Depression, and the Origins of Pentecostal Political Activism." *Journal of Policy History* 17, no. 3 (2005): 308–38.

Swint, Kerwin. *Mudslingers: The Twenty-Five Dirtiest Political Campaigns of All Time*. New York: Union Square Press, 2008.

Tan, Amy. "Two Kinds." In *The Joy Luck Club*. New York: Penguin Book, 1989. 132–48.

Tanabe, Karin. "Newt Discusses Meghan McCain." *Politico*. October 27, 2011. Accessed June 30, 2012. www.politico.com.

Tannen, Deborah. "Fighting for Our Lives." In *The Argument Culture*. New York: Ballantine Books, 1999. 1–26.

———. *Talking Voices: Repetition, Dialogue, and Imagery in Conversational Discourse.* 2nd ed. New York: Cambridge UP, 2007.

Taylor, Paul S. "The San Francisco General Strike." *Pacific Affairs* 7, no. 3 (1934): 271–78.

"Temperance Topics." *Natchitoches Populist*, June 10, 1898. Library of Congress. Chronicling America.

"The States: Governors." *Time*, November 12, 1934.

"The State of the News Media." *Project for Excellence in Journalism.* Washington DC: Pew Research Center, 2007, www. stateofthemedia.org/2007.

Time. "Untitled." 124 no. 4, (July 23, 1984): 1. March 5, 2012. ehis.ebscohost.com.zeus.tarleton.edu:81/ehost/search/advanced?sid=ae7acf92- c5ea-48dd-9896-59a57057ef5c%40sessionmgr110&vid=1&hid=116.

Tomlinson, Marian D. "Frances E. Willard Centenary." *ALA Bulletin* 33.7 (July 1939): 518. JSTOR.

"Topics of the Time." *The Century*, July 1895. Cornell University Library. The Making of America.

Tuchman, Gaye. "Women's Depiction by the Mass Media." *Signs* 4, no. 3 (Spring 1979): 528–42.

Tucker-McLaughlin, Mary, and Kenneth Campbell. "A Grounded Theory Analysis: Hillary Clinton Represented as Innovator and Voiceless in TV News." *Electronic News* 6, no. 1 (2012): 16.

Tyler, Patrick E. "Hillary Clinton, in China, Details Abuse of Women." *New York Times*, 6 September 1995, A1.

"Uppie's Goddess." Review of *Southern Belle*, by Mary Craig Sinclair. *Time*, November 18, 1957.

Van Engen, Marloes L., Rien van der Leeden, and Tineke M. Willemsen. "Gender, Context and Leadership Styles: A Field Study." *Journal of Occupational and Organizational Psychology*. 74 (2001): 581–98.

Vaughn, Steven. *Holding Fast the Inner Lines: Democracy, Nationalism, and the Committee on Public Information*. Chapel Hill: University of North Carolina Press, 1980.

Vickers, Brian. *In Defense of Rhetoric*. Oxford: Clarendon Press, 1988.

Vitanza, Victor J. *Negation, Subjectivity, and the History of Rhetoric.* Albany: State University of New York Press, 1997.

Walker, Jeffrey. "Aristotle's Lyric: Re-Imagining the Rhetoric of Epideictic Song." *College English* 51 (1989): 5–28. JSTOR.

———. *Rhetoric and Poetics in Antiquity*. Oxford: Oxford University Press, 2000.

Watson, Molly. "It's My Political Party and I'll Cry If I Want To." *The Times*, January 9, 2008. Accessed July 1, 2012. journalisted.com.

Whitney, Craig. "Prague Journal; Shirley Temple Black Unpacks a Bag of Memories." *The New York Times*, September 11, 1989.

Willard, Frances E. "The Dawn of Woman's Day." In *Let Something Good Be Said: Speeches and Writings of Frances E. Willard*, edited by Carolyn De Swarte Gifford and Amy R. Slagell, 125–37. Urbana, IL: University of Illinois Press, 2007.

———. *What Frances E. Willard Said*, edited by Anna A. Gordon. Chicago: Fleming H. Revell Co., 1905.

———. *A Wheel within a Wheel. How I Learned to Ride the Bicycle with Some Reflections by the Way*. New York: Fleming H. Revell Co., 1895.

Wilson, Marie C. *Closing the Leadership Gap: Why Women Can and Must Help Run the World*. New York: Viking, 2004.

Wittig, Monique. *The Straight Mind and Other Essays*. Boston: Beacon Press, 1992.

Wolf, Naomi. *The Beauty Myth*. New York: Doubleday, 1991.

Yagoda, Ben. *Memoir: A History*. New York: Riverhead Books, 2009.

Young, Dannagal. "Political Entertainment and the Press' Construction of Sarah Feylin." *Popular Communication*. 9 no. 4 (October–December 2011): 251–65. Accessed March 29, 2012. doi: 10.1080/15405702.2011.605314.

Young, Iris Marion. "Feminist Reactions to the Contemporary Security Regime." *Hypatia* 18 (Winter 2003): 223–31. Accessed May 1, 2012.

YouTube. "Clinton Wells Up: 'This Is Very Personal.'" Last modified January 07, 2008. Accessed February 13, 2013. www.youtube.com/watch?v=pl-W3IXRTHU.

———. "Hillary Clinton 3 AM Ad." Last modified May 15, 2008. Accessed February 13, 2013. www.youtube.com/watch?v=7yr7odFUARg.

Yuval-Davis, Nira. *Gender and Nation*. London: Sage Publications, 1997.

Zelizer, Barbie. *Covering the Body: The Kennedy Assassination, the Media, and the Shaping of Collective Memory*. Chicago: University of Chicago Press, 1992.

Zerubavel, E. *Time Maps: Collective Memory and the Social Shape of the Past*. Chicago: University of Chicago, 2003.

Žižek, Slavov. *The Sublime Object of Ideology*, London: Verso, 1989.

Index

Black, Shirley Temple: ambassador to Ghana, 31–32, 37, 42, 43–44; ambassador to Czechoslovakia, 31, 34; breast cancer, 35, 36, 37, 39; chief of protocol, 31–32, 43; Vietnam, 39

Clinton, Hillary Rodham: 2008 presidential campaign, 49, 109, 176, 178, 193; appearance, 112, 114, 115, 118, 119; first lady, x–xi, 153–154, 156, 171n1, 171n11, 171n13, 178, 179, 182, 183–184, 184–185, 186, 186–187, 204; national healthcare reform, 153, 183, 184; "Women's Rights are Human Rights", 154, 156, 157, 159, 165, 166, 169, 171n1, 171n11. *See also* leadership

Ferraro, Geraldine : 1984 presidential campaign, x, 71, 85, 93, 100, 101; 1984 vice-presidential nomination acceptance speech, 73–84; 1984 vice-presidential concession speech, 85, 86n8, 88n77; appearance of, 93, 100; Mary Gross, 94, 95, 100; portrayal on *Saturday Night Live* , 91, 94, 95, 95–96, 100, 101, 102. *See also* Walter ("Fritz") Mondale; leadership

leadership: *ethos* , xi, 5–6, 15, 24, 32, 37, 44, 49, 71, 73, 82–83, 155–156, 159, 159–161, 163–164, 167, 168–169; political, ix–x, vii, viii, 5, 7, 49, 50, 58–59, 71, 73, 74–75, 75–76, 82, 85, 91, 102, 112, 128, 129, 131, 155, 157–159, 159–161, 163–165, 169–170, 175–176, 178, 179, 183, 186–187, 193, 205; global, 62, 64, 66, 155, 156, 159, 167, 168; language, ix, viii, 38, 54, 57, 58, 60, 63, 67, 69n56, 71, 72, 73, 78, 80, 81, 82, 83–84, 85, 86n1, 108, 125, 127, 131, 134, 135, 145, 147, 148, 149, 155, 157, 159, 163–164, 167, 201, 204; presidential, x, 49, 71, 72, 72–73; vice-presidential, 49, 52, 71, 72, 73, 85, 91, 96; women, ix, x, 49, 50, 51, 52–53, 60–61, 64–65, 66, 67, 71, 82, 85, 91, 102, 111, 113, 125, 128, 129, 131, 141, 149, 155, 158–159, 163–164, 166–167, 168–169, 175, 176, 177–178, 179, 183, 186, 187, 194, 195, 202, 205. *See also* Hillary Rodham Clinton; Geraldine Ferraro; Meghan McCain; Aimee Semple McPherson; Sarah Palin; Margaret Thatcher; and Frances Willard

McCain, John: 2008 presidential campaign, 51, 78–79, 85, 87n15, 91, 96, 102; Sarah Palin, 78, 78–79, 79, 85; *Saturday Live*, 98, 99; Meghan McCain,

109, 117, 118. *See also* Meghan
McCain; Sarah Palin

McCain, Meghan: appearance, 109–110,
115–116; blog, 105, 111–112, 118, 119;
Glenn Beck, 106, 107, 110, 111–112;
Ann Coulter, 108–109, 117, 120n14,
120n36; Laura Ingraham, 106, 107,
108, 109, 111, 112, 118,
120n16–120n17, 120n19; Rush
Limbaugh, 106, 107, 116. *See also*
leadership; John McCain

McPherson, Aimee Semple : 1934
California governor's race, ix, 19, 21,
26, 27, 28–29; Angelus Temple, ix, 19,
22, 23, 24, 26, 28; ministry of, ix, 19,
21, 22–23, 26–27, 28, 29. *See also*
Upton Sinclair; leadership

Mondale, Walter ("Fritz") : 1984
presidential election, 76–77, 92–93, 95,
96, 102, 203; Geraldine Ferraro, 76–78,
81, 85, 91–94, 95, 96, 101

Obama, Barack: 2008 campaign, 49,
88n77, 129, 130; 2012 campaign, 148,
149; blog, 129; Jill Biden, x, 125, 137,
142, 145, 146, 147, 148, 149; Michelle
Obama, x, 125, 131, 133, 136, 137, 142,
144, 145, 146, 147–148; political
emails, 125, 129

Palin, Sarah : 2008 presidential campaign,
vii, 74, 85, 89n81, 91, 96–97, 102; 2008

vice-presidential acceptance speech, 52,
73–84; appearance, 98, 100, 101, 118;
portrayal on *Saturday Night Live* ,
97–99, 101; Tina Fey, 94, 97, 97–99,
100, 101, 102. *See also* John McCain;
leadership

rhetorical action : feminist, ix, 2, 15, 32,
34, 38–39, 41, 69n56, 101, 105–106,
112, 116, 117, 154, 157–159, 162, 164,
170, 172n23, 186, 187; invitational, ix,
32, 33, 36, 39–40, 41; legal, 155, 159,
160–161, 164, 171n10; masculine, ix,
viii, xi, 14, 53, 59, 68n33, 86n7, 112,
171n11, 176, 181, 185, 187, 194, 195,
197, 198, 200–201, 203, 204;
transnational, xi, 53, 66–67, 69n41,
69n56, 157–158, 170, 172n23

Sinclair, Upton, 20–21, 24–28

Thatcher, Margaret: global leadership of,
62, 66; Iron Lady, 61, 62, 200; language
of, 51–52, 62, 66, 70n67. *See also*
leadership

Willard, Frances : *A Wheel within a
Wheel* , 1–2, 2, 3–4, 5, 8, 9, 10, 15;
Woman's Christian Temperance Union
(WCTU), ix, 1, 2, 3, 6, 8. *See also*
leadership

About the Editors

Michele Lockhart, PhD, teaches business communications and English at Texas Woman's University. Her research interests include political rhetoric, media in politics, and technical and business communications. Dr. Lockhart holds degrees in broadcast journalism, political science and public administration, and rhetoric. Her previous professional experience includes serving as an analyst for the U.S. Government Accountability Office (GAO), a broadcast journalist and bureau chief, working on a gubernatorial re-election campaign, and writing speeches for an elected official.

Kathleen Mollick is an associate professor of English at Tarleton State University, where she serves as the director of the writing program. She has presented papers on topics related to composition studies, presidential discourse, and twentieth-century American literature at the Conference of College Composition and Communication, the Rhetoric Society of America, and the Southwest/Texas Popular Culture Association Conference. She has been published in *Composition Studies*, *CCTE Studies*, and she edits *The Popken Writer*, an anthology of first-year writing at Tarleton State University in Stephenville, Texas.

About the Contributors

Diane M. Blair is a professor at California State University, Fresno. She teaches and researches in the areas of rhetorical criticism and theory, American public address, and feminist theory and practice. She has published several articles and book chapters on women and politics, including the rhetorical performances of U.S. first ladies. Her research has appeared in the scholarly journals of *Women's Studies in Communication*, *Rhetoric and Public Affairs*, the *Western Journal of Communication*, and *Communication Quarterly*, and in edited volumes of *Civil Rights Rhetoric and the American Presidency* and *Leading Ladies of the White House: Communication Strategies of Notable Twentieth Century First Ladies*. She served as President of the *Organization for Research on Women and Communication* from 2010–2012.

Kristie S. Fleckenstein is professor of English at Florida State University where she teaches graduate and undergraduate courses in rhetoric and composition. Her research interests include feminism and race, especially as both intersect with material and visual rhetorics. She has published in a variety of venues, including *College English*, *College Composition and Communication*, *Rhetoric Review*, and *JAC*. She is the recipient of the 2005 CCCC Outstanding Book of the Year Award for *Embodied Literacies: Imageword and a Poetics of Teaching* (SIUP, 2003), and the 2009 W. Ross Winterowd Award for Best Book in Composition Theory for *Rhetoric, Image, and Social Action in the Composition Classroom* (SIUP, 2009). Her current project explores photography as a resource for visual rhetoric in nineteenth-century debates about racial identities.

William Carney is director of composition at Cameron University in Oklahoma, where he teaches freshman writing, technical writing, and rhetoric courses with a historical emphasis. His interests include the history of rhetoric, American sermons, and English as a second language. Professor Carney has published in such venues as the *Community Literacy Journal*, *Intercultural Communication Studies*, *the Journal of Language Teaching and Research*, and in edited collections.

Sara Pauline Hillin is an associate professor of English at Lamar University in Beaumont, Texas. She teaches courses in composition, rhetoric, and pedagogy. Her research interests are political rhetorics, feminist rhetorics, and composition theory and pedagogy.

Rebecca Richards is an assistant professor of English at St. Olaf College. She is also affiliated faculty of women's and gender studies, media studies, and the writing program. She is finishing a book manuscript, *From Daughters of Destiny to Iron Ladies: Transnational Feminist Rhetorics and Gendered Leadership in Global Politics*. Her work appears in journals like *Feminist Teacher*, *Rhetoric Review*, *Composition Studies*, and various textbooks. This essay builds upon her recently published article "Cyborgs on the World Stage: Hillary Clinton and the Rhetorical Performances of Iron Ladies," in *Feminist Formations*. Rebecca received her MA and PhD in rhetoric, composition, and the teaching of English from the University of Arizona. Before working in academia, Rebecca was a children's book editor, a high school French teacher, and a freelance writer.

Nichelle McNabb is an associate professor of communication studies at Otterbein University. She has published articles in journals such as *Communication Teacher* and the *National Forensic Journal*. She also co-authored an article on intercultural teaching activities with Liberty University Press. She has had several top papers at the Central States Communication Association.

Rachel Friedman is an assistant professor of communication at Embry-Riddle Aeronautical University in Daytona Beach, Florida. She has published articles in *Communication Teacher*, the *Journal of Cross-Cultural Communication*, and *Advancing Women in Leadership Journal*. She also co-authored an article on teaching intercultural communication activities with Liberty University Press. She often attends the Central States Communication Association conference and the National Communication Association conference.

Alison N. Novak is a PhD candidate in the Department of Culture and Communication at Drexel University. She studies media coverage of the millennial generation's participation in politics as well as online communication in political resistance movements.

Janet Johnson has a degree in rhetoric from Texas Woman's University. She currently is a clinical assistant professor in emerging media and communications at the University of Texas at Dallas. Her research interests include rhetorical analysis, political rhetoric, and social media communications.

Nancy Myers, an associate professor of English at the University of North Carolina at Greensboro, specializes in the history of rhetoric and composition pedagogy and served as 2010–2012 president of the Coalition of Women Scholars in the History of Rhetoric and Composition. Her recent publications include essays in *Rhetoric, History, and Women's Oratorical Education: American Women Learn to Speak* (Routledge 2013); *Rhetoric: Concord and Controversy*, (Waveland 2012); *Silence and Listening as Rhetorical Arts* (SIUP 2011), as well as entries on Sappho and Hillary Rodham Clinton in *Feminist Writings from Ancient Times to the Modern World: A Global Sourcebook and History* (ABC-CLIO 2011).

Mary Tucker-McLaughlin is an assistant professor at East Carolina University where she teaches multiplatform and broadcast journalism. She received her PhD in mass communications at the University of South Carolina. Her research interests include representations in television news and online platforms, grounded theory methodology, and collective memory.

Kenneth Campbell is an associate professor in the School of Journalism and Mass Communications at the University of South Carolina. His research interests include media history, representation of minorities, and collective memory. He received his PhD from the University of North Carolina at Chapel Hill.

Maria Daxenbichler is a PhD student in American studies at the University at Buffalo. She received her MA from Leipzig University, Germany. Her research interests include race and gender studies, American political discourse, and transnational history.

Rochelle Gregory, PhD, is currently the honors coordinator and an English instructor at North Central Texas College in Corinth, Texas, where she teaches first-year composition, technical writing, and sophomore literature. Her research interests include disability studies, visual rhetoric, and composition theory and history.